A birthday gift
to
My Husband

THE AUTOBIOGRAPHY

OF

THE REV. WILLIAM JAY;

WITH

REMINISCENCES OF SOME DISTINGUISHED CONTEMPORARIES,
SELECTIONS FROM HIS CORRESPONDENCE, AND
LITERARY REMAINS.

EDITED BY

GEORGE REDFORD, D.D., LL.D.,

AND

JOHN ANGELL JAMES.

IN TWO VOLUMES.

VOL. II.

NEW YORK:
ROBERT CARTER & BROTHERS,
No. 285 BROADWAY.

1855.

STEREOTYPED BY
THOMAS B. SMITH
216 William St. N. Y.

PRINTED BY
E. O. JENKINS,
114 Nassau St.

CONTENTS TO VOL. II.

PART III.—CONTINUED.

REMINISCENCES OF DISTINGUISHED CONTEMPORARIES.

PART IV.

SELECTIONS FROM THE CORRESPONDENCE OF THE REV. W. JAY.

PART V.

LITERARY REMAINS.

CONCLUDING OBSERVATIONS.

BY THE EDITORS.

PART III.—CONTINUED.

PRACTICAL ILLUSTRATIONS OF CHARACTER,

IN

A SERIES OF REMINISCENCES

BY

WILLIAM JAY.

"Clothed in sanctity and grace,
  How sweet it is to see
Those who love thee as they pass,
  Or when they wait on thee."—COWPER.

"Mark the perfect man."—DAVID.

REV. RICHARD CECIL, M.A.

Mr. Cecil was a very popular preacher when I went to London, though I always thought his popularity was not equal to his desert. I greedily seized every opportunity in my power of hearing him, and never without impression. The impression was not so much of the pathetic as of the serious and solemn. He did not excel so much in the soft and tender, as in the striking and powerful.

He was perfectly free from all affectation of oratory; but everything about him in the pulpit, his figure, his looks, his hand sometimes laid across his loins from pain, his firm and decisive enunciation—all was dignified and impressive, and never failed of commanding attention. Conscious of the divinity of his mission, and the importance of his message, he always seemed to feel what he once expressed, when with a powerful voice he said, "*I must be heard.*"

For the sake of excitement and effect, especially upon the mass of his hearers, he was sometimes, after the manner of the Nonconformists, with whose works his education made him familiar, quaint in his sentences, and sometimes also in the plan and division of his sermons. Indeed, his excellency lay not so much in the clear and orderly arrangement of his subject, as in the fillings up and exemplifications. There was also nothing very consecutive in his discourses; no one train of thought being pursued at length, or fully argued out; and this, I remember, Mr. Wilberforce rather complained of, saying, one day, after he had been attending him, that he seemed too much to follow after things by starts, and sometimes failing to overtake them. This was rather severe, especially for him; and I could not but think that the *senator* had been hearing rather than the *Christian;* and that for once, if possible, the talent and the eloquence to which he had been accustomed made him forget what is most profitable to a common congregation.

The eloquence of the senate, the bar, and the schools will never be the effective eloquence of the pulpit. All eloquence there which does not arise from feeling, and produce it, is sounding brass and tinkling cymbal; and any profound argumentation, or long-continued illustration, will fail in keeping up the attention, or in securing the remembrance, in ordinary hearers. "The words of the wise are as goads and as nails." What preponderates must be weighty; what pierces must be pointed; what is carried away must be portable; and all cannot equally carry.

Mr. Cecil had always a number of striking remarks, reflections, and sentiments, which would be remembered from their own impressiveness, independently of a more lucid or connecting arrangement. He seemed much at home in treating historical passages; in representations of common life; in brief sketches of character; and in hitting off, with a stroke, a particular feature, so distinctly and strongly, that there was no mistaking the individual to whom it belonged.

He had few anecdotes, but these always told, and were brief and pertinent, and always offered their assistance, instead of being introduced for their own sakes. But he abounded peculiarly with Scripture facts, which, without a formal quotation, he aptly interwove in the texture of his discourse, with singular propriety and telling effect. If a figure would go with him a mile, he did not compel it to go twain. He never evaporated the spirit of a metaphor, in numerous subtle particles of allusion. He seldom used an entire comparison; but rather, as he passed along, by a glance snatched from it a significant circumstance which helped his subject without drawing off attention to itself. Instead of glossing a passage of Scripture as he repeated it, or explaining it after he had repeated it, he admirably threw out the meaning and force of the words previously, and then announced them as a beautiful and powerful illustration, confirmation, and clinching of the argument he was treating.

Among many other excellences in his preaching he was always brief. I never heard him surpass forty minutes. This is an excellency which did not distinguish our forefathers; and it is not, I fear, very likely to be a characteristic of the moderns, especially our younger preachers, who show in their long harangues the confidence they have in their own ability and acceptance.

The late Dr. Bogue is reported to have one day said to some of his students, "Do you suppose that people have nothing to do but to listen to your emptiness by the hour?"—a rebuke too pettishly given, and too severe. But there is propriety in Lamont's remark, "There is no excuse for a long sermon: if it be good, it *need* not be long, and if it be bad, it *ought* not to be long." Queen Anne, after hearing Dr. South, said, "You have given us an excellent sermon, Dr. South: I wish you had had time to make it longer." "Nay, please your majesty," said he, "I wish I had had time to make it shorter." Whitfield and Wesley, and most of the early Methodists, were short. Why do not many of their successors follow their example?

No man distinguished more in his mind, and in his preaching, between the essential parts of Christianity and the subordinate and circumstantial, than Mr. Cecil. With what a crushing force has he been heard to repeat the language of Jeremiah, "He that hath a dream let him tell a dream; and he that hath my word let him speak my word faithfully. What is the chaff to the wheat?" With him "neither circumcision availed anything, nor uncircumcision, but a new creature."

I believe the following incident has been published; but I was in London when it occurred, and knew it before it spread. A female, who had more of the form of godliness than of the power, one day said to him, "Sir, have you heard that I am going to turn from the Dissenters to the Church?" "Madam," he replied, "you are turning from nothing to nothing."

Hearing a person censuring a churchman for going to hear the Gospel in a meeting (the only place in the village where it then could be heard), he exclaimed, "Did ye never read what David did when he was an hungered, and they that were with him; how he entered into the house of God, and did eat the shewbread, which was not lawful for him to eat, neither for them that were with him, but only for the priests?"

He had his own fixed views and convictions (and

without these candor is only indifference), but he was moderate enough to think it no sin to attend occasionally in Argyle Chapel; and one day calling upon me, he asked where he could take two sittings for his daughters? adding, "You know I am an Episcopalian, and wish my children to go to church, that is, *if* the one thing needful be heard there. But they must take heed *what* they hear, as well as *how* they hear. If *the story* be not told in a cathedral, they must follow it into a barn; for they *must* hear it, and hear it with care." And what practical proof can we give of our belief either of the truth, or the importance of evangelical principles, if it be nothing to us whether we hear the words which cause us to err, or those by which we may be saved?

With this man of God I had some acquaintance in London, but he frequently came to Bath for some weeks together for recreation or health, and then I had much intercourse with him. His conversation was equal to his preaching. It was singularly original, vigorous, pertinent, instructive, and edifying; and none of it could easily be forgotten. In the pleasure of the companion you felt also the presence of an oracle.

I remember his admonishing me against having too great a plenitude of matter in a sermon—an admonition which, I fear, I have not sufficiently followed.

He also advised me, as I was acceptable, and found people much disposed to hear, to beware of checking it by disappointment in frequently putting up others to preach. But how is this in many cases to be avoided? Can a minister slight his brethren when they come in his way? "But they may decline his invitation;" and this would be often wise even for themselves; for when people hear under a baulked expectation, they seldom hear with pleasure or profit.

"Be," said he, "*never to be had.*" Many other hints I received from his rich mind and acute and judicious observation, by which I ought to have profited more. I thank God that I ever heard the *preacher*, or was in company with the *man.*

Who can be ignorant of his "Remains"? Is there a work of the same size that abounds with such riches of understanding and wisdom, and genius and truth? By what a multitude of inimitable passages has Mr. Poynder enriched his three volumes of "Literary Extracts!" How much of his excellency has his daughter secured and made known in her Memoirs of Mrs. Hawkes!

REV. SAMUEL PEARCE, A.M.

I HAD not a great deal of intimacy with Mr. Pearce, but I knew him and heard him sufficiently to appreciate him, and to make me thankful that I had not to depend on report for his character or preaching. It may seem saying much, but I speak the words of truth and soberness,—when I have endeavored to form an image of our Lord as a preacher, Pearce has oftener presented himself to my mind than any other I have been acquainted with: not, however, as he *began* his ministry. Then he was too rapid, and had a kind of tiptoe motion in the pulpit; but after awhile, when his delivery was distinguished by mildness and tenderness, and a peculiar unction derived not only from his matter but his mind. I cannot accurately convey the appearance and impression he made, yet I can see the one, and feel the other, even at this great distance of time.

If, after days of drought, in a summer's evening, you have viewed from your window the rain from heaven, not falling in a pouring torrent, but in a kind of noiseless distillation, every drop soaking in, and sure to be useful, and you thinking of "the smell of a field which the Lord hath blessed"—that emblem would aid you a little in conceiving of the mode and effect of his address. He was a man of a most affectionate disposition and candid temper, having much of the meekness of wisdom and the wisdom of meekness. He was the first Baptist minister I ever heard use the Lord's prayer, which he did as he prayed before my sermon, when I preached at Battersea for Mr. Hughes. There, too, I had my last interview with him. Mr. B——e had sent his carriage to town for two others and ourselves, and it was to take us back the next morning; but preferring to be by ourselves we privately took boat, and returned by water. In our conversation I well remember asking him what views of heaven he found the most attractive and affecting? He replied, "These have varied, (perhaps owing to some change in my condition or experience,) at different times; but for a good while past, I think my most delightful view of heaven has been derived from it as a place and state of blessed and endeared society, with Jesus at the Head. Hence I have frequently touched upon it in my sermons, and have more than once preached from such texts as these:—'I beheld a great multitude,' &c., and 'by our gathering together unto him.' 'He will present us together with you,' &c." Thus we reached the stairs of Blackfriars Bridge, and parted to meet no more till *adieux* and *farewells* are a sound unknown. But what a savor does communion with such a man leave upon the spirit! And how blamable are we in not turning our social moments to more account! for we never know but our *present* intercourse may be our *final*.

What a noble and deserved Memorial of him did Fuller publish, and what a beautiful motto did he prefix to the work!—"O Jonathan, thou wast slain in thy high places!" Who was not, therefore, mortified to find, in a new edition by his son, this exquisite motto exchanged for a good, but common-place passage of Scripture? Fuller, all polemic as he was, had no little genius and sensibility; and sometimes he had expressions which verify Shakspeare's remark,—

"One stroke of Nature makes the world our kin!"

N. B. The son promised, in case of a new edition of the Life, to replace the beautiful motto.

Pearce seemed beatified before his time. How young he died! and with what prospects of usefulness before him! and with what qualifications to serve his generation! What can we say to these things? Nothing. "Be still, and know that I am God."

But there is something peculiarly mysterious and affecting in the removal of such men, and in the midst of these days especially,

1st. When contrasted with the continuance to long life of many of the worthless and injurious. And,

2dly. When viewed in connection with the disposition and influence to do good, and the numberless calls for their exertion. Alas for this dark world of ours! We have had a few burning and shining lights, and can we see the most luminous among them extinguished without concern? We want all their talents, and all their zeal; and shall they perish and *no* man lay it to heart? or pray, "Help, Lord, for the godly man ceaseth, for the faithful fail from among the children of men"?

When the Reminiscent informed Dr. Davies of the death of Dr. Williams of Rotherham, he burst into tears, and said, "I am almost ashamed to be alive, when so many great and good men die."

The hoary head is a "crown of glory," if it be found in the "way of righteousness;" and Job speaks of it as a privilege; "Thou shalt come to thy grave in a full age, like as a shock of corn cometh in, in his season." Be it so, and let all whose days are lengthened be concerned to "bring forth fruit in old age." Yet, is protracted life always the mark of Divine approbation and distinction? May not the produce remain longer on the tree because of its slow ripening? May not persons go late to rest, because the business of the day is not yet discharged? Do not some live because they are not fit to die?

Of one thing we may be assured, that, whenever we are summoned, we shall not be detained for want of means of removal.

> "Dangers stand thick through all the ground
> To push us to the tomb;
> And fierce diseases wait around,
> To hurry mortals home."

Though I was not a personal witness of the following occurrence, I cannot deny myself the pleasure of recording it, from the testimony of one who was. Mr. Pearce was preaching on a public occasion; the sermon was excellent and well arranged; but after he had appeared naturally to have ended it, he broke forth afresh; and what was added, though excellent, seemed not to grow out of the particular subject of the discourse.

When it was over, Mr. Fuller, who had heard it, said, "Mr. Pearce, will you allow me to ask a question? I much liked and admired your sermon, but did you make intentionally any alteration of or addition to it, in the close? because, valuable as it was, it seemed not of a piece with the former parts." After a pause, Mr. Pearce said, "Well, if I must answer, the case was this:—When I was uttering the last two or three sentences, I saw running up to the crowded place a poor man, wiping his face and head, and eager to hear. I thought this poor creature had come from a distance, and it would be cruel to let him go away without hearing a word of the Saviour; and so my pride yielded to my pity, and I tried to be useful, by adding a few things, regardless of connection or order." And what said—not fastidious critics—but lovers of souls, and angles, and God, the Judge of all?

In confirmation of Mr. Jay's exalted judgment of this eminent minister and Christian, we could add something from our own recollection, but prefer the insertion of a few words from the pen of the Rev. W. Ward, missionary to India, and a brief description of Pearce's character by the Rev. Andrew Fuller.

Mr. Ward says, in a letter to a friend, dated January 5, 1799, "I am happy in the company of dear brother Pearce. I have seen more of God in him than in any other person I ever knew. O how happy should I be to live and die with him! When well, he preaches three times on a Lord's day, and two or three times in a week besides. He instructs the young people in the principles of religion, natural philosophy, astronomy, &c. They have a Benevolent Society, from the funds of which they distribute £40 or £50 a-year to the poor of the congregation. They have a Sick Society for visiting the afflicted in general; a Book Society at chapel; a Lord's-day School, at which betwixt two and three hundred children are instructed. Add to this, missionary business, visiting the people, an extensive correspondence, two volumes of mission history preparing for the press, &c.; and then you will see something of the soul of Pearce. He is everywhere venerated, though but a young man; and all the kind, tender, gentle affections make him as a little child at the feet of the Saviour."

Mr. Fuller says, "There have been few men in whom has been united a greater portion of the contemplative and the active; holy zeal, and genuine candor; spirituality and rationality; talents that attracted almost universal applause, and the most unaffected modesty; faithfulness in bearing testimony against evil, with the tenderest compassion to the soul of the evil-doer; fortitude that would encounter any difficulty in the way of duty, without anything boisterous, noisy, or overbearing; deep seriousness, with habitual cheerfulness, and a constant aim to promote the highest degree of piety in himself and others, with a readiness to hope the best of the lowest; not breaking the bruised reed, nor quenching the smoking flax."* Mr. Pearce died October 10, 1799, at the early age of thirty-four, universally admired, beloved, and lamented.

* Memoirs of Pearce by Fuller, pp. 208 and 245.

REV. ROBERT HALL, A. M.

WITH this very eminent man I became acquainted when, before my settlement in Bath, I was preaching for Lady Maxwell, at Hope Chapel, at the Hotwells. Being so near Bristol, I had opportunities of hearing him, and also of visiting him in his own house, and meeting him in various companies. He was then co-pastor with Dr. Evans, of the Baptist church in Broadmead, and co-tutor with him in the academy. He had been for some time before noticed, but he was then exciting peculiar attention, and rising into great fame.

In speaking of him as a preacher, I have one advantage which Mr. Foster had not; viz., an early, as well as a late, acquaintance with him; so that I can view him comparatively in different periods of his history.

His preaching, when I first knew him, was certainly intellectually greater and more splendid than it was for many years before his death. This was the case with sermons I well remember, from these texts,—"Ye err, not knowing the Scriptures nor the power of God;"—"The wrath of man shall praise thee, O Lord;"—"The spirit of life in Christ Jesus hath made me free from the law of sin and death;"—"The inheritance of the saints in light," &c. These sermons, considered only as the productions of genius, rose above any I ever heard from him years afterwards. This, however, was not the effect of any declension of ability; and, therefore, he still occasionally brought forth a discourse far above the level of his usual performances, as if to show he had not become unequal to his former doings; but from mere pious considerations, and a growing wish to accommodate himself to the common apprehension, and to general usefulness. Another reason, too, had some influence; viz.,—the increased number of his sermons after he became a sole pastor, which allowed not so much time to elaborate and polish.

Mr. Hall sometimes expressed himself as if he believed his real conversion was subsequent to his first awful visitation (*insanity*). We do not admit this; but it is well known that he became more and more spiritual and evangelical; and that at first, while he drew the admiration of all, he awakened the fears of some. Nor need we wonder at this, when we take into the account the occasional (though not criminal) sportivenesses and levities he betrayed; his freedoms in conversation, when, for the sake of a contest, in which he was always pretty sure of victory, he defended things which he did not believe; and that, for awhile, he avowed *materialism*, and denied the common notion of the Trinity, by contending for a Duality of persons in the Divine Essence. With regard to the latter, the scheme had all the difficulties supposed to attach to Trinitarianism, without some of its scriptural supports. Hence, many have questioned whether he was in earnest in his belief of so strange a doctrine; but I have heard him avow it with firmness; and I remember spending an evening with him in Bath, in a company that included a Sabellian, two Trinitarians, and himself as a Dualist; and when the Reminiscent, afraid to enter into the metaphysical part of the discussion, ventured to mention the baptismal form of words as a difficulty, and to ask whether it was not very strange that "in the name of the Father and of the Son," should intend *personality*, and "in the name of the Holy Ghost" only a mere *power* or *influence*; and, also, whether it was not strange to baptize any one "in the name" of an abstraction, he acknowledged that it presented a difficulty, but incautiously said, he did "not think it right to hang a Divine person on one text." This was obviously improper and unbecoming, and he ingenuously acknowledged it, as soon as it was noticed by one of the company; and nothing, in his after-years, was further from his disposition than to treat anything sacred lightly; though it must have been always *difficult* for him to refrain from *jeu d'esprit* on many subjects, with his amazing force and quickness of imagination.

Some *individuals* (for there was no *party*) complained and frequently absented themselves when Mr. Hall preached, and there was considerable probability that the number would increase. I speak from personal knowledge at the time, and as one who, standing out of the scene, could observe and judge with less bias than those who were thus drawn into an unpleasant dispute and division. In the painful breach that took place between Mr. Hall and Dr. Evans, I must think that Dr. Evans was perfectly blameless of the *motive* which some of Mr. Hall's friends were led, by some circumstances, to impute to him. I am fully persuaded that nothing could be further from the spirit of Dr. Evans than an uneasiness at the growing fame of his associate. He loved and esteemed him almost to idolatry. I happened to be in Bristol for a Sabbath but a little while before the breach. I attended Dr. Evans in the morning; preached myself in the afternoon; and heard Mr. Hall in the evening. As we were going to the evening service, Dr. Evans leaned upon my arm, and all his conversation was of the wonderful man we were going to hear; and it was all full of what some would have deemed excessive honor and praise. "His eloquence," said he, "is unequalled, and his powers of mind seem bordering on infinite. If some are not so satisfied with regard to his piety, I have had better opportunities of knowing him, and whoever shall live long enough will see the excellency of his character. I find him distinguished, not only by his talents, but by his grace also." But, on the other hand, as from *this* motive, Dr. Evans did not hail Mr Hall's invitation, (and never did use means to *procure* it, as some have surmised,) I believe he had no objection to Mr. Hall's removal on *another ground*, viz., the danger of a schism, owing to some respectable persons who were suspicious of his orthodoxy, occasioned by appearances likely to operate on *some* minds. A rent in, or even a considerable secession from, such a respectable and kindly mother church, was to be earnestly deprecated; but the evil would be prevented by Mr. Hall's translation to another sphere, and what seemed so suitable as Cambridge for the exertion and display of his mighty mind?

There is little doubt but Mr. Hall, in process of time, saw this. He spake cordially of Dr. Evans before his death, and he has now joined him in a world where mistakes and infirmities are known no more. Yet we cannot help remarking with lamentation, what trifling causes give rise to surmisings, and strifes, and discords, even among good men, which a little seasonable explanation would hinder or heal. But there is nothing new under the sun. Paul and Barnabas contended, and parted for a season; but this was overruled for good, and caused the Gospel to be spread in several currents, which would otherwise have been confined to one; while it served to prove the excellency of their principles in their eventual reconciliation and harmony. But how ought we to rejoice and praise God that a man of his extraordinary ability and influence so soon had his "heart established with grace;" fully preached the peculiar doctrines of the Gospel; and through the whole of his after life acknowledged and defended their *importance*, as well as their *truth*. His path was like the shining light, which, though it may be a little hazy in the dawn, yet shineth more and more unto the perfect day, and sets in cloudless glory.

It is needless to dwell on Mr. Hall as "the eloquent orator." But in his preaching, there was not only eloquence which charmed numbers who sought for nothing else, but the fervor of the man of God. It was impossible to hear him and not be impressed with his earnestness, and concern to do good, rather than to be admired; and the entire forgetfulness of himself in his subject.

His powers of conversation were equal to those of his preaching. Some have thought they even surpassed them. I remember Mr. Foster, when he had been introduced to Mr. Hall, remarking that, after being in his company, you might be comparatively disappointed in hearing him preach; for, after hearing him speak off-hand upon any subject with such ease, and force, and purity, and precision, and exquisiteness, you might be naturally led to expect something proportionally greater after much study and preparation.

Some men's minds seem to resemble a reservoir, large and deep; yet, having *been* filled, capable of *being* emptied. But Mr. Hall's mind always intimated a mighty spring; not made, but created; always full, yet pouring forth streams of clear and living water. There was not only a constant plenty, but a constant freshness of communication. Who ever heard him repeat any image, or maxim, or saying of his own? Perhaps the following is *not* an exception:—A minister has stated in print that, in a conversation with him not a great while before his death, he called Dr. Owen "a continent of mud." I am sure I heard this from him more than thirty years before, and I had often repeated it. Might not the report of an old sarcasm have been taken for a fresh one? And what was related by another be mistaken for what was so unlikely to be *repeated* by himself?

As to the reflection itself, it always surprised me. I think he could only have read some of the doctor's least valuable works, and in an unfavorable mood. A voluminous writer he was, but surely he was anything but a dull one; and even in the presence of so great an authority, I must judge for myself, and rather join with Newton and Cecil, who pronounced him "the prince of divines." How searching and quickening are some of his treatises! what specimens also of fine reasoning have we in them! how much does he carry us always with him! and how little are we able to question his conclusions as we peruse them! We say not this of all his numerous publications, but we could specify many of his works which, for their practical bearing, and experimentality, and evangelical sentiment, and the savor they diffuse of the Redeemer's knowledge, we are ready to say are incomparable; and we wish many of our young divines were more familiar with them. I have a little work of his, I believe very little known, (of which I have never seen any other copy,) "Evidences of the Faith of God's Elect." It was written for the encouragement and comfort of his wife under her doubts and fears, and was given me many years ago by Mr. Wilberforce, who much commended it; only wishing, for the sake of some readers, that it had been differently entitled. So I remember he did also with regard to Fuller's unanswerable publication, "The Calvinistical and Socinian Systems Compared," remarking, that if the word "evangelical" or "orthodox" had been used instead of "Calvinistical," many would have read that wonderful performance whose narrow and prejudiced minds had been revolted by a term unnecessarily adopted.

Mr. Hall, like Dr. Johnson, professed to believe in preternatural appearances; and certainly, from his manner when speaking of such subjects, his credence seemed to be sincere.

The first evening I ever spent with him was at the house of Mr. W——y, near the Bristol Bridge. Of course, he was the *lion* of the company. The party broke up late, and the latter part of the conversation turned upon apparitions. He defended his belief, not only in the possibility, but in the actuality, of these appearances, with much ingenuity and ability, and seemed to convince himself, if not others; and when we were to separate, he refused to go home at that midnight hour unless some of us accompanied him. His arguing and fear certainly *seemed* more than oddity or affectation.

Mr. Hall was fond of referring to Satanic power. In his sermon on this subject, taken imperfectly in short-hand, finding a difficulty in his view of such agency, as immediate, personal, and individual, without admitting omniscience and omnipresence, he seems to solve it by pleading for an infinite number of agents. Is not this strange?

It is remarkable how he noticed little incidents and circumstances which seemed likely to escape the observation of so great a mind, and what proof he gave of it in adverting to them long after. How many instances of this have I witnessed! No one could express a compliment or a commendation more tersely and perfectly. I remember his saying of Dr. Ryland, "Sir, I would as soon take Dr. Ryland's word as Gabriel's oath." At another time he said, "Sir, he's piety itself; and if there was not room for him in heaven, God would turn out an archangel to make room." I one day asked his opinion of a female who attended his ministry at Leicester. "Sir," said he, "she has the manners of a court, and the piety of a convent."

He was at the tabernacle the first time I ever preached in Bristol, and when I was little more than seventeen. When I came down from the pulpit, as I passed him, he said, "Sir, I liked your sermon much better than your quotations." I never knew him severe upon a preacher, however moderate his abilities, if, free from affectation, he spoke with simplicity, nor tried to rise above his level. But, as to others, nothing could be occasionally more witty and crushing than his remarks. One evening, in a rather crowded place, (I was sitting by him,) a minister was preaching very *finely* and *flourishingly* to little purpose, from the "white horse," and the "red horse," and the "black horse," and the "pale horse," in the Revelation. He sat very impatiently, and when the sermon closed he pushed out towards the door, saying, "Let me out of this horse-fair."

One day, when he had heard another of those self-admiring, pompous nothings, and was eagerly asked by a lady how he liked his sermon, he answered, "Ma'am, I always thought he was predestinated to be a fool; and he has now made his calling and election sure."

I was once in the library at the academy, conversing with one of the students, who was speaking of his experience, and lamented the hardness of his heart. Mr. Hall, as he was near, taking down a book from the shelf, hearing this, turned towards him and said, "Well, thy head is soft enough; that's a comfort." I could not laugh at this; it grieved me; for the young man was modest, and humble, and diffident. *He* must have felt it severely; and I have no doubt but Mr. Hall's reflections smote him afterward for this *apparent* harshness and offence. There is no just excuse for such things. We must not fling about arrows, and, if any of them pierce, say it was in sport. Should not only ill-nature, but wit or humor, expose us to this evil, we know the prayer,—"Set a watch, O Lord, upon my mouth: keep the door of my lips."

A minister, popular too! one day said to me, "I wonder you think so highly of Mr. Hall's talents. I was some time ago travelling with him into Wales, and we had several disputes, and I more than once soon silenced him." I concluded how the truth was; and, some weeks after, when his name was mentioned, Mr. Hall asked me if I knew him. "I lately travelled with him," said he, "and it was wonderful, sir, how such a baggage of ignorance and confidence could have been squeezed into the vehicle. He disgusted and wearied me with his dogmatism and perverseness, till God was good enough to enable me to go to sleep."

Though the Reminiscent so much admires all Mr. Hall's writings, nothing strikes him so powerfully as his "Reviews." Who does not wish we had more of them? The Reminiscent also is compelled to acknowledge, contrary to the opinion of some dissentients, that he believes Mr. Foster has done justice to Mr. Hall's character as a divine and a preacher.

I cannot forbear inserting Mr. Hall's character of Popery:—

"Popery, in the ordinary state of its profession, combines the form of godliness with the total denial of its power. A heap of unmeaning ceremonies, adapted to fascinate the imagination and engage the senses; implicit faith in human authority, combined with an utter neglect of divine teaching; ignorance the most profound, joined to dogmatism the most presumptuous; a vigilant exclusion of Biblical knowledge, together with a total extinction of free inquiry, present the spectacle of religion lying in state, surrounded with all the silent pomp of death. The very absurdities of such a religion render it less unacceptable to men whose decided hostility to truth inclines them to view with complacency whatever obscures its beauty or impedes its operation. Of all the corruptions of Christianity which have prevailed to any considerable extent, Popery presents the most numerous points of contrast to the simple doctrines of the Gospel; and, just in proportion as it gains ground, the religion of Christ must decline. Popery still is what it always was; a detestable system of impiety, cruelty, and imposture, fabricated by the father of lies; and though we are far from supposing that, were Popery triumphant, it would allow toleration to any denomination of Protestants, the professors of evangelical piety would assuredly be among its first victims."*

---

* Rev. Robert Hall, Works, IV., 230.

REV. JOSEPH HUGHES, M. A.

No institution since the Apostolic era will bear a comparison with the British and Foreign Bible Society, whether we consider the period and circumstances of its origination, the supreme importance of its design, the catholicism of its basis, the principle on which alone it depends for its success, the unbroken harmony of its numerous adherents, the magnitude of its undertakings, the immensity of its achievements, or the bearing of its operations on the great moral questions which agitate the world.

To meet its growing and rapid demands, and to support its operations, especially by public meetings, three secretaries were appointed to defend, advocate, and recommend its claims. These were John Owen, chaplain to Bishop Porteus, Dr. Steinkopff, a German Lutheran divine, and Joseph Hughes, a dissenter. The wisdom of the appointment appeared strikingly obvious. No three individuals could more have suited each other and their work.

Mr. Hughes had another relation to the Society. He not only attended from the first its formation; but may be, in some respects, acknowledged (as Mr. Owen in his history states) as influencing the commencement of it. This was enough to ennoble and immortalize him; but he would always say, "By the grace of God I am what I am."

A good Life of this deservedly-esteemed man was published soon after his death by the Kev. Dr. Leifchild. In that work, my opinion of him, generally expressed, is to be found.* My acquaintance with him is there also noticed. It was long and very intimate. We indulged in a peculiar freedom of mind towards each other; and there seemed to be but a single religious difference between us, and this was not an essential one. It did not, therefore, diminish our mutual regard. Some, perhaps, would deem *it* impossible to be the means of increasing it. But love and liberality have secrets which strangers intermeddle not with. And is there no pleasure in knowing that we are able to distinguish things that differ; that we have candor enough to allow others to think and judge for themselves; and that, instead of being "overcome of evil," we can overcome evil with good"? And is not bigotry such an evil?

He was a man of great simplicity of manners, and of freedom from affectation and all airs of superiority; and, though decidedly a Dissenter and a Baptist, not only from education but conviction, yet he had a most catholic spirit; and I do not wonder that the exercise of it, in some instances, awakened the suspicions of bigots, who feared that, because he was not rigid, he was not decided; and that, where there was no exclusiveness, there was no conviction.

He kept himself unspotted from the world, and was not only sincere, but "without rebuke until the day of Christ."

* See the addition to this paper, at its close.

As a preacher he possessed materials and qualities which did not produce the advantages in his ministrations which might have been expected. I remember the Rev. Mr. Hinton of Oxford (his *alter idem*, and who was exceedingly attached to him) once asking this question—"Whence is it that our valued friend, who has such an unblemished reputation, and stands so high in public esteem, and has so much more learning than falls to the share of many of his brethren, and has such an easy command of words, and such an affluence of imagery, and such a readiness of utterance; should make so little impression in preaching, compared with persons so inferior to him, in these and other attributes?" "Send this question," said I, "to all the tutors in our academies; bring it forward also in every company of preachers; and show the propriety of learning from example as well as from precept, and from failure as well as from success, how to excel."

Some would, perhaps, ascribe a little of his want of popularity to his personal appearance. This was not prepossessing; but other preachers have succeeded without this species of attraction and impression. In part his failure arose from his voice, which was inharmonious and weak, and, when elevated to the full, had a kind of dry shrillness, and allowed of no inflexions. But his style is the most faulty. Foster, in one of his letters to him, says, "Hall spoke much of your attainments and talents, but exceedingly condemned what you know I always hate, the want of simplicity in your style." It was this want of simplicity, rather than a want of right feeling, that made him fail in the pathetic. His metaphors were glances rather than comparisons. His beauties were too delicate to be striking, and required some degree of previous cultivation and taste to perceive and admire them. His discourse contained too little of the phraseology of the pulpit to be satisfactory to many of the common yet pious hearers, who were most familiar with the words which the Holy Ghost useth, and whose ears were most attuned to the language of their orthodox ancestors. And why should such hearers be disappointed or perplexed? And what is there less instructive and edifying in the diction of our old divinity than in the terms of those who would rather remind us of Johnson and Addison, than of Leighton, Flavel and Whitfield?

It was too much Mr. Hughes' aim, not only as a writer but as a preacher, to render his language correct and refined, rather than bold and free. His concern here was *extreme;* and what Gray said of the *penury* of his "Churchyard" peasant may be applied to the *fastidiousness* of our preacher—

> "*Fastidiousness* repressed his noble rage,
> And chill'd the genial current of his soul."

A dread of little mistakes and improprieties, like the sword of Damocles, hung over his head, and prevented the relish of the banquet he would otherwise have enjoyed.

A preacher's great and obvious attention (and where it is great it will usually *be* obvious) to minutenesses in his composition and address weakens the sympathy of his audience, and often hardly allows of a frigid approbation of what is deserving of praise. On the other hand, when a man is absorbed in his subject, little improprieties, should they occur, will either be unperceived, or as being more than atoned for, will be disregarded by a riveted audience.

And what should be the anxiety of a man of God to gain admiration or to secure profit? To be favorably noticed for memory by two or three who have little more to recommend them than mere intellect; or to have numbers hanging upon his lips, and "wondering at the gracious words which proceed out of his mouth," to the use of edifying? To appear the chaste classic from the schools, or the able minister of the New Testament full of grace and truth?

I always considered Mr. Hughes as one of the founders of the Tract Society, and also as the first suggester of the British and Foreign Bible Society. Had he been distinguished by nothing else, surely this would have been sufficient to ennoble and immortalize him. One structure has made an architect; one poem, a poet; one battle, a hero. But what one exploit can be compared to that which led to the establishment of a society which has translated the Scriptures into all languages; and is filling the earth with the knowledge of the Lord, as the waters cover the seas. And how much did he who was honored in the suggestion of this Godlike Institution aid it afterwards by his Secretaryship, by his travels, and labors, and those addresses on the platform which so much excelled the effect of his sermons!

Mr. Hughes was the first from whom I heard anything of the extraordinary powers of John Foster. He was then a student leaving Bristol Academy, where he had been only one year. Mr. Hughes prepared the way for the spread of his fame; and for this he had the best opportunities, especially on his settlement at Battersea; and having access to a variety of distinguished characters residing at Clapham Common. He was not mistaken in his estimate of this peculiar and original genius; but lived to see his opinion abundantly confirmed by the voice of the public. Mr. Hughes himself sold several hundred copies of the Essays when they first came out.

Mr. Hughes had the honor of being appointed to preach Mr. Hall's funeral sermon. But how strange was the choice of his text on so peculiar an occasion,—"All the days of my appointed time will I wait, till my change come," Job, xiv. 14. It was as appropriate to a private believer, as to one of the most extraordinary of human beings. But he had prepared a funeral sermon from those words which he had preached a fortnight before at Hackney. "In all labor there is profit." How much do we often lose by sacrificing to ease? An old discourse seldom answers the purpose of a new occasion:

First. As someting already prepared is learnt off, there will be relaxing of study and exertion.

Secondly. There will be less suitableness and pertinence to the event to be noticed and improved. And,

Thirdly. There will be less liveliness and freshness of feeling in the preacher's address.

Mr. Hughes was little known as an author. He published several single discourses,—a sermon before the Society for the Propagation of the Gospel in the Highlands and Islands of Scotland,—a sermon on the Sabbath,—and a sermon on the death of the Duke of Kent. He published also an essay on the excellency of the Scripture—his best performance.*

* This was no doubt the essay which prepared the way for the

There were few men for whom I entertained a higher regard, or with whom I exchanged so much thought.

APPENDIX BY THE EDITORS.

The Rev. Dr. Leifchild, in his Life of the Rev. Joseph Hughes, thus introduces Mr. Jay's opinion referred to in the preceding article.

"With the Rev. W. Jay of Bath Mr. Hughes was more than ordinarily intimate. As far as two men, of somewhat different intellectual habits and theological views could love one another, they did so love to the end of life. Let the survivor speak for himself, with his own characteristic *naïvete* and force:—

"'Mr. Hughes was often and much at Bath formerly, supplying several years at Argyle Chapel for six weeks together while I was in town. I have been intimately acquainted with him for upwards of forty-three years, and have exchanged more mind with him than with any man I ever knew, except my friend and tutor, Cornelius Winter. With regard to religious things, we only differed as to Baptism; and if we did not love each other the more for this difference, I am sure we did not love each other the less. We disagreed, too, a little with regard to composition and preaching; he too squeamish, and I too careless; he laboring for correctness, and I for impression; (in grasping which I sometimes erred;) he too satisfied if he could abide criticism; and I too careless of critical judgment, if I could secure effect. Yet though he was often kindly finding fault with me when we were alone, he was always seeking opportunities to hear me, and I cannot be ignorant how much I shared his commendation as an author and a preacher. I am thankful for my intimacy with him. My esteem of him always grew with my intercourse. *I never knew a more consistent, correct, and unblemished character.* He was not only sincere, but without offence, and adorned the doctrine of God our Saviour in all things.

"'His mind was full of information; his conversation singularly instructive, and very edifying; and while others *talked* of candor and moderation, he *exemplified* them. In his theological sentiments he was firm, yet sober and liberal; and not too orthodox (as I have

---

formation of the Bible Society, of which we have taken notice in the Appendix to this article.

often known this) to be evangelical. But why do I write this? You know it as well as I, and will describe it better.'

"Mr. Jay's opinion that the conception of the British and Foreign Bible Society originated in the mind of his friend, Joseph Hughes, is fully confirmed by the memoir from which the above extract is taken; and from which we must beg to present the following elucidation of a fact which has sometimes been obscured, if not actually denied.

"The Rev. F. Charles, a clergyman of the Church of England, but frequently officiating among the Calvinistic Methodists in Wales, paid a visit to the Metropolis. He represented, with all the characteristic ardor and pathos of his native country, the dearth of Bibles in the native language of the Principality. He told of a scanty supply which had once been obtained from 'The Society for promoting Christian Knowledge,' but which by its inadequacy had served rather to increase than allay the anxiety of the inhabitants; as the thirsty earth but pines and languishes the more for a few big drops only from the cloud which had been expected to shower down an abundance of moisture. This individual being present as a visitor at the Committee Meeting of the Tract Society, expatiated on the subject of a supply of Welsh Bibles, (Mr. Joseph Tarn, a member of the Committee, having previously introduced him,) and urged it most earnestly upon the attention of the meeting. To supply Bibles was not the professed object of the Society; yet he could hardly have been introduced to a circle of individuals in the whole world more disposed to listen to his representations, to sympathize with his feelings, and to respond to his calls. The whole meeting instantly felt the desirableness of the object; but the mind of the Secretary (Mr. Hughes) was warmed with the subject, his previous train of reflections was recalled and quickened into motion, and wrought, it may well be believed, into a high degree of energy. His views, probably, in connection with those of the members present, went much further than the specific object proposed to them—the supply of the Welsh. The precise language in which he expressed his views, it is now difficult, if not impossible, to ascertain; and we must, therefore, be contented with the fact. Some, indeed, of the individuals present at that meeting who survive recollect nothing particular; others retain a sense of his distinct and emphatic utterance of this remark—'Why not Bibles for the whole country—*for the whole world*?'

"The minutes of that meeting which were revised by himself and Mr. Tarn, under a concern to leave a perfectly accurate account of what had transpired, record that such an object of solicitude, 'AT THE SUGGESTION OF THE SECRETARY,' (*Mr. Hughes,*) was deemed worthy of attention, was suitable for the notice of that body, and should be placed on record for consideration at their next meeting. This fact he himself, though careful of not having too much attributed to him, always admitted. It appeared in several printed accounts, while most of the members of that Committee were living; and all had access to the minutes as well as himself, and was never questioned. A variety of particulars in his correspondence, as well before as after this period, *and the part immediately* and thenceforward assigned to him in all ulterior proceedings, confirm the idea. It may, therefore, be safely concluded that the elements of the New Institution were first of all deliberately conceived in his mind;—that there its original seed was planted by the hand of its Almighty Author. The facts above related occurred in the memorable morning of December 7, 1802. The views and feelings of all present accorded with the suggestion or suggestions made to the effect above noticed.

"Mr. Hughes was requested by the Chairman, in the name of the rest, to embody the sentiments then delivered in a written address, to be read to them at a future meeting convened for the purpose. He readily complied; and, after several meetings of the same kind, the address, with some few emendations, was ordered to be printed with a view to its immediate circulation. It was printed at first in *quarto*, the intention being to circulate chiefly among persons in high station—individuals whose countenance might shield the magnitude of the scheme it proposed from the charge of wildness or utter impracticability. It was subsequently printed in octavo, and went through several editions.

"This pamphlet, which was entitled, '*The Excellence of the Holy Scriptures: an Argument for their more general dispersion at home and abroad,*' was the earliest public act of preparation for the establishment of that first and greatest of our National Societies. A document so momentous in its results, so excellent in itself, and so intimately connected with the subsequent history and everlasting renown of our friend, requires some further notice from the pen of his Biographer. A more important production, viewing the train of consequences to which it has led, and is still leading, surely never issued from the British press, saving only the Holy Bible itself."

After giving a very complete analysis of Mr. Hughes' work his Biographer thus concludes:—

"The publication of this pamphlet marks an era, undoubtedly one of the most propitious in the religious history of our country; and which will be pointed to and signalized in future ages as the date of one of the most popular, most useful, and most important Institutions that ever blessed the world.

"The publication of Mr. Hughes' Essay took place early in 1803; and for something more than a year the project was contemplated with serious, and, it may be believed, with much prayerful thought, by pious and benevolent men of various Christian denominations. At length its first general public meeting was called, on March the 7th, 1804. Granville Sharpe, Esquire, in the Chair."—Memoir of Rev. Joseph Hughes, A.M., pp. 142, 194, 207, 209.

REV. JOHN FOSTER.

I HAD many opportunities of seeing Mr. Foster, from the time he was a student at Bristol to the period of his death. He was thrice settled near me, viz., at Downend, at Frome, and at Stapleton. His wife had relations in my congregation; and he sometimes passed a Sabbath in Bath; but I could never induce him to preach for me. He declined commonly by saying (with complacency and pleasantry), "You know neither you nor your people would ever ask me again; I am never desired to preach a second time."

The first interview I had with him was at the house of Mrs. Hannah More. It was attended with the incident which I mentioned in my Reminiscence of this extraordinary and excellent woman,—the producing for the opinion of the party of the tract entitled "*The Shepherd of Salisbury Plain*," as the first of a series which, it was hoped, would tend to supplant the worthless and mischievous trash in immense circulation, and to furnish something not only harmless, but useful, in its stead. It was at a breakfast; the company was select, yet rather numerous. But all I remember with regard to Foster was his taciturnity; for I know not that he uttered a single sentence. As, like myself, he had risen from (what is called, I know not why) penniless life, and had, as yet, seen little of society, it might have been supposed that he was rather restrained, when among persons above the class in which he had moved; but even then, he had such a consciousness of his talents as would have secured him from such influence.

Some time after this, Mr. Henry Thornton, M. P. for the Borough of Southwark, being in Bath, and having heard of his powers, desired me to engage him some day to dine with him. I did so; and, mortifyingly, he again showed his indisposition to talk; and our most excellent entertainer was not much formed to make his company easy, and free, and communicative; for his manner was peculiarly cold, distant, and reserved. Foster said (yet I think very untruly), that *he sat as if he had a bag of money under his arm;* but at this time Mr. Foster had a kind of silly prejudice against persons of affluence, however their wealth had been obtained. This lessened in time; and when he thought of espousals, he seemed to think *property* "was good and profitable to men;" not that, in his choice, he overlooked wisdom and goodness, but showed that he thought these were not the worse for being endowed.

And this leads me to observe, that I never knew a man possessing such a capacity for every kind of conversation who spoke so little, unless he had an individual or two; not (as he used to express it) to talk *upon*, but to talk *with*.

An observable circumstance was his omission of Scriptural expressions in his prayers; for I can hardly remember his ever using any. This could not have been from his ignorance of the Scriptures, for from a child he had known them; and, if it were designed, what could have been the motive for the omission? As this applied very much to his sermons, as well as to his prayers (as may be seen in his skeleton lectures), I ventured to ask him once concerning it, when he rather lamented than justified the practice, and said the fault was principally in his memory, and that he feared to repeat such expressions, lest he should fail or boggle in the accuracy of the sacred diction.

This leads me to remark another thing. In his account of Mr. Hall's prayers, he has gently censured him for too much of personal references and specifications. The remark being rather bold and novel, and coming from such a pen, I hoped it would have excited notice, and produced a friendly discussion in some of our religious periodicals. For myself, I had always wished that less of the practice prevailed in our public devotions. I say *public devotions;* for the family altar, and the private closet, admit these, and often require them; and *there* they are not only allowable, but desirable. But against the public and frequent introduction of minute and specific cases pertaining to individuals, there lie, I think, four objections:—*First*, it often perplexes and embarrasses the preacher to bring them forward *properly*. Few have the command of that fluency which enables them to express incidents with readiness and with ease; and there is frequently danger in extempore prayer, lest the faculties should be employed where the affections only should be exercised; and this difficulty should not, if possible, be increased. *Secondly*, it excites improper and unreasonable attention and inquiry in the minds of the hearers. This is especially the case with the more curious and inquisitive. The devotion of many of these is at an end as soon as such personalities are brought in; and their minds are immediately hunting through the congregation or the neighborhood to ascertain the family, or the individual, to whom the minister has alluded Yet some in their devotions introduce, not only a particular fact, but its circumstantial attributes; the thanksgiving is not only for a *safe* delivery, but for that of a *son* or *daughter;* and the prayer is not only for a *safe* journey, but by *land* or by *water;* and the recovery is implored, not from *sickness*, but from *dropsy* or *fever;* and so of the rest. *Thirdly*, there is frequently in these references a kind of adulatory, complimentary strain. This is sometimes so gross, that, if it be not very trying to those for whom it is designed, it must be offensive to those by whom it is heard. Hence expressions must be sought which *tell* in favor of the individual; and, when several are to be noticed at the same time, great caution must be observed not to use more respectful terms in speaking of one than of the other. So averse have I been to this, and so afraid of it in my own case, that I have commonly, especially with younger ministers, when they have been preaching for me, taken them aside before they entered the pulpit, and begged them, either not to refer to me personally at all, or in only general terms. *Fourthly,* a difficulty arises from the multiplicity of cases. And which of these can be passed by without offence? Yet how can all be distinctly referred to? I had, when preaching in the great congregation in Blackfriars Road, ten or twelve notes at a time. Who had memory enough to retain them all? And what time would all these particularizations have taken up?

And "God is in heaven, and we upon earth; therefore, our words should be few."

I always dissented from Mr. Foster's recommending preachers (sanctioned by his own practice) to lay aside the language of what he called religious technicalities; and speaking of divine things in the same phraseology as that in which they would speak of other things. Would the substitution be easy? Would the advantage repay the endeavor? Has it ever succeeded where it has been tried? I have known attempters who have injured their acceptance and usefulness, especially among those who heard our Saviour gladly. And is the improvement of the mass of hearers to be forgotten, in trying after two or three dry-minded, perhaps captious, speculatists, or individuals, looking only for literary display, when they hear the Gospel, as well and as much as when they hear or read anything else?

Three things should be remembered. *First,*—that many, and let the main of these be poor, suppose they have not the same things, if they are delivered in new and strange words. *Secondly,*—the terms and phrases to be laid aside are generally the language of our translation (the only Bible the many have); and, of all our divines, the most eminent and the most known. *Thirdly,*—is the new image preferable to the old currency? Is reformation equal to renovation? Is *favor* as significant as *grace?* Is *forgiveness* a full substitute for *justification?* Does *a promise* supersede "*an everlasting covenant, ordered in all things, and sure*"?

No one seemed to delight more in a simple, consistent Christian, or "an Israelite indeed, in whom was no guile," whatever was his condition or religious party, than Mr. Foster; but he was very indignant at the inconsistencies of many professors. I was one day visiting with him at the house of a gentleman, who, though a deacon of a Christian church, was too much carried away with the pride of life. The mansion was decorated with every kind of ornament, and the table furnished with every luxury. As we were entering the sumptuous dining-room, Foster pinched my elbow, and said, "Is this the strait gate?"

In preaching, his delivery all through was in a low and equable voice, with a kind of surly tone, and a frequent repetition of a word at the beginning of a sentence. He had a little fierceness occasionally in his eye; otherwise his face was set, and his arms perfectly motionless. He despised all gesticulation, and also all attempts to render anything emphatical in announcement; looking for the effect from the bare sentiment itself, unhelped by anything in the delivery, which he professed to despise. He contended that all eloquence resides essentially in the thought, and what is eloquent in *any* mode of expression would be so in *every* mode. Yet he was singularly slow in composition, and fastidious in the structure of his sentences. But, upon the admission of his own principle, how needless was the solicitude of his practice? But in *what* do any of our professions and our practices ever perfectly accord?

He declined all explicit divisions in sermons, and he was never found using the numerals "first," or "second." The notes of his discourses (I have seen many of them) seemed to consist of some leading sentences, as places from which he started to enlarge. These sentences, to change the metaphor, were seminal, and contained much matter which *he* could deduce from them; and the seemingly detached parts had some real connection or relation in his own mind.

An anecdote here may be instructive. I remember dining with him in company, when the gentleman who entertained us (the conversation happening to turn upon preaching) remarked the propriety of an obvious and numerical arrangement; stating that, whatever may be the case with educated and intellectual individuals, the greater part of an audience do not perceive what is relative unless it be expressed; nor are they able, without methodical assistance, fully and easily to receive and secure what they have heard. Mr. Foster not seemingly assenting, the gentleman proceeded to ask, what no one could deny, whether that which escaped in the mere act of hearing could do much good; and whether that was not more likely to be beneficial which remained on the mind, and would be thought of alone and repeated in company. He added, "Now, sir, here is a preacher present who heard you deliver in Bristol a few days ago a sermon which he much admired; but when I pressed for a sketch of it, he said he could not recall or relate it. But, sir, I will call in my gardener. * * * John, did you hear Mr. —— last Sunday?" "Yes, sir." "Did he not preach from such a text?" "He did, sir." "Do you remember anything of the sermon?" John, after a little reflection, replied, "Why, sir, he introduced the subject by observing what a difference there was between pretension and reality in religion,—that there may be a form of knowledge and a form of godliness without the power,—and how necessary it was to remember and be able to distinguish this, especially with regard to ourselves. He then said the text contained three things. These he stated and severally explained. He then called upon us to examine ourselves, and I shall never forget (it thrills through me now) how he closed with Bunyan's words, 'Lo, I saw there is a way to hell by the gate of heaven.'"

But though Mr. Foster despised the usual order and arrangement, yet he did not leave things general and indefinite in their bearings; and there was often a pointed force and appropriateness of reflection, which *seemed* suddenly called forth without design, and which fell terribly on the conscience. This may be seen in the *Lectures* which have been published; for though they are posthumous, and none of them were entirely the discourses which he delivered, they fail not to give a just impression of his usual preaching. They also show (though too sparingly) that he held what are commonly called the peculiar doctrines of the Gospel. Of these doctrines, as a Christian, he felt the truth and importance; yet not sufficiently by believing to enter into rest, and feel that peace which passeth all understanding, keeping his heart and mind through Christ Jesus; or *fully* to enjoy the blessedness of the people who know the joyful sound, and walk all day in the light of the Lord's countenance. His mind seemed too much surrounded with gloomy, rather than cheerful, images; nothing appeared to satisfy him, in civil or religious concerns; and he commonly was not indulged with the peculiar associations which well suited and pleased his mind and heart.

It is needless to speak of his endowments, which have become so generally known from his works, and so justly rated. His *Essays* have excited universal admiration, and have obtained for him a very high and established position, in the estimation of all readers of judgment and taste. These *Essays* first came to my hand on the morning of a day devoted to rural jaunting and recreation; and though I was bound to be attentive to my companions, and was always fond of natural scenery, (some fine specimens of which we were visiting,) yet, having opened the work in the carriage, I was tempted to go astray more than once in the day, to dip into the contents, which I could not leave until the morrow.

Mr. Wilberforce thought his *Essay on Popular Ignorance* much inferior to its predecessors; others have thought the same. I confess I could never see any reason for this. But priority has here an advantage; and if an author does not surpass in a second attempt, he is supposed to come short of himself. The *Lectures*, without being sermons or expositions, abound with thought; but the reflections are to subtile, or profound, for the seizure of common attention or intellect; and what degree of impression or effect did *they* produce?

I love not to draw comparisons between good and great men, but I have commonly thought he was superior to his illustrious contemporary; not in every respect, by any means, especially in learning, and composition, and eloquence, but in a kind of unlabored penetration, an iron grasp and hold of whatever he seized, a bottomless profundity of thought, and a fulness of all kinds and degrees of illustration, nothing of which ever seemed derived *ab extra*, but all springing from his treasures within. And I found, when in Scotland, that Dr. Chalmers and others conceded the same *partial* pre-eminence.

I have sometimes thought of the one as having

more genius, and the other more judgment; the one as having more comprehensiveness of mind, the other more force and condensation; the one having more of intuition, the other of acquirement; the one more discursive, the other more consecutive; the one more distinguished by depth, the other by height. But all this is of little significance; they were both great and extraordinary men; I knew enough of each to feel competent to describe them perfectly; and, if they were to be weighed, I should strive to hold the scales.

It is worthy of observation that, though Mr. Hall, as a preacher, was so much more popular than Mr. Foster, (we were always hearing of the one, and scarcely ever of the other,) yet, since the decease of both, quotations from the sermons (I mean the unpublished) of the former are seldom to be met with; extracts and whole skeletons from the ordinary preaching of the latter have been, and continue to be, in various modes multiplied.

In God's hand it is to make great, and to give strength "of every kind" to all; and superior talents are never given in vain. They have their use and their value; but, lest we should idolize them, and think them essential, we often have them (unlike the instances before us) unassociated with piety, and God doing his work without them, "that the excellency of the power may be of him, and not of them." Admired, therefore, and valuable, in their way, as natural and acquired endowments and attainments are, they are not grace; and Paul would say to us, "Covet earnestly the best gifts, and yet I show unto you a more excellent way." Many without splendid endowments have been the power of God to save, and will have to present a number of converts, their joy and crown, in the day of the Lord Jesus. How lamentable is it to reflect how little this master-genius effected, at least in the higher species of good; and how every religious interest he served was diminished, rather than increased, by his labors!

The biography of Scripture is impartial, and faithfully records the errors and miscarriages of God's greatest and dearest servants; and *need* we, *should* we, overlook the errors and imperfections of wise and good men now? especially when they have excellences which will bear a gentle censure without snuffing them out? And is not this the more necessary where persons are elevated, and their example the more likely to be seen and influential; where morals, like fashions, always work downwards? We should not readily concede the dispensableness of attending on the means of grace and ordinances of religion to any. Man is not purely intellectual, nor is reason the only attribute of his nature. His mind must be approached through the medium of sense; and his fellowship with things unseen and eternal must be maintained, or aided, by those which are seen and temporal. And those eminent degrees of the divine life which some might suppose render attendance in the sanctuary and at the Lord's Table needless, always attach the possessor more to them. But, if some individuals could supply the place of such attendance from their own stores, yet it is otherwise with the mass of persons. Without these excitements and advantages, the very appearance of religion would soon cease among them. Therefore, how desirable and dutiful is it that we should sanction and enforce such usages, even for the sake of the public welfare, by our own example. However defective the public services may be, they conduce to some profit. Nothing tends so much to socialize, and civilize, and to produce decorum and cleanliness: so that by the want of these you may always infer the spiritual destitution of a neighborhood.

When residing in the vicinage of Bristol, and disengaged from office, Mr. Foster usually heard Mr. Hall, (and what marvel?) but no other minister; nor, I believe, did he even then commune at Broadmead; and, when residing for some time at Burton-on-the-Water he always heard the pastor, yet left the table of the Lord; and Mr. C—— (Coles) complained, and said what a distress it occasioned to himself, and what a stumbling-block it proved in the way of some of the members. I presume (but I am not certain) that in the several places where he officiated as the pastor himself he administered the Lord's Supper; but, as to the other ordinance, he never dispensed it, or attended the administration; and, in several attempts, Mr. Hughes, his most familiar friend, assured me, he never could get him to express himself upon the subject; but had a full persuasion that with the *Friends* he did not believe in the perpetuity of water baptism.

I never knew a person (with the exception of Mandeville and Rochefoucault) who had such views of the badness and depravity of human nature. He seemed to regard it as a mass of entire corruption, and especially of *aversion* in *everything* towards God; so that he saw nothing in it capable of being altered, or *improved* into something better; and religion was not with him a transformation, by the renewing of the mind, but a perfect production and substitution of other powers, through the power of God. His views also of ministerial and missionary labors, far from being sanguine, were scarcely hopeful; and his expectation of a better state of things did not arise from the blessing of God on the use of the means we possess, but from an express interposition of almightiness coercing its effects.

And who can commend his wish to break up all church institutions and orders, leaving religion to individual influence and exertion? Or at most to domestic? In several of these things he was joined and aided by another remarkable and talented character, a member of my congregation, Mr. Thomas Parsons, of whom I have spoken in my published funeral sermon.

But is it wise to abandon the present methods of doing good, because of their defectiveness, instead of gradually endeavoring to improve them? Who knows what may be the result between the giving up of the old means and the establishment and prevalence of the new; for the change may not be easily, and therefore not speedily accomplished; and who can be certain of its greater benefit and usefulness? We actually know what is now doing, and may hope for greater things than these, by the blessing of God upon our wise and active use of our present instrumentalities. "To him that hath shall be given, and he shall have more abundance; but from him that hath not shall be taken away even that which he *seemeth* to have."

Mr. Foster, though great in all his productions, appears to me greatest in his *Reviews.* The more I read them, the more I am astonished at the quickness and clearness of his perceptions; the power of his discrimination; his detection of sophistry; his love of fairness, rectitude, and truth; his sly, yet just sarcasms; his stinging satire; his abomination of pedantry and pretence. Nor is my admiration abated by comparison, when I read the contributions of Macaulay, Jeffrey, and Macintosh; and nothing surprises me more than that the purchase of the two volumes of his contributions has not been rapid and extensive enough to induce the editor to send forth the large remainder, now shut up in the *Eclectic Review*.

But the production of his pen the most spiritually important, and the most adapted to awaken the conscience and to urge the heart to God, (perhaps, too, the best written,) is the *Essay* prefixed to Dr. Doddridge's *Rise and Progress of Religion in the Soul.* Why is not this more known? Why is it not published separately?

Yet, as to himself, the choice of that work for this prefix (for the subject was at his option) was remarkable. As in scenery he could not endure the old forms in which gardens were laid out, in squares, and parterres, and yew-trees cut into formal figures, but something bordering on rude, in which *nature* was seen rather than art; something rather wild than neatly cultured; ever yielding freshness and having no bounds. So it was as to his taste with regard to publications; especially also as to the commencement of religion. He conceived that it began by some one powerful emotion or impression, and never from any plan or scheme laid out in long and regular perspective. He would say, "I love a scene in which nature keeps much in her own hands."

Mr. Cottle (Foster's friend, and, I am happy to say,

my own also) once showed me a letter of Mr. Foster's, concerning this prefixed *Essay*. It may be curious and gratifying to subjoin a copy. It will serve, as the receiver remarked, to show the complex motives and manner in which important productions originate and are perfected.

"My dear Sir,—Dr. Chalmers some three years since started a plan of reprinting, in a neat form, a number of respectable religious works, of the older date, with a Preliminary Essay to each, relating to the book, or to any analogous topic, at the writer's discretion. The Glasgow booksellers, Chalmers and Collins, the one the Doctor's brother, and the other his most confidential friend, have accordingly reprinted a series of perhaps now a dozen works, with essays, several by Dr. Chalmers, and several by Irving, one by Wilberforce, one by Daniel Wilson, &c., &c. I believe Hall and Cunningham have promised their contributions. I was inveigled into a similar promise more than two years since. The work strongly urged on me for this service in the first instance was Doddridge's "Rise and Progress;" and the contribution was actually promised to be furnished with the least possible delay; on the strength of which the book was immediately printed off, and has actually been lying in their warehouse as dead stock these two years. I was admonished and urged again and again; but, in spite of the mortification and shame which I could not but feel at thus occasioning the publisher's certain positive loss, my horror of writing, combined with ill health, invincibly prevailed, and not a paragraph was written till towards the end of last year, when I did summon resolution for the attempt. When I had written but a few pages, the reluctant labor was interrupted and suspended by the more interesting one of writing those letters to our dear young friend, your niece (Miss Saunders). Not, of course, that this latter employment did not allow me time enough for the other; but by its more lively interest it had the effect of augmenting my disinclination to the other. Soon after her removal, I resumed the task, and am ashamed to acknowledge such a miserable and matchless slowness of mental operation that the task held me confined ever since, till actually within these few days. I believe that nothing but a strong sense of the duty of fulfilling my engagement, and of not continuing to do a real injury to the publishers, could have constrained me to so long a labor. It is most mortifying to think of so slender a result of so much time and toil. The article is, indeed, of the length of one half of Doddridge's book; but many of my contemporary makers of sentences would have produced as much with one fifth part of the time and labor. I have aimed at great correctness and condensation, and have found the labor of revisal and transcription not very much less than that of the substantial composition. The thing has been prolonged, I should say spun out, to three times the length which was at first intended, or was required. It has very little reference to the book which it accompanies, has no special topic, and is merely a serious inculcation of the necessity of religion on young persons and men of the world. In point of merit, (that, you know, is the word in such matters,) I rate it very moderately, except in respect to correctness and clearness of expression. If it do not possess these qualities, a vast deal of care and labor has been sadly thrown away. I suppose the thing is just about making up, to be sent from the publisher's warehouse. I shall have a little parcel of copies, and shall presume to request the acceptance of one in Dighton-street.

"My dear Sir, I am absolutely ashamed to have been led into this length of what is no better than egotism, when I was meaning just five lines, to tell what has detained me from the pleasure of seeing you.

"My dear Sir,

"Yours most truly,

"John Foster."

LADY MAXWELL AND THE REV. JOHN WESLEY.

I HAVE mentioned in another place my meeting with Lady Maxwell in Bristol, and her engaging me to preach at Hope Chapel, at the Hotwells. (1789.)

This place of worship had been founded, and the cause advanced, by Lady Hope and Lady Glenorchy. The former (whose name it bears) died before its completion. This was also the case with her successor, Lady Glenorchy, on whose death it came into the hands of Lady Maxwell. She finished it, and opened it for the service of God; and had it supplied for some time by a succession of ministers, and managed by a selection of gentlemen from the several congregations in Bristol, two of whom in succession always attended on the Sabbath, to arrange the affairs of the infant interest. But this plan was soon found very inconvenient and troublesome. It seemed desirable that the place should have a fixed minister. The trial was made, and it commenced with the Reminiscent.

Lady Maxwell was a very holy and pious woman, with a considerable tinge of enthusiasm in her constitution. Her Memoirs have been published in two volumes. Some of her religious views were peculiar, or not easily explained. She had a notion of communing with the

Persons in the Divine Nature *individually* and *separately*, i. e., one day more particularly, if not exclusively, with the Father, another with the Son, and a third with the Holy Ghost. Has not Dr. Owen a little verged toward this in his work on communion with God? But here it was not only admitted, but pleaded for, as of great importance, and reaching the very *acme* of Christian experience.

Her ladyship was peculiarly attached to Mr. Wesley. Her doctrines, unless in the above articles, accorded entirely with his; but as these were not precisely the sentiments of the two foundresses of the place, who were Presbyterians, she determined it should not be said that she availed herself of her privilege to introduce them; and, by a very scrupulous delicacy, admitted none of Wesley's preachers to officiate there, and not even himself.

The place had not been long opened when I undertook the service. A congregation was to be raised. Though young and immature, my labors were acceptable and useful; and while there, the Lord gave me three converts, all of whom entered the ministry and labored well. Here I remained for near twelve months; and, being pressed by her ladyship as well as the congregation, here I should perhaps have continued, but for a dispute with a good female whom her ladyship left to manage the secular concerns of the place. It regarded her interfering with the ecclesiastical also. In this disagreement we were both to blame. Two things I learned from it,—

First, To prefer the government of females in the family rather than in the church; and,

Secondly, To observe on what slender things often

hinge the most important events of our lives. This disagreement determined me to accept the invitation I had just then received from Bath.

During my stay at Hope Chapel, I had the honor and pleasure of dining at her Ladyship's house with the venerable Mr. Wesley. He kindly noticed me, and inquired after Mr. Winter, adding, "Cornelius is an excellent man." This was the more candid, as Mr. Winter, in a letter, a copy of which I have, had testified freely against some of Mr. Wesley's opinions. At the first interview there were in the company the Rev. Mr. More, one of Mr. Wesley's biographers, and several other preachers in his connection; and among these was a Captain Webb, deprived of one eye at the battle of Bunker's Hill, who held forth commonly without doors in regimentals. As I wished to hear Mr. Wesley talk, nothing could be more mortifying than the incessant garrulity of this fanatical rhodomontader; and I much wondered Mr. Wesley, who had such influence over his adherents, did not repress, or at least rebuke, some of his spiritual vagaries and supernatural exploits. Did this master in Israel think it harmless to tolerate a kind of visionary agency, and suppose that it was little for the common people to believe too much rather than too little?

At my second interview, among others was the Rev. Mr. Easterbrook, the vicar of Temple parish; one of the best men I ever knew; and at whose death, it is said, some respectful notice was taken of him in every pulpit in the city. He denied himself to an extreme to give to him that needeth, and was always going about doing good. As evidential of his liberality of mind, as well as of heart, when Mr. Hoskins, a dissenting minister, opened for preaching a large room in his extensive parish, he himself attended the opening; and embracing him before the people as he came out of the pulpit, he said, "I thank you, my brother, for coming to my aid." This very good man (for so he was) erred a little on the side of credulity and superstition. A few weeks before, an extraordinary service, with fasting and prayer, had been held in his church, attended by several ministers in the Methodist connection, to dispossess a supposed demoniac. This was John Lukins, who had exhibited some strange appearances, and uttered some kind of singular sounds, which his friends were unable physically to account for. The man was present at the service, and the spirit supposed to be in him was addressed, and in the name of Christ was ordered to come out of him. After some shrieks and contortions he became gentle, and exhibited nothing more of his former malady. I knew the man afterwards, and more than once relieved him. The case naturally excited even public attention, and gave rise to several pamphlets; the chief of which was written by an eminent surgeon in Bath, in whose native place Lukins was born.

I should not have related this, but it unfortunately engrossed the conversation for nearly the whole of the afternoon, and because, to my great surprise, Mr. Wesley seemed to admit the reality of the possession and dispossession, and to consider it as nothing less than a wonderful work of God. After tea I went with him in his carriage into Bristol, and heard him preach from Ephes. v. 8—"Ye were sometimes darkness, but now are ye light in the Lord; walk as children of light." It was the only opportunity I ever had of hearing this truly apostolical man. The whole scene was very picturesque and striking: several preachers stood in the large pulpit around him; the sermon was short, the language terse and good, but entirely devoid of expansion and imagery, while the delivery was low and unanimated. This surprised me. Was it the influence and effect of age? If it was originally the same, how came he to be so popular among the rude multitudes which always attended him, and so hung upon his lips? Whitfield's voice and vehemence, and strong emotions, will in some measure account for the impressions he produced, even regardless of the grace of God which accompanied them. How popular and useful was Berridge! yet he had nothing of the vulgar orator in his manner; it was plain and unimpassioned. This was the case also with many of the original corps of evangelists.

—— HOLMES, ESQ.

WITH this gentleman I became intimately acquainted early in my ministry. He then resided at Ide, in the vicinage of Exeter. He had good natural talents; was well educated; read the Scriptures familiarly in their original languages; and could speak French fluently. He was also, without assuming the ministerial office, occasionally a preacher. For though he had retired from merchandise, in which God had prospered him, he did not consider himself as thereby justified in living a life of ease and indolence; but as the more bound (as in some respects the more able) to do good; and to serve his own generation according to the will of God, especially in their spiritual interests.

He possessed an ample fortune, kept his carriage, and lived in a genteel style becoming his circumstances; but expended nothing in gay extravagance, and saved up nothing by sordid hoarding. He viewed himself as a steward, used his property as a talent, and kept in mind the day of account.

I pass by his private benefactions, in which he never sought to be seen of men, to notice two or three things of a more public nature, by which being dead he yet speaketh; and in which, I hope, he may be instructive and exemplary.

Observing the people in the villages so exceedingly ignorant and irreligious, he found out individuals of good character and decent capacity, and employed them as schoolmasters during the week, and as preachers on the Sabbath, and supported them at his own expense. He was the means of re-opening some meetings which error had shut up, of repairing others that were decaying, and of enlarging others that had become too small.

He erected, exclusively at his own cost, a large and commodious chapel at Teignmouth; and principally, if not entirely, supported it for some years. When he resolved on this, there were no pious individuals in the place. I only remember (and I had opportunities of knowing) one person who made any pretension to serious religion. And here I differed from my friend, thinking that, in all cases of this kind, we should first make trial of the will of God, and see if there is a disposition to hear, and then build. But the founder said he was strongly impressed with the importance of the measure, and was fully persuaded in due time much good would be done by means of it. His expectation, however, was not immediately accomplished. Some years passed before there was any considerable appearance of success. It must, indeed, be allowed that, for a good while, the preaching was not much suited to the station, or adapted to convert or to edify. But in process of time things changed for the better; a good congregation was raised, and the church made to prosper, and continues to be a flourishing interest. I preached at the opening. My subjects were, Psalm xciii. 5, "Holiness becometh thine house, O Lord, forever,"—and 1 Sam. i. 13, "Now Hannah she spake in her heart; only her lips moved, but her voice was not heard; therefore Eli thought she had been drunken."

Owing to its being opened on the Lord's day, ministers could not attend without leaving their own places. One brother only was there, but he took no part in the service, except the introductory prayer. Being a hypochondriac he had left his pastoral office. I never had the pleasure of seeing him again. But I heard afterwards of his misfortune, shall I call it?—or happiness? He was a man of sober years, and was going to be conjugated to a dame of discretion; but happening to pass a fortnight with her at the house of a relation previously to their union, they gained such a mutual increase of knowledge, as induced them to be satisfied to remain *in statu quo*.

The first six sabbaths I remained to officiate. Mr. Holmes himself preached in the afternoon, and I in the morning and evening. We came from his house on the Saturday, and returned on the Monday. Our accommodations were always at the inn.

Mr. Holmes had children by his first wife, but they all died young. His second wife was the daughter of the Rector of W——n. She had then two brothers in the church, evangelical preachers, but afterwards turned away from the truth. I trust she was a good woman; but though she had married a rich Dissenter, her heart was left behind. I could perceive, the six weeks I resided in the house, that she did not relish what her husband was doing out of the Establishment; and I foresaw what would be the consequence if she survived him. The event took place, and the apprehension was realized. It is desirable when persons marry, to marry as much as possible in their own religious community. To justify a contrary course two things are at least necessary.

First. That they hold the sentiments in which they differ with moderation, and feel them to be subordinate; and,

Secondly. That they consent to attend the same place of worship. Worshipping together cherishes and promotes social and devout affections; and has a lively and favorable effect upon children and servants. What evil consequences have I often seen arising from husbands and wives, fathers and mothers, always repairing to separate sanctuaries, or worshipping alternately at different places!

I do not herein condemn myself. I married the daughter of a clergyman, but there was no separation in our devotions, or differences in the training of our children. We united with each other much more as Christians, than Episcopalians and Dissenters; and never had we, in a long and happy union, one word of discord, or even dispute.

I happened, in my way to the opening of a Meeting-house at Tavistock, to spend a week at Painton. The people at Teignmouth hearing of this sent a deputation to urge me to preach for them on the following Sabbath, as it was the very day of my opening their sanctuary thirty years before. This I did, and was pleased to see the state of things so prosperous and promising. Two days after, when I had reached Totness, as the chaise was at the door to take me forward to Tavistock, I was recalled home by a messenger announcing the apprehended death of my youngest daughter, whom I had left perfectly well. I was only in time to see her expire. How much do times and places derive from association and recollection! What have been my feelings in passing through Totness since!

To proceed with this Reminiscence: On my return from the dedication of the chapel at Teignmouth to Bath, Mr. Holmes brought me in his carriage as far as Taunton, where I took coach. He had made engagements for me to preach in my way back at Chudleigh, Tiverton, Wellington, and Taunton. At Taunton I preached for Mr. Reader, then the Tutor of the Western Academy. He was a very pious and spiritual man; but had for some time past been led inordinately to the study of the Revelation of St. John. His wife assured me, that sometimes for near an hour at a time would he be agonizing with God in prayer, when he found difficulties in the Book, and could get no satisfaction from human authors. Hence he too much concluded that what came into his mind after these prayers was the meaning of the Holy Ghost, and this made him too positive in his interpretations. As out of the abundance of the heart the mouth speaketh, his reference to the Apocalypse was almost incessant. My friend apprized me of this addiction, and desired me to observe, as we were approaching his house, how long it would be before he brought forth his favorite topic. Within a quarter of an hour, the name of Mr. Newton was incidentally mentioned; when he said, "Ah, Mr. Newton is a very good man, but God will correct him before his death." Wherefore? it was asked. "Because of his indifference," said he, "towards the blessed Book of Revelation." I asked wherein he had shown this indifference. "Sir," said he, "when I had finished my exposition of that Book, I sent him a copy for his acceptance, and begged his opinion of the work; and this," said he, pulling his letter out of his bureau, "is his answer."—"'Dear Sir,—I am much obliged by your kindness in sending me the volume on the Apocalypse; but you must excuse me for not criticizing the contents, for which I have neither leisure nor ability. I hope God has for some years given me a word in season for him that is weary, but he has not given a capacity to open the seals,—I am, &c., John Newton.'"

Now, I do not go the length of South, nor admire the unhallowed wit that says,—"The Revelation always finds a man mad, or leaves him so;" yet we may learn from this good man; and what I say concerning him, I speak as with affection, so I speak only what I could verify. This kind of prophetical zeal gave a kind of new and unhappy turn to his preaching. It injuriously affected the congregation—

"The hungry sheep look'd up and were not fed;"

and sinners heard less of repentance towards God, and faith towards our Lord Jesus Christ, than before.

We are not ignorant of *his* devices who is not only the accuser of the brethren, but the tempter too. Had he addressed this excellent man with anything obviously erroneous or sinful, he would have said, "Get thee behind me, Satan." But it was otherwise when he approached him in a sacred attire, with the Bible in his hand, and this text in his mouth,—"Blessed is he that readeth, and they that understand the words of this prophecy."

Would it not be well if professors, and especially preachers, were not only to think of the difficulty (not to say impossibility) of deciding many things in dispute—but remember their little value comparatively if demonstrated,—" What is the chaff to the wheat?"

After preaching for this good old man, and returning into his house, he said, " Sir, I did not like what you said of candour this evening." I answered, " I think I sufficiently guarded it, and distinguished it from indifference with regard to essential truth." " Sir," said he, " you have had many apostates to hear you, and they will think too favorably of you." While he was thus speaking Mr. (afterwards Dr.) Toulmin was introduced into the parlor, asking me to preach for him, like Robinson, saying, his pulpit was open to all good men. At this, Mr. Reader pounced upon me—a confirmation of what he had said; nor did he ask the applicant to sit down, or even speak to him. And is this the meekness of wisdom? If we cannot love persons as Christians, are we to refuse them civilities as men? Is this the way to win souls? Not that I was disposed to preach for him. I never officiated but twice in an Unitarian pulpit; and in each instance I took care not to be asked under any ignorance of my sentiments. I said, "The thing with me is not *where* I preach, but *what* I preach. I must speak according to my own principles. Allow me this liberty and I will comply. I shall not go out of my way to insult or oppose; but I cannot forbear to deliver what my conscience tells me I should deliver from the same text in my own place."

Having said all that honesty and fairness required, I spoke with freedom; but one of the two ministers who invited me the first time went out in the middle of the discourse, and the other before I began had rather cautiously intimated that "it were always better to avoid abstruse doctrines, and teach our people how to keep God's commandments and find their way to heaven." I told him, I always made this *my* ultimate aim. Yet I felt not at home. I seemed not to be among my own people, and was not a little embarrassed in the intercessory part of my prayer for the ministers; for under what character could I pray for them as *Pastors?*

I was only once after this coldly asked, and I refused; for, besides the difficulty I had felt in the performances, I considered how liable it was to misconstruction; and how careful we should be not to offend against the generation of the upright. Upon the same principle Mr. Hall acted. He had occasionally, when he came to Bristol, preached for Mr. E——n the Unitarian minister; but after awhile, with godly prudence, he declined; and saved from surmise, fear, and distress, some who, if not his most intelligent, were yet his most pious and prayerful hearers. The last sermon he preached there was against Atheism!

I see in his Diary, Mr. Toplady (who lived not far from Exeter), though a beneficed clergyman, was most cordially intimate with Mr. Holmes. Here I insert two short extracts taken from Mr. Toplady's Posthumous Volumes, page 279 and 285.

"Spent about an hour and a half with good Mr. Holmes, whom I found in great distress, on account of his only surviving son being given over in a fever. During our interview, God so opened my mouth and so enlarged my heart, that I trust both my friend and myself found our spiritual strength renewed, and were sensibly and powerfully comforted from above."

"After breakfast, rode to Exeter, where I dined at Mr. Holmes'. Found that dear and excellent man not only more resigned to the will of God, but even more cheerful than I could have conceived. Mrs. Paul of Topsham, and Mr. Lewis, a worthy Baptist minister, dined with us. Our conversation at table was on the best subjects; and I found our Christian discussions sensibly blessed to my soul. After tea, myself and four more followed the remains of Master Holmes to Cade, about two miles out of the city, where they were interred. Mr. Cole, curate of the parish, read the funeral service. I preached a sermon suitable to the solemn occasion to a large auditory, and one of the most attentive ones I ever saw," &c.

—— WELSH, ESQ.

I AM the more inclined to speak of this good man, because I *believe* no account of him, even in a funeral discourse, has been published. I can assign no reason for this; but, as we proceed in this brief narrative, the omission will raise our wonder, and show us that the excellency and usefulness of persons are not to be always estimated by the noise they make or the notice they excite at the time. I say "*at the time*," because as the thing is only partial, so it is often only temporary. In due season, and in a way which *marks* the providence of God, he brings forth their "righteousness as the light, and their judgment as the noonday." How many of the Nonconformists are now admired, whose names were even cast out as evil! When Cowper wrote, he seemed forbidden to mention Whitfield by name.

> "Leuconomus, (beneath well-sounding Greek,
> I slur a name a poet must not speak)."

Is there a man now in the kingdom but considers him an upright, honest man, who lived only to do good? But Bunyan! poor Bunyan! that ignoramus, that fanatic, that rebel, that traitor to his country, insulted on his trial, infamously condemned, cruelly imprisoned for twelve long years; what, where—is he now? His book is acknowledged the first of allegories, and his statue is in one of our parliamentary niches!

Good men should be willing to leave their reputation, like everything else, with God; and it is well if, when little is said of *them*, their works praise them in the gate. By these "the *memory* of the just is blessed."

Mr. Welsh was a considerable banker in London. One of the partners in the firm was Mr. Rogers, the father of the poet. His wife was a daughter of the famous Thomas Bradbury, of political, polemic, and facetious memory; and she had much of her father's humor about her. She often mentioned some of his witticisms. I wish I had recorded them. Two of them at this moment I just remember. One day, meeting with a man who was going to push him from the wall, saying, "I don't choose to give the wall to every fool I meet,"—says Mr. Bradbury, "I do, and so pray take it." Another day he was at the coffee-house, where several gentlemen were reading the papers, and one of them having read that, the Sunday before, a man who was violating the Sabbath fell from his horse, and fractured his leg and thigh; upon which he said, turning to Mr. Bradbury, "I suppose, Mr. Bradbury, you deem this a Divine judgment?" "Why, sir," said Mr. Bradbury, "if you deem it a Divine mercy, we will have no dispute about it."

The church over which the Reminiscent has so long and happily presided owed very much to the zeal and liberality of Mr. Welsh. He unceasingly nursed it in its infant state; and, when it had only a small and incommodious place to assemble in, he principally, at his own expense, fitted up the old Roman Catholic chapel, which had been left very much in ruins, from the Protestant riots in 1780. He also, from their having only a successional and uncertain supply of preachers, recommended to them an able pastor, who could feed them with knowledge and understanding, and engaged to support him till the congregation should be capable of bearing the burden themselves.

Mr. Welsh commonly passed some weeks, if not months, annually in Bath; and nothing in these visits afforded him more pleasure than to observe the cause he had so patronized increasing and prospering; and this was the case even after the loss of my predecessor, the Rev. Thomas Tuppen, whom he had introduced, and especially after the opening of our new chapel in Argyle-street, and which even then required to be enlarged.

But this was not all, but comparatively little, of what Mr. Welsh accomplished. I was once passing the evening with him; he was in a very solemn and feeling mood; and after awhile he said, with tears, "I am growing old, and I ought, and I wish, to do something more to glorify God, and serve my generation according to his will, than I have done; and I have the means." Several schemes passed under our review; and at last he mentioned what (as I entirely approved of) I did all in my power to enforce. I will simply specify the case.

At this time our country was in a state very different from its present condition. It was generally under the greatest of all curses, the curse of an unregenerate ministry, especially in the smaller towns and villages, where many of the people, though in a land of vision, and with an Established Church, were yet perishing for lack of knowledge.

We, therefore, thought (for it was the King's business, and required haste) that it was desirable immediately to search out, and educate, a number of young men of gifts and grace for the ministry, and place them in a kind of domestic academies. These seminaries were not to be in opposition to any larger and higher establishments, but rather in addition to them. They were to give these young men a less literary training, but a more theological and practical; or with a fuller reference principally, though not exclusively, to divinity and preaching. These students were to be placed for some years under the care of ministers of piety, experience, and competent learning, residing in separate localities; and where they could be, even during their tuition, employed in teaching the poor, and ignorant, and vicious; and, while employed, to be also improved, and *actually* prepared for their work, like those who are taught to run by running, and to walk by walking, and not by mere rule and lesson.

Of seven tutors, Mr. Welsh chose three, engaging to support several students under each. Cornelius Winter was one of them. He had, indeed, been engaged in such work before, though without any *regular* and *certain* provision for expense, like Professor Frant, at Wells, in *his* work of *faith* and labor of *love*.

The Reminiscent was not one of Mr. Welsh's students, but belonged to an earlier class, under Mr. Winter's care, and principally supported by John Thornton, Esq., Sir Richard Hill, and others.

Mr. Welsh married a second time, late in life, the

half-sister of Dr. Evans of Bristol. He lived to a good old age, and died very suddenly. I had preached before him in the morning, from the words of our Lord to the Church of Ephesus—"To him that overcometh will I grant to sit with me on my throne." It was the last sermon he heard; and, one hour after, rising from dinner to return thanks, he fell down upon the floor, and expired:—

> "A soul prepared needs no delays;
> The summons comes, the saint obeys;
> Swift was his flight, and short the road,—
> He closed his eyes, and woke with God!"

To conclude this brief and imperfect memoir. We read of "the spirit of judgment and the spirit of burning." This is a fine and an advantageous union; fervor enlightens prudence, and prudence qualifies fervor. Therefore, says the Apostle, "let your love abound yet more and more in all knowledge and in all judgment." As if he should say, "Be not weary in well-doing, but in your benevolence exercise discretion as to time, and place, and means, and manner; and as your ability is always but small, endeavor to make a little go a great way." I cannot but think a more judicious course of usefulness could not have been chosen than that which Mr. Welsh encouraged; and, though some were disposed to blow upon it at first, and though more may now deem it too humble for *modern* Dissent, how many opportunities have I had, and thousands more, of witnessing its blessed effects, in turning sinners from darkness to light, of evangelizing heathen neighborhoods, and even in forming congregations, whose beginning, indeed, was small, but whose latter end greatly increased!

And here, without the least wish to check or undervalue superior degrees of literary attainment, may not the Reminiscent be allowed to ask a few questions? Is there no distinction between an educated and a learned ministry? If (and the Apostle says, "Christ sent me not to baptize, but to preach the Gospel"), if the chief design of the ministry is to preach, and faith cometh by hearing, should not everything in the preparation be made to bear principally upon *it?* And is *this* unceasingly and obviously the case in all our existing institutions? Are mathematical and classical acquirements, especially in their higher degrees, equally necessary in *all* stations, and for *all* teachers? Are there not cases in which these distinctions may relatively even disqualify, more than help; *first*, by their aptness to draw away the preacher too much into the pursuit of things in which he excels, and in which, therefore, he delights? and, *secondly*, by betraying him into a manner of address less intelligible, familiar, and impressive, to the mass of his audience? Is not a minister of the Gospel to be the teacher of religion, the subjects of which are matter of pure testimony and not of reasoning, and therefore little depending on talent and science; for "by faith we stand"? Is there no difference in the department of preparation between a kingdom which is "not of this world," and one which is? Is the minister to be laboriously qualified to meet the casual intellectual few, rather than the *certain many*, that may attend his teaching? Is the church the proper and express sphere for the highest cultivation of genius and literature? Or for studying and striving for degrees and titles derived from the arts and sciences? Far be it from the Reminiscent to domineer or dictate; but may he not again ask, Is there any mode of address so little likely to be popularly useful as that of a dry, cold intellectuality? Is there no difference between the press and the pulpit? May not that which is proper for the one be unsuitable for the other? Is there no difference between a treatise and a sermon? I will buy the former, if it be published, and read it with pleasure; but I will never hear the latter, if I know it. Can a discourse adapted to general improvement safely admit more than a certain portion of intelligence and argument? Can that be felt that is not understood? And that carried away which is not portable? And is there no danger of rendering the Scriptures in time a mere book for criticism, and to be treated scientifically, without regarding it for the sole purpose for which it was given,—to guide our feet into the path of life, and to answer the inquiry, "What must I do to be saved?"

But to return. Let us redeem our time, and use our resources and abilities, whatever they may be; and let us never forget that, if we have not ten talents, we have one, and that the man with one talent was the unprofitable servant, and therefore the wicked servant, and therefore the *punished* servant. He hid his talent in a napkin. And let us see what a *single* individual may accomplish, when (as it is said of the builders at the Temple) he has a mind to work. What good did this man effect by the natural and simple instrumentality which he set in motion? Why, "there is joy in the presence of the angels of God over one sinner that repenteth." He that saves one soul from death does more than he who rescues a country from civil bondage. And how many were here turned from the error of their way, and made partakers of that "godliness which is profitable unto all things, having promise of the life that now is, as well as of that which is to come!" Yes; and how *extensive* was the good done to all these! for it not only saved their souls, but blessed their bodies, and the labor of their hands, and their relations and families. And, then, how *perpetuated* was this good! The subjects of it themselves were the medium of it to others; and now, even now, it is operating in various influences and effects, and will continue to operate till the last day.

And by what was he rendered most a benefactor? By the consecration of a measure of his substance to the service of his God and Saviour. One is almost afraid to speak in favor of money, lest avarice should hail the remark, and capture the praise, and apply it to perverted purposes. But, the truth is, that while the love of money is the root of all evil, the use of it may be made the root of all good. In one respect, it is the most important of all agencies, because it can employ in its service *all* other instrumentalities—labor, genius, eloquence, learning, and even piety itself. The lawful acquisition of it, therefore, should never be neglected; a penny of it should never be wasted; nor a farthing of it be sordidly or needlessly hoarded up. "Charge them," says the Apostle, "that are rich in this world, that they do good, that they be rich in good works, ready to distribute, willing to communicate." Again, he says, "To do good, and to communicate, forget not, for with such sacrifices God is well pleased."

Thus did Mr. Welsh. He was in a good degree his

own executor, and had the satisfaction to see the seed he had sown ripened and reaped. Nor was it a small sum which he only in this one instance employed in defraying the expenses of the tuition and boarding of such a number of students from year to year.

But what shall we say of some, yes, even professors of religion, who perhaps began with little, accumulated much, did nothing with their abundance while they lived, and secured by their accursed treasures the depravity and destruction of their descendants when they died! Shame be to those pliant ministers who, in compliment to their connections, will preach funeral sermons for such characters,—unless they take for their text, "But whoso hath this world's goods, and seeth his brother have need, and shutteth up his bowels of compassion from him; how dwelleth the love of God in him?" There are two suppositions concerning these men. The first is awful, and we shrink back from it. "Lo, this is the man that made not God his trust, but trusted in the multitude of his riches."—"With these words," say the Jewish Rabbi, "the angels sing down to hell the soul of the wealthy sinner, when it leaves his body." We do not believe this; we have a better opinion of those heavenly beings than to suppose they rejoice and sing at the misery of any creature, though they may acquiesce in it. But says Young—

"Hell's loudest laugh—the thought of dying rich."

The second is perplexing. It regards the supposition, (how hard to be realized!) that those persons who die in such affluence are received up into glory.

We naturally think that grief and shame can never enter heaven; and yet Christians are never more happy here than when they are most ashamed, and mourn after a godly sort, under a sense of the Divine goodness. It seems improbable that those saints who died so rich will then be free from certain reflections. There is a relation between the present and the future; and not a relation of sequence only, but one of cause and effect; and "whatsoever a man soweth, that shall he also reap; he that soweth to the flesh shall of the flesh reap corruption, but he that soweth to the spirit shall of the spirit reap life everlasting." No one can deny that there will be in another world a consciousness of our state and conduct in this; but the consciousness must affect us according to the nature and quality of the recollections themselves. In that world things will be seen clearly and perfectly; and, in the morality and holiness of heaven, there must be righteousness in our feelings, as well as in our conceptions. What, then, we should be ready to say, must such an individual think and feel, when he knows what a power of every kind of usefulness his wealth gave him, and remembering what good he neglected to do with it;—in the poor he might have fed and clothed; the children he might have educated; the academical institutions he might have endowed; the Gospel he might have extended; the souls he might have saved! And when, in addition to this, he reflects upon the evil his property is now doing, surrounding his children and dependants with temptation, providing for their evil passions, so much going to the gaming table, so much in riotous living, so much swallowed up in the pride of life; the evil still extending and multiplying, and operating in its effects, perhaps, for generations to come! and when he remembers, how the Book he was constantly reading and hearing charged him to be *a good steward of the manifold gifts of God!* and when he sees face to face, Him, who, "though he was rich, yet for our sakes became poor, that we through His poverty might be made rich," who was always going about doing good, and who said, "It is more blessed to give than to receive," and gave His life a ransom for us. We leave the subject,—"*Consider of it, take advice, and speak your mind.*"

ROBERT SPEAR, ESQ.

SOME considerable notice of Mr. Spear appeared after his death in the papers and magazines. There was also a larger memoir of him by Dr. Raffles in a quarterly periodical. The writer was very adequate for such a work, as far as talent was concerned, but he was not intimately acquainted with the person who was the subject of it. And when I was in Edinburgh, where Mr. Spear died, Dr. Stewart, with others, who all well knew and much esteemed him, wished a fuller and more particular account of him could be sent forth; and desired the Reminiscent to undertake it; but this he declined from some peculiar circumstances in the family, and also from too much engagement, and too little leisure and health at the time.

Mr. Spear, under the blessing of Providence, had risen to affluence by his own exertions and skill. He was a cotton merchant, residing at Manchester. He stood very high in the commercial world for ability and integrity, for fairness and honor. And I remember a very clever American, who had long known him and had large dealings with him, saying, that, while he preferred English merchants to those of any other nation, he preferred Mr. Spear to any even of his own nation.

Having met at Cadiz with a quantity of cotton of a fine and superior kind, he very advantageously purchased the whole; and soon introduced the growth into Georgia, where he sent and employed an agent of his own from Manchester to encourage the culture, and purchase the produce. He loved not speculation, yet in his line of business it could hardly be avoided. He, therefore, laid down this rule for his own government therein,—that he would keep a certain sum appropriated to this purpose, and that it should be no more than he thought he could afford to lose, without injuring his *family* or his *temper*.

"He that maketh haste to be rich shall not be innocent;" and "they that will be rich fall into temptation and a snare, and into many foolish and hurtful lusts." But when the acquisition of property is not made an absolute aim, but is a consequence left with the providence of God, in the discharge of duty, it will not be found so commonly corruptive and injurious. And Mr. Spear knew it became him not to be slothful in business; and God blessed the labor of his hands. But as riches increased, he set not his heart upon them; but viewed them as a talent for which he was responsible, and by which he was "to do good and to communicate." And who can estimate the measure and degree of his benevolence and beneficence? His bountifulness was *impartial.* He loved all who loved our Lord Jesus Christ in sincerity; and aided many institutions and charities which belonged not to his own immediate connections. His beneficence was also very *extensive.* He devised liberal things. He gave largely to the Bible Society, and to the London Missionary Society. With regard to the latter, at the first public collection at his own chapel in Mosley-street, Manchester, designing it to be secret, he slipped a £300 note into the plate, which was only discovered accidentally. He contributed generously to several of our academies for the education of young men for the ministry, and as (owing to the spiritual destitution of the people, especially in the villages and smaller towns) many laymen were engaged in teaching,—to render them more acceptable and useful, he remunerated an able minister to instruct them in the evenings, as they had leisure; and even from this humble source of improvement issued several able preachers, who in time became pastors of churches.

There was another thing with which I was struck, (for after my intimate friendship with him I knew much of his liberal measures,) and I mention it as rather original as well as exemplary. He looked out and employed in several parts of the peopled locality pious men and women whose houses were to be day-schools to which any children might come, at any time, as they could be spared from their home or their labor; while the owners were to be always present and ready to teach them.

While thus going on, Law's "Call to a Devout and Holy Life" fell into his hands, and unduly impressed him. The book might be useful to some, but it may lead others astray, by not distinguishing things that differ, as to their order and place in the scheme of the Gospel. It has too little of evangelism in it, and is sadly wanting in that "free spirit" by which the subjects of Divine grace are upheld in their goings, and enabled, with enlarged hearts, to run in the way of his commandments. It is John preaching the baptism of repentance, rather than Jesus proclaiming the glad tidings of the kingdom of God.

Some mistaken zealots, too, at this time, urged him to leave his secular calling, and dedicate himself entirely to the service of God; as if he was not entirely serving Him while trading for God, and by means of it doing so much good to men. What we do *by others* is as much our agency as if we did it in our own persons. By nothing can a man be so useful as by property, for this enables him to employ every kind of instrumentality, even to piety itself. Few, comparatively, have it in their power to gain substance largely. When, therefore, a man has the opportunity and the means of attaining it, he should not needlessly resign it, amidst so many calls for pecuniary assistance, and especially if he can trust his benevolent bias. When a tradesman called upon the rector of St. Mary Woolnoth, and told him he was going to leave off trade, for he had gained enough for himself and family.—"Why, then," said Mr. Newton, "now be the Lord's journeyman, and carry on business for Him." And says Isaiah, "Her merchandise and her hire shall be holiness to the Lord; it shall not be treasured nor laid up; for her merchandise shall be for them that dwell before the Lord, to eat sufficiently, and for durable clothing." This is the text from which I should have preached his funeral sermon had he died at Manchester, but he died at Edinburgh. The title would have been "The Christian Merchant."

But there were some who pleaded, and in a measure prevailed, that he should forsooth leave the world, and go about personally relieving the poor, and consoling the afflicted, and distributing tracts, and preaching the

Gospel to souls perishing for lack of knowledge. In these excursions he sustained considerable losses in business, which he acknowledged afterwards to me might have been prevented, had he remained at home, with God's blessing, in his calling.

On two other grounds these erratic efforts were wrong; for, first, though he was exceedingly qualified for business, he was (not for want of talent, but *suitable* talent) as unfit for his new work, especially teaching. And, secondly, he had a tinge of lowness of spirits, which required active scenes of employment, rather than solitude and study, to which he was much driven by his supposed calls. Accordingly, he soon began to fall under dejection, which was rapidly increasing, and from which he was with difficulty rallied by the visit of and travelling with the Reminiscent and his wife. Few in doing good ever more fulfilled the command, "Let not thy left hand know what thy right hand doeth."

He was generally a man of much reading and reserve, so that it was impossible to know the interior riches of his character but by being much with him, and observing him when he was a little off his habitual guard. I hardly ever knew a man who seemed to make so much conscience of his speech. He was cautious and careful in the extreme, not to err or mistake, especially in relating things which he had heard, and in speaking of persons. He daily made David's resolution and prayer his own:—"I said I will take heed to my ways, that I offend not with my tongue.—Set a watch upon my mouth, keep the door of my lips."

It was a pleasing trait in his character that he loved to raise those of low degree; and to set forward in life industrious and deserving individuals. A clerk or a person in his employment, who for a few years had acted confidentially, and diligently, and respectfully, was sure to be aided and elevated; and, therefore, he was always well served.

For his second marriage he chose a beautiful and pious female in humble life. To prepare her for her superior station, he placed her under the care of the Reminiscent and his wife, and to be educated with our daughters. He married her from our house, and it was on this occasion I preached and published my Sermon on "The Mutual Duties of Husbands and Wives." The acceptance and commendations which this discourse met with (for it soon went through six editions), encouraged and induced me to become more familiar with the press; and to issue in time a large number of publications. Several other events also arose from my connection with this excellent man; such as a relative alliance; and especially my acquaintance and connection with the family of Mr. Bolton of America, from which such important consequences to me have resulted.

Such a concatenation and dependence is there in occurrences and circumstances, which may seem to be casual, but are really providential: "And whoso is wise and will observe these things, even they shall understand the lovingkindness of the Lord." Life should never be separated from the agency of God in all; but in retracing it how often do we find a particular event, otherwise not distinguished, pregnant with results, the birth of which fills us with surprise and astonishment; and teaches us that "the way of man is not in himself."

In general we see that the generation of the upright is blessed, but this implies imitation and conformity. The seed of the righteous have many advantages, arising from the prayers, instructions, examples, and influence of their pious parents; but these *may* be disregarded, and even turned into a curse; for "where much is given, much will be required;" and "to him that knoweth to do good, and doeth it not, to him it is sin." And if there are children who have forsaken the guide of their youth, and are, after all their early opportunities and advantages, walking in ways that are not good, who shall read this page, let them tremble at the thought of separation from, and of condemnation by, those parents who so anxiously sought to save them!

MISS ELIZA PROTHEROE.

I HAVE never entered into the dispute concerning the comparative powers of the sexes. We naturally and unavoidably judge of the whole by parts, and of course by those parts which come within the circle of our observation. Either (which I have no reason to believe) I have met with a series of very favorable *exceptions*, or I ought to think highly of the female character. I am sure I cannot be mistaken with regard to many with whom I have been intimately acquainted in various seasons and circumstances of my life. I have found in them a kindness, a tenderness, a purity of affection, a disinterestedness of friendship, a readiness to oblige, to serve, and to sacrifice; and these, with their gentle manners and lively conversation, and sprightly correspondence, (next to the influence of the dearest of all connections,) have been my peculiar excitement and solace, under anxious duties and trying afflictions, and a tendency to depression of spirit, to which, though perhaps little suspected, I have been always liable.

As my children had all left me by death, marriage, or professional engagement; and, as my beloved wife had some growing indispositions which limited her activities, I much wished for what I soon obtained, in a very valuable and inestimable friend. This was Miss

Eliza Protheroe, whose uncle was member of Parliament for Bristol, and whose cousin is member for Halifax.

I knew her first by visiting her as a minister, when she was suffering under an enervating malady, which had much reduced her. She was then under medical care in Bath. Upon her recovery she left this place for Cheltenham; but she soon returned, and we had frequent interviews with her. These prepared Mrs. Jay and myself for a more intimate connection. So she accompanied us to the sea as our only companion; and this excursion of six weeks together gave us such an insight into her qualities, that after our return home she soon became an inmate under our roof. She was well brought up, genteel in her manners, very intelligent, an excellent reader, pleasingly sociable, with a degree of the humorous and comic in her conversation. Above all she was truly pious, entirely free from everything low and mean, and singularly unselfish and generous, never seeming to be so much in her element as when denying herself to do good to others. What a treasure did we find in her! What a companion, helper, and comforter did she prove! And what a mutual regard did we all increasingly feel towards each other!

The most pleasing weeks I ever spent on earth were passed in four successive excursions to Plymouth, in the north of Devon. No little of the exquisite pleasure I experienced was derived from the mixed sublime and beautiful scenery, and from the solitude and tranquil retirement; but how much of it did our associate contribute in our mutual walks and readings, and discourse! And not only so. Here I prepared my Lectures on the Christian Character for the press, and wrote the long preface prefixed to it. And here also I wrote many of my Morning and Evening Exercises, one of which, as I wrote them, I daily read at our family worship. These familiar compositions, which have had such an extensive circulation, I owe much to her stimulation and encouragement; without which I much question whether I should have persevered.

Watts tells us,

> "We should expect some danger near
> Where we possess delight;"

and Cowper tells us,

> "Full bliss is bliss divine."

My entirely esteemed wife, while at Plymouth, was unable fully to enjoy the attractions of the retreat, and the week after our return home from the last visit, she was seized with apoplexy and paralysis, and which, though life was spared, broke up much of my domestic happiness. Our friend was so attached and devoted to us, that she was ready to die for us—yea, I cannot but think this was the case, in a great degree at least; for, in consequence of my affliction, I immediately wrote to her at Cheltenham, whither she had gone for a few days to see her mother; upon which she instantly hastened back while under a medical process and considerable indisposition, and much mental suffering from affection and fear; so that the day after her arrival she was seized with delirium, and after a week of frenzy, she expired. At the time my wife was insensible, and, so, ignorant of an affliction that would have exceedingly added to her own, and which did add so much to it, when she became capable of learning the event. As for myself, I hardly felt more at the death of my own daughter, by whose side she lies in my own family vault.

After several natural relations, Moses says, "Or thy friend which is as thy own soul." Is this is an anticlimax? or does he mean to say that sometimes friendship arises above kindred?

"The tear
That drops upon this paper is sincere."

Few deaths could have afflicted me more. It was the termination of a life of perfect unselfishness, no little of which had been lived for the welfare of myself and mine. "Scarcely for a righteous man will one die, yet for a good man some would even dare to die." Power may cause a man to be feared, learning, to be admired, wealth, to be flattered; but goodness naturalizes one heart in another and renders it "more blessed to give than to receive." Mrs. Jay was equally affected when recovered enough to be able to hear the report of our loss.

"Friend after friend departs.
Who has not lost a friend?
There is no union here of hearts,
That finds not here an end.
Were this frail world our final rest,
Living or dying none were blest.

"There is a world above,
Where parting is unknown;
A long eternity of love,
Form'd for the good alone;
And faith beholds the dying here,
Translated to that glorious sphere."

MRS. SMITH.

WITH this very excellent woman I had a long and intimate acquaintance. My youngest daughter, of whom I was bereaved in the bloom of her youth, was named Statira after her. During many of my annual visits to Surrey Chapel, I spent with my wife much of the time I could spare from my services in London at her house at Woodford. Her name was then Pool, and her husband was a merchant, and had been prosperous, and was rich. She was a woman of a superior understanding, and had a cultivated mind. She had lived in the levities and gaieties of genteel commercial society, (generally the most vain, profane, and vapid,) and so she knew enough of the ways and friendships of the world, to be, in a measure, weaned from them; or at least to be fully convinced of their vanity and vexation of spirit; while she felt her need of something better than earth could offer, without knowing what it was, or where it could be obtained.

With these views and feelings she came with her husband to Bath; and as they were acquainted with Mr. H. Thornton, M. P. for the Borough, she inquired of him where he would recommend them to attend. He answered, "You know I am a Churchman, but there are persons who may be occasionally heard to advantage out of the Establishment." *He* knew what was *then* the state of Bath, and he also perceived the state of her mind. What he said induced her to visit Argyle Chapel; and the first sermon she heard the Reminiscent preach, brought her in sight of the relief and satisfaction she had ignorantly, but really been seeking after. She now made herself known, and a mutual and growing friendship ensued.

Upon her returning home to Woodford, her lamentation was that she could not hear the truth which had made her free indeed. But one of her servants rather casually heard the Rev. George Collison of Walthamstow, and eagerly informed her mistress that she had found a minister who preached just like the minister they had heard at Bath. She forthwith the next Sabbath ordered out her carriage, and went to hear him herself. She much relished the preaching of this man of God; and from thenceforth made it the place of her constant attendance.

From the commencement of her religious career, she had morning and evening prayer, with the female domestics of her household; but her husband was not as yet favorable to the establishment of *family* worship. But when is a woman whose heart is right with God, at a loss to carry a good point, for want of motives, methods, or means?

Some months after, Mr. Thornton and the Reminiscent were to spend a week together as their guests. So she said to her husband, "These friends who are coming, always have the worship of God in their families; and they will expect it here, and will think it very strange, if they should not find it." He replied, "Well, then, we must conform to their custom *while* they are here." So I was desired to conduct the service every morning and evening, reading the Scriptures, now and then dropping a very few words, and always praying *short* and as *wisely* as I could. But no sooner had we departed than Mrs. Smith said to her husband, "Will it not appear very odd to the servants, if we now give up this exercise? Will they not think that we have been endeavoring to appear to our friends more religious than we really are? And do you not think the performance itself is likely to do good, if not to ourselves, yet to our domestics?" So the practice was allowed to be continued, on the condition of *her officiating.* This she was qualified to do; but she took it up, not by choice, but as a trial, and from a sense of duty, arising from a peculiar condition of things. She always had a form of prayer before her, but she occasionally interspersed some expressions of her own. And would not this be the best way of using forms of devotion? I once heard Mr. John Shepherd of Frome, recommending it from his own example and experience.

Are Christians ever useless? When blessed themselves they prove blessings to others; and in various degrees, in some way or other, serve their generation by the will of God. Who can tell the good this woman accomplished in her own place and neighborhood by her example and influence, in visiting the rich; feeding and clothing the hungry and the naked; instructing the ignorant; establishing schools; and forming a club for the poor females to aid them in their illnesses and lyings-in, whose meetings she accompanied with moral and religious addresses, without however excluding their little homely and innocent festivities?

When she was bereaved of her husband, as her means remained, the widow equally sustained and carried on what the wife had begun and established.

Some years after she married again. It was to a very accomplished gentleman, a serjeant-at-law, a fellow of the Antiquarian Society, a scholar, and the father of the authors of the "Rejected Addresses," "Horace in London," and various celebrated novels.* At first his doctrinal sentiments widely differed from her own. This created great difficulty on her side; and for some time a refusal of marriage was the result. At length some peculiar circumstances led her to yield, though not *perfectly* in accordance with her convictions. But God overruled it for good in more evangelizing his sentiments, and bringing some of his *daughters* into the way of life. Yet the connection was not without its trials. It occasioned the loss of a large part of her property. But herein again her gracious principle continued to operate and show itself. Though she much reduced her establishment, she resolved that her charities, sacred and civil, should not suffer. These continued the same. In what are not the subjects of divine grace a *peculiar* people? Trying events befall them, and evince that they are not conformed to this world, but transformed by the renewing of the mind; and so proving "what is that good, and acceptable, and perfect will of God."

It is pleasing to know that her husband, whom she had once characterized, in a letter to the Reminiscent, as "having all the wisdom of the Greeks, and their

* I once dined with these gifted young men; and was sorry to remark that, if religion was not the object of their contempt, it was not the one thing needful.

foolishness too,"—after awhile received the kingdom of God as a little child, died in the faith of the Gospel, a member of the Independent Church at Wandsworth, looking for the mercy of our Lord Jesus Christ unto eternal life. Not many wise men after the flesh are called; but there have always been a few to falsify the prejudice that the religion of the cross is fit only for the vulgar and illiterate.

JOHN POYNDER, ESQ.

My acquaintance with this good and distinguished character has continued for considerably more than fifty years. It commenced from a letter I received desiring me to inform him from what author I had given an extract in my sermon preached upon the formation of the London Missionary Society. This inquiry was prefatory to something else,—and he soon expressed his gratitude to God that he ever heard that discourse, as "it had had such an effect upon him as he hoped would never wear away." And this was the case; for from that period he was found a decided, avowed, consistent, undeviating, and zealous follower of the Lamb.

After this letter, upon my going to London to fulfil my annual appointment at Surrey Chapel, I had my first personal interview with him. The meeting was affecting; and we exchanged some pleasing thoughts and feelings. After this we seized every opportunity to meet and converse; and though, as he was a Tory, and a firm Churchman, and I a Whig, and a moderate Dissenter, and we, therefore, differed in some of our political and ecclesiastical views, this instead of gendering alienation rather endeared us the more to each other. Harmony is better than unison,—"Yes," says Lord

Bacon, "and it is so not only in *sounds* but in *affections.*"

Hence during my annual weeks of labor in London he frequently heard me, and has given most ample proof of his kind approbation of my services, by his multiplied quotations from my preaching and publications in his three volumes of "Literary Extracts." In these three volumes, he shows much reading, judgment, and taste; yet they would have borne abridgment or reduction. It is natural for persons when they read to remark and transcribe. But what strikes them peculiarly at the time, owing to its novelty, or something in their own circumstances or feelings, may appear very differently afterwards; and the wonder is that, in the cool review, more freedom was not here used in selection, and articles *weighed* rather than *numbered.*

Though these volumes are large, they are not all his issues from the press. His publications were numerous, in all of which usefulness was the obvious design and tendency. As a *Christian*, many of them turned on religious subjects: The Evangelization of our Eastern dominion; The Paganism of Popery; The Sanctification of the Lord's Day, &c.

As an *East India proprietor* he spoke much in favor of the abolition of Sutteeism, or burning of widows. In this work and labor of love, many of his speeches were very able and eloquent, and several of them were published. Several years before his death he had the satisfaction of seeing his exertions crowned with success. He was equally earnest and persevering in opposing the accursed tax arising from the idolatrous worship of Juggernaut. But he died without seeing this foul stain wiped off from our government; and "hope deferred made the heart sick." But he had roused the public indignation, and awakened a cry that he knew must be heard in due time.

Never was there a warmer advocate of evangelical truth, and the doctrines of the Reformation.

Never was there a more determined enemy to Popery, and its half-sister Puseyism.

Never did man more strive to serve his generation by the will of God.

And, as to his private and relative character, who ever excelled him as an attached husband, a devoted father, a faithful friend, or a helper of the needy?

Behold what may be done by a single individual when disposition, ability, and opportunity concur.

"The memory of the just is blessed."

N. B.—I wrote this brief sketch the very day I was informed of his death, lest at my time of life I should be prevented from bearing even a very inadequate testimony to this man of so much varied worth.

RAMMOHUN ROY.

I WAS but little acquainted with the rajah, but I feel inclined to notice him, not only because I was struck with him as a man of prodigious powers of mind, and treasures of knowledge, and readiness of address; but because I think justice has not been done to him in another and far more important view.

I first saw him at the Mansion House, London, to which I was invited to meet him by the then Lord Mayor, with whom, as an author, I had had considerable dealings. The dinner was early and the company select, though not entirely religious; and I was allowed to bring any of my acquaintance with me. Several accompanied me, one of whom, John Poynder, Esq., could turn the intercourse to account, in conversing with the rajah on a subject in which he was then so zealously laboring, and did not labor in vain, (the abolition of Sutteeism,) and which the rajah himself before he left India had nobly advocated.

Of course this man was the lion of the company. He spoke freely on several topics, especially of Mahometanism, which he considered as an improvement on Paganism, and of some considerable advantage to Christianity itself, whose professors were yielding to a kind of idolatry in worshipping masses and relics.

He also expressed himself with regard to Mahomet himself, as possessing greater talents and some better qualities than had been commonly ascribed to him. This was not suffered to pass without some hesitation and dissent, especially by the Rev. Mr. Melville.

The Lady Mayoress asking his opinion of the comparative estimate of the sexes, he promptly replied, "*Physically* considered, men are superior to women. *Morally* considered, women are superior to men. *Intellectually* considered, they are on a level, admitting the same opportunities and advantages;" a confession which, if not questioned, was deemed remarkable, as coming from a quarter where females are commonly, if not universally, undervalued and degraded.

When he spoke of the Gospel, he frankly avowed his full belief of it, adding, "But I consider this no merit of mine, for I found it impossible to peruse the Book itself, and not be convinced that it was the work of a being of perfect wisdom and benevolence." The Rev. Mr. Dale, who sat next me, could not help expressing rather audibly his approbation and admiration of the sentiment, and the manner in which it was delivered; and Mr. Melville, who principally led the discourse with the rajah, acknowledged, as I went away with him, that he had a much more favorable opinion and hope of him than he had before.

The following Sabbath-day evening he came with the Lord Mayor and the rector of St. Olave's to hear the Reminiscent. He gave proof of his liking, not only the preacher, but the subject, by coming into the house afterwards, and soliciting a copy of the discourse to print for distribution among his friends. As the sermon was taken down in short-hand, I was able to comply with the desire. I procured him a transcription, and he printed it at his own expense. (The sermon is to be found in the seventh volume of my works.)*

I fear this is too personal to be excused; but it tells upon what I have in view; for though the discourse was not strictly doctrinal, it contained allusions and statements, only to be found in "the truth as it is in Jesus."

He had engaged to accompany Mr. Poynder to Surrey Chapel again the Sunday after; but, before its arrival, he wrote him a note, (which I keep, and value as an autograph,) saying he was afraid he should not be able to attend, owing to a degree of indisposition, and the pressure and heat of the congregation; but lamented the loss the less as he should soon have an opportunity to hear, so he expressed it, that truly evangelical minister in Bath.

This was denied him, as, the week before his intended visit to Bath, he died in Bristol. There he was by invitation, at the house of a lady belonging to Lewin's Mead Meeting, where he attended on the morning of the Sabbath, but heard an evangelical clergyman at Clifton in the evening. During his short stay in Bristol, a party of several distinguished individuals met him. Among these was John Foster,† who, upon my inquiry, said that nothing on this occasion very striking or definitive came from him. He probably began to feel the approach of the disorder which so rapidly carried him off.

* See page 100 of that volume.

† Mr. Foster's interesting account of this interview, and of the rajah's death. we shall subjoin to this article.

Soon after his private interment in the premises of his friend, an extolling account of him was published by Dr. Carpenter, assuring the public that he was a Christian, in the Socinian translation of that word. Here I am persuaded he was mistaken. He was this on his conversion to Christianity in India, when he only considered Christ as a moral Teacher, and wrote accordingly. But we have reason to hope and conclude, that, on his coming to this country, his views varied and were approaching evangelical sentiments. At first, (and it was not wonderful, with such talents and reasoning powers,) on emerging from heathenism, he felt difficulties with regard to some of the more mysterious doctrines of the Gospel, but there is no little proof that his mind was beginning to open to the cross and grace of our Lord Jesus Christ. He commonly in London attended the preaching of an orthodox clergyman.

Earl Gainsborough was not only much pleased with him, but much encouraged concerning his state and character by the rajah's visit to Barham Court. When he dined with Mr. Poynder he begged to be allowed to attend his evening family-worship, after the company was gone; and next day he came also to attend his morning-worship; and expressed much delight at the blending with prayer, the reading of the Scriptures and singing. Mr. Poynder engaged the Rev. Mr. Knight to conduct these services, by means of which this pious and judicious minister became acquainted with this prodigy; and he also had good hope concerning him, both from his interviews and correspondence; for the rajah often addressed notes to him respecting passages of Scripture, (with the solutions of which he seemed satisfied,) and often called upon him; and in his last interview with him, finding him very serious and tender, he said to him, "Sir, I trust you do not less prize Christianity since you came amongst us." He rose; and taking him by the hand said with tears, "Mr. Knight, I feel such a regard for the truth and importance of Christianity, that I think I could die for it."

This account, we presume, will not be satisfactory to some; they will ask for more evidence; and we could have wished we had been able to furnish more. We cannot be too anxious and inquisitive, where our *own* religious state is concerned, but with regard to others, there is a charity, which with the due allowance "hopeth all things, believeth all things, endureth all things." We may know what heresy is without being able to ascertain the state of a heretic. We know not what disadvantages *he* has been under; what struggle he has had with difficulties and doubts, to which others have been strangers; and what prayers he has offered, which, though they cannot be lost, may not be immediately and consciously answered. But we know who hath said, "Seek and ye *shall* find." "He that doeth His will shall know of the doctrine whether it be of God;" and "Then shall we know, if we follow on to know the Lord."

Why cannot we admit, in connection with Christian safety, doctrinal sincerity as well as moral deficiencies? And why cannot we imagine that where there is less enlightenment, there may be more excellence of another kind to balance it—more humbleness of mind, more benevolence, and more active zeal? I have met with instances in which, where there was little speculative and systematical clearness and accuracy, there has been much of that wisdom which is from above, and which is first pure, then peaceable, gentle, and easy "to be entreated, full of mercy and good fruits, without partiality and without hypocrisy." When the blind patient in the Gospel first looked up, he only saw men as trees walking; but he was under the operation of a Divine Restorer; and a second touch enabled him to see everything clearly. How little of the Gospel salvation did Peter know at the time; yet upon his confession, our Lord pronounced him blessed; and affirmed that flesh and blood had not revealed this unto him, but his Father in heaven.

From this case we are led to another reflection. How readily and eagerly are the advocates of religious parties induced to claim and avow extraordinary men as belonging to them; as if their faith stood in the wisdom of men, and not in the power of God. But let no man glory in men. We should be thankful when any of superior intellect and endowment are found walking in the truth; but we are not to have the faith of our Lord Jesus Christ with respect of persons. The poor and the common people are generally the evangelized. These "things are hidden from the wise and prudent and revealed unto babes." Not many wise men after the flesh are called; and these are often in our churches more glaring than useful members; yea, it is well if they do not become Diotrephes by their gifts.

Mr. Foster gives the following interesting particulars of the rajah's visit to Bristol, in a letter to Mr. Hill, dated October 8th, 1833:—

"The most remarkable thing of late is the visit, so soon to end in the death, in the house behind our garden, of the Rajah Rammohun Roy (the title of rajah, of no very definite import, was conferred on him by the King of Delhi, the remaining shadow of the great Mogul). I had entertained a strong prepossession against him, had no wish to see him, but could not avoid it, when he was come to the house of my young landlady, Miss Castle.

"My prejudice could not hold out half an hour after being in his company. He was a very pleasing and interesting man; intelligent and largely informed, I need not say—but unaffected, friendly, and, in the best sense of the word, polite. I passed two evenings in his company, only, however, as an unit in large parties; the latter time, however, in particular and direct conversation with him, concerning some of the doctrines of the Indian philosophers, the political, civil, and moral state of the Hindoos. In the former instance, when the after-dinner company consisted of Dr. Carpenter and sundry other doctors and gentlemen, Churchmen and Dissenters, he was led a little into his own religious history and present opinions. He avowed his general belief in Christianity as attested by miracles, (of which I had understood that he made very light some ten or a dozen years since,) but said that the internal evidence had had by much the greatest force on his mind. In so very heterogeneous a company, there was no going into any very specific particulars. Carpenter, in whose company I have since dined at Dr. Pritchard's, very confidently claims him as of the 'Modern Unitarian' school. * * * * It may be that he was finally near about in agreement with that school, but I do not believe that they have any very exact knowledge of his opinions. * * * * Here he went to several churches, and to hear Jay on a week-day at Bridge Street, as well as sometimes at Lewin's Mead, where the family in which he was visiting constantly attended. There is, or a few days since there was, a great perplexity how to dispose of his remains. He had signified his wish not to be committed to any *Ecclesiastical* burying-ground, but, if it might be so managed, deposited in some quiet corner of the mere *profane* earth. His principal London friend (a Mr. Hare, from India) thinks it the most desirable that he were conveyed to India. During the greater part of his short illness (it was an affection of the brain) he was in a state of such torpor as to be incapable of any communication. Dr. Pritchard, who attended him during the latter days, says he did not utter, while he was with him, ten distinct sentences. As far as I have heard, there was *nothing* to indicate the state of his mind. There were actions (of his hands, &c.) which his own attendants said were the usual ones that accompanied his devotional exercises. To me and several of our order of friends, who were, the latter evening to which I have referred, (at Mrs. Cox's,) in such close and interesting conversation with him, then apparently in perfect health, but then within hardly two days of the commencement of his fatal illness, it was emphatically striking, nine or ten days after, to think of him as no longer in our world."—Foster's Life, Vol. II., p. 218, &c.

REV. THOMAS TUPPEN.

He was my predecessor in the pastorate of the congregational church in Bath. He was originally in trade; and in his earlier days had deviated from the paths of righteousness and peace. Living, then, at Portsmouth, he went to hear Whitfield, who was to preach on the neighboring common, and (which was so often the case under the ministry of that extraordinary herald of the Gospel) the word came to him not in word only, but in the demonstration of the Spirit and with power. He had gone to hear, not so much from curiosity, as from the worse motive—to oppose, insult, and interrupt. "I had," said he, "therefore, provided myself with stones in my pocket, if opportunity offered, to pelt the preacher; but I had not heard long, before the stone was taken out of my heart of flesh; and then the other stones, with shame and weeping, were dropped one by one out upon the ground."

The change then commenced, was carried on, and evinced itself to be of God by its continuance and its effects. In process of time the receiver of the Gospel became also the publisher; and was ordained over a church in the place where he resided. Some years after he ruptured a blood-vessel; and resigned his charge, as unable to meet safely its numerous services; but after a considerable suspension, his recovery allowed of his taking another sphere, with less public duty. Mr. Welsh, a rich banker from London (as may be seen in my Reminiscence of him), who had much aided our rising cause, brought him to Bath while the interest was young and weak; and engaged to support him till the congregation should be able to meet the expense.

Here his labors were peculiarly acceptable and useful. Many were awakened unto his ministry, and added to the growing church; which was soon required to enlarge the place of her feet. He was therefore excited and encouraged (much by Lady Glenorchy) to take ground and build; Argyle Chapel was the consequence. But the founder, though he set his heart upon it, lived not to see it opened for the Lord's service. This was performed by the Reminiscent, who had been introduced by Mr. Tuppen to his people as an occasional supply during his sickness, and recommended to them as their pastor when he was dying.*

* In the Life of the Countess of Huntingdon, Vol. II. p. 75, is the following notice of Mr. Tuppen:—The congregation assembling in Argyle Chapel, Bath, originated in the secession of a few pious individuals who did not approve of the forms of the Established Church, and who formed themselves into a church on independent principles. The first person to whom application was made to preside over this infant church was the Rev. Thomas Tuppen, who had been a preacher in Mr. Whitfield's connection, and afterwards minister of the Tabernacle at Portsea; he arrived in Bath in the year 1785, when the interest rapidly increased; from about twenty-five persons who at first attended him, the number rose in a few years to seven or eight hundred. The place in which they worshipped being now too small for the congregation, a new chapel was begun in 1789, and opened October 4, 1789; but Mr. Tuppen's health was

He was a man of great seriousness and exemplary piety; he talked little, but his speech was always with salt and ministered grace to the hearer. Mr. Cecil once said, a minister should not be "a man to be had,"—and Mr. Tuppen was most observant of this rule of any man I ever knew. This grew not so much out of disposition as out of circumstances, as he had had only a common education, and never had the advantage of any regular preparation for the ministry, and yet was very thirsty of improvement. Through desire he separated himself, seeking and intermeddling with all wisdom. He was a most laborious student, and by assiduous and self-denying application, he gained much general information; acquired a tolerable knowledge of the original languages; excelled in theology; and became one of the most distinguished preachers of the day, in his own connection. He, therefore, lived very retired, not only from society at large, but also from his own congregation; and to such

then so much reduced that he was never able to preach a single sermon there—he could only attend the services of the day which were performed by the Rev. William Jay, who has been the minister of the place ever since.

During the few years that Mr. Tuppen exercised his ministry at Bath, his manner of preaching was very striking: he was often heard to say, "If the attention be gained, half the business is done."

It was never his wish to empty other places where the Gospel was preached in order to fill his own; for, after observing the largeness of his own audience, he would often inquire whether the other places were full. When he was answered in the affirmative, he seemed to be much pleased, and would say, "Well, we may now hope something is doing."

After a lingering illness, which he supported with great resignation and patience, he entered into his rest on the 22d of February, 1790, aged 48.

a degree as would not have been justified or excused, but for the value he attached to time, and the necessity he felt for diligence.

This is not always the case: I have been sorry to have observed in no few instances the reverse of this. Where the iron has been blunt, less strength has been put to it; and where there has been no advantage of preparatory fitness, preachers have been *less* anxious and active in their exertions. It is one of the benefits of training for the ministry that, however imperfect it may comparatively be, it creates a habit of order, a tone of application, and a heedfulness of time and opportunity. I have known individuals of no enviable talents, and of no previous acquirements, who have even given less time and attention in preparing their three sermons for the week, than Robert Hall, with all his powers and education, employed in preparing one, and that only his week evening lecture before the Lord's supper. And are there not people who prefer this remissness, and lounging, and sauntering in a preacher, provided he favors them with a portion of it, in what they call pastoral visits, than in letting his profit appear unto all men, in giving himself to reading, meditation, and prayer?

Mr. Tuppen's face was peculiarly intelligent; his eye remarkably piercing; and his look frequently insufferable. The skeletons of his sermons (for he wrote none at full length) were written with uncommon neatness, order, and precision; and generally filled two octavo pages. They were in long hand with a few contractions. His library was arranged according to Locke's Common Place Book; so that when he had to preach on any particular subject, he could turn to any volume; and every volume where that subject was treated in a way of proof, illustration, or improvement. Whenever he added a book to his collection, he thus immediately arranged its topics for reference; and this rendered the work easy, which would, if done at once, have been a tiresome task.

He was a widower, and had only one child, a son, residing with him, and articled to a solicitor in Bath. This son had more than his father's natural talents, and was a good scholar, and gave much promise of rising above many in his profession. He also seemed much inclined to walk in those ways which are pleasantness and peace. When, therefore, he had arrived at age, on his birthday he wrote a paper, entitled "Rules for my Conduct." It began thus: "I am now come of age, and hope for the favor and blessing of God upon my future years. But in order to this, I know I must adhere to certain principles and rules; the first of which is *piety*. 'Behold the fear of the Lord, that is wisdom, and to depart from evil, that is understanding,'" &c. But alas! this goodness was as the morning cloud, or early dew which passeth away. These hopeful appearances were in a few months blighted, and in a few more entirely destroyed.

"Evil communications corrupt good manners; and a companion of fools shall be destroyed." This fine youth became acquainted with some sceptical, or as, by a patent of their own creation, they call themselves, free-thinking young men; gave up the Sabbath; forsook the house of God which his father had built; abandoned the minister to whom he had been greatly attached; and boldly "left off to be wise and to do good." But as his fall was rapid, so his new course was short. Swimming on a Sunday for amusement and experiment, he caught a chill which brought on a consumption. This for months gave him warning, and space for repentance, but it is to be feared this grace of God was in vain. During the gradual decline, he refused all intercourse with pious friends or ministers; and when his good nurse entreated him to call me in, as I lived close by, and there had been such an intimacy between us, he frowned and rebuked her, and ordered her to mind her own business. On the last day of his life, unasked, I ventured into his dying chamber. He was sensible; but exclaimed, "O Voltaire! Voltaire!" He then raised himself up in the bed, and wringing his hands again exclaimed, "O that young man! that young man!" I said, "My dear sir, what young man?" With a countenance indescribable, he answered,—"I will not tell you."

How was my soul agonized, for I had loved him much, and had endeavored in every way to render myself agreeable and useful to him. But "one sinner destroyeth much good." What have I seen in a long ministry of the dire effects of evil associates, and licentious publications! He kept moving about, and grasping the bed clothes; and after a disturbed silence muttered something about his seeing fire, and then abruptly expired. On the last circumstance I laid no stress; it was probably from a sparkling of the eye, affected by the imagination or disease; nor did I publish a narrative of the event from the press or the pulpit; or attempt to make of it an imitation of Dr. Young's "Centaur not Fabulous." In many cases we know too little for explanation or decision; and it is our wisdom to "be still, and know that He is God," both as to the exercise of his mercy and justice. We are to avoid rash judgments, but it becomes us to hear and flee.

Should this solemn and true statement fall under the notice of any youth who has had godly parents, and a religious education; and not only outward advantages but serious convictions and resolutions; from all which he has turned aside,—surely here is enough to awaken his reflection and alarm, and to enforce the language of inspired wisdom and love :—"My son, if sinners entice thee, consent thou not. Enter not into the path of the wicked; and go not in the way of evil men. Avoid it, pass not by it; turn from it, and pass away. For they sleep not except they have done mischief; and their sleep is taken away unless they cause some to fall. And thou mourn at the last, when thy flesh and thy body are consumed; and say, How have I hated instruction and my heart despised reproof! and have not obeyed the voice of my teachers, nor inclined mine ear to them that instructed me! Rejoice, O young man, in thy youth; and walk in the way of thine heart, and in the sight of thine eyes; but know thou, that for all these things God will bring thee into judgment."

—— YESCOMBE, ESQ.

THE only history of this rather singular character I derived from himself; and, as far as my information goes, it principally turns upon his two conversions, the one from Protestantism to Popery, and the other from Popery to Protestantism.

Of his family I am ignorant, though I think he once mentioned that he had a brother who commanded a government packet to Lisbon. As it is a considerable time since his death, I may have mis-remarked a few trivial circumstances; but I am certain, from the impression the case made upon me at first, my repeated relation of it since, and my lengthened acquaintance with him, that the following statement is essentially correct.

He was travelling in Wales. In the neighborhood of Abergavenny he met with a Romish priest, who immediately and sedulously sought an intimacy with him. He succeeded; and they soon became familiar friends, as, though a nominal Protestant, he knew very little of the rudiments of his own profession. He was shortly, by the zeal and art of his new associate, drawn over to Popery, and fell so entirely under the control of this man, that he was prevailed upon to deliver up his Bible, (of which, alas! he had made little use,) and to live a kind of monkish life in a sort of mountain cave; and though he had often witnessed the occasional intemperance of this priest, he went weekly, and regularly, and solemnly, to confess before him for penance and pardon.

In process of time, in his complete devotedness to Popery, he thought of entering the monastery of La Trappe, the inmates of which were so renowned for denying themselves even the use of the speech which God has given us for enjoyment and profit. But, as the convert was required, as the term of his admission, that he should divest himself, in favor of the holy body, of all he had, he hesitated a little, and resolved to judge by a personal inspection. For this purpose he set out to visit the institution, and "he must needs go through" Bath. On the Thursday evening, walking by Lady Huntingdon's chapel, he heard the singing after the prayers, and went in, and continued during the whole of the sermon. The preacher was the Rev. Mr. Kemp of Swansea. I forget the text; but, in the course of his subject, he spoke against the errors of Popery, especially transubstantiation, and idolatrous worship of the Virgin Mary. His remarks so powerfully struck Mr. Yescombe, that, after the service was over, he went into the chapel house, and asked to see the minister, and said he wished much to have some conversation with him. Mr. Kemp was surrounded with friends, who were taking their leave of him, as he was setting off for London early the next morning. He therefore excused himself from a conference; but learning that the applicant's desire arose from some impression of what he had just heard, he recommended him, mentioning my name, to call upon myself. This he did on the day following. He apologized for calling by mentioning his recommendation, and stated the occasion of it in the doubt which had been raised in his mind from the sermon he had heard, avowing himself to be a Roman Catholic. If true, I was glad of such an opportunity, and lifted up my heart to God, that I might continue and complete these doubts, and make him know the truth, that the truth might make him free.

And this I have every reason to hope was the case; and after several interviews (not without prayer) he expressed with gratitude and tears his full conviction —brought me his beads and books, constantly attended my ministry, and communed with us in the dying of the Lord Jesus, spiritually and by faith eating the flesh and drinking the blood of the Son of God.

He soon now furnished himself with a Bible, and indescribable was the pleasure he found in it, after never having dared to look into it for sixteen years. How often and significantly would he say with Jeremiah, "Thy word was found, and I did eat it;" and "Thy words were to me the joy and rejoicing of my heart."

Yet he said, as he was single, and had now been so long accustomed to *solitude*, and from habit enjoyed it, he hoped he might still be allowed to live much in retirement; and this he did, occupying two rooms away from all interruption and intercourse; walking with God, and confessing himself a stranger and pilgrim on the earth.

He always called me "Father." I had many pleasing and profitable interviews with him, and saw him growing in grace and in the knowledge of the Lord and Saviour till he reached the end of his faith, and that end was peace.

Three inferences are derivable from this brief memoir: *First.* We see the spirit of Popery, and its fear of the Scripture. If we could separate the zeal to make proselytes from the cause, how worthy would it be of imitation!

Secondly. Let young persons when they travel be careful of the company they keep, lest they get a snare to their souls, and be led away by the error of the wicked.

Thirdly. See on what little, and, to us, casual circumstances important events hinge; and how the purposes of him are accomplished "who worketh all things after the counsel of his own will."

I bless God that, in the sixty-three years of my pastoral life, I lost no one of my flock by perversion to Romanism; while I received into my communion two converts from Popery, who walked in the truth, and "adorned the doctrine of God their Saviour in all things."

DR. THOMAS COGAN.

DR. COGAN, celebrated as a physician, author of "Views on the Rhine," and many other well-known works, was originally a Dissenting minister, educated at Homerton Academy, and officiating first at Southampton. But changing his sentiments, and abjuring his Calvinistical Creed, like an honest man he informed the church of his new convictions, and resigned his pastorate. For some time he was subsequently a preacher at the Hague, but afterwards he was led, as the condition of a matrimonial alliance, to study medicine, and practiced as a physician at Rotterdam. When the French poured into Holland, he feared, (as he had offended them by some public strictures,) and fled to this country with the Prince of Orange, Mr. Hope, the Malvers, and others.

He took a farm at Wraxal in Wiltshire, but soon found that the scientific agriculturist could not succeed so well as his plain practical neighbors. He then fixed his residence in Bath, and occupied a house of his own opposite the Reminiscent's Chapel. He had married in Holland. His wife, being an orthodox Presbyterian, communed with our church. He always attended the Unitarian Chapel; but in the evenings he was seldom absent from Argyle Chapel. When my subject was of a more general and practical nature, he was pleased and sometimes flattering; at other seasons he was silent and never seemed offended, was never censorious or severe. He allowed the liberty he assumed; but I presume he thought we were not very well off in Bath, for he said more than once that, of the two ministers he heard, one of them preached about God, as if there had been no Christ; and the other about Christ as if there had been no God; but he hoped from the pulling on each side he should be kept upright.

I sometimes found it trying to preach before such a superior man and so often; but I am perfectly conscious I never yielded to the temptation of pleasing, by altering my matter or style.

Though he passed, and wished to pass, generally as an Unitarian, he did not give that community in all things his preference or commendation. He wished they would resign reading their discourses, as less exciting and impressive; and often spoke of republishing a pamphlet, entitled—"Reading not Preaching." He complained of their disuse of the awful terms of Scripture, such as *fury*, *vengeance*, *the lake of fire and brimstone*, observing they were words employed by the only wise God himself, and were adapted to strike the careless, and arrest the thoughtless. He disliked their glossing Scripture when read or quoted, and wished the language of revelation to be always left to speak in its own unmixed simplicity. He also acknowledged that they never seemed to ascribe importance enough to the mediatorial work of the Messiah; especially to his sufferings and death, as the (in some way or other) medium of Divine forgiveness.

He had the habit of too many of his party, and

which may be deemed worse in its cause and effects than pure error itself; viz.: the speaking lightly of Divine things, and even sporting with them. Walking with him one day down Pulteney street, he said, "This long, even street, puts me in mind of the dull eternal Sabbath." He often joked about Satan. He kept back his attack on the agency and even existence of his infernal majesty in the last volume of his works, because he knew his more orthodox friends would never forgive him for the offence. He mentioned that, when he was in Holland, a minister put forth a pamphlet deemed by many atheistical in its tendency, yet he was not anathematized by the Synod to which he belonged; but afterwards when he published again, denying diabolical influence and existence, they immediately suspended him,—as if not caring what became of God, if they could but retain the devil. But it was not a bad thing he uttered, when in the fields I met him after a return from town, (though it was a little inconsistent with his avowed opinion,)—"When I am in London I believe in the devil, and when I am in the country I believe in God." He was a great and consistent admirer of Nature, and I believe drew more of the materials and excitements of his devotion from wood and lawn than from Bethlehem and Calvary.

He was truly generous and benevolent; as a companion he was most amiable and interesting; never obtruding or insinuating his sentiments among those who differed from him. Like other great men, he was not so ready with his tongue as with his pen, or so definite and lucid in his speech as in his writings. Nothing indeed can surpass the crystal clearness apparent in his works, for which see his "Treatise on the Analysis and Influence of the Passions;" his "Theological Disquisition on the Characteristic Excellences of Christianity."

The following is rather a curious circumstance. One evening at Argyle Chapel, he sat in the same pew, and close by the side of Mr. Wilberforce. After the service Mr. Wilberforce, coming into the vestry, asked me who that very agreeable-looking man was, who sat at his left hand. "Sir," said I, "that gentleman is your opponent who has just published an answer to the chapter in your work on Hereditary Depravity." "Indeed!" said he, "had I known it I would have shaken hands with him, for he is a fair and able disputant." Two days after this, dining at his house with Mr. Toller, of Kettering, (who was his guest,) Dr. Cogan soon asked,—"Who was that odd and very movable gentleman, who sat last evening at my right hand?"—"What, sir, did you not know that that was Mr. Wilberforce?"—"Was *that* Wilberforce! I should much have liked to have been introduced to him; for though I have written against his sentiments, no one can admire his character more, as one of the best of men, and one of the greatest philanthropists;"—and went on justly eulogizing him.

Not being inclined or qualified for controversy, I never entered into dispute with him, but I sometimes dropped a few words from experience or observation, to which he listened, and which seemed to strike him, especially when I spoke of persons who had recently died in confidence, peace, and comfort, commending and recommending those truths which they said were all their salvation and all their desire. And when I mentioned what I had lately met with, viz.: a female, young and beautiful, agreeably espoused, with two lovely babes, with everything that could render life desirable, dying of a consumption, (which destroys so many of our roses and lilies,) and when reduced by the lingering disease almost to a shadow, she asked an attendant to hand her the looking-glass,—after glancing at which she returned it, saying with a smile—

"Then while ye hear my heart-strings break,
How sweet my moments roll!
A mortal paleness in my cheek,
But glory in my soul!"

and soon expired,—he could not avoid weeping.

When also I sometimes mentioned instances (and, blessed be God, I could mention such instances under my own preaching) of persons converted from a sinful course to a life of morality and holiness; and where the change has not been produced by practice, but the practice has been the effect of the change; and sin has not only been left but loathed; and duty has not only been performed but delighted in; his pause and manner have seemed to say, "Why, *we* hear and see nothing of this!"

He went to see his learned brother, the Rev. Edward Cogan, (whose name so often appears as a contributor in the "Gentleman's Magazine,") and who was the pastor of the Presbyterian church at Walthamstow. Before his return he died. I know not the manner or circumstances of his departure; but have been informed only, that he ordered his tombstone to be inscribed with these words: "I am the resurrection and the life: he that believeth in me, though he were dead, yet shall he live; and he that liveth and believeth in me shall never die. Believest thou this?"

I cannot help observing, that while Dr. Cogan was in Holland, from the existence and usefulness of the Humane Society there, he recommended the institution of it in this country to his friend Dr. W. Hawes of London, an elder of Dr. Rees' church. In consequence of which, that gentleman had the honor of establishing a similar Society here, by means of which so many lives have been restored and given back to their agonizing connexions.

Shall I remark—when Dr. Hawes called upon the Reminiscent to engage him to preach for the Society, our discourse naturally turned upon the subject of suicide; and he expressed it as his opinion that self-murder *commonly* sprung, not from *infidelity* or *insanity*, but from some *impression* intolerable for the moment, but which might have been diverted or dissipated by some timely change of company, place, or action; and the event been prevented. And who has not felt a temporary gloomy depression, which, had it been increased tenfold, or fivefold, (and it might have been easily so increased,) but might have sought relief by any means within reach?

He also remarked, contrary to a common opinion, that those who once attempt self-destruction, repeat the attempt, and commonly succeed at last; but that *they* had found comparatively few of those they had happily resuscitated chargeable with the repetition of the offence.

I remember Dr. Cogan saying, he was once, when abroad, walking with a young Portuguese lady, and saw at a distance a fire surrounded with a number of persons; and when he was disposed to notice it, she pulled him on, saying, "O, I suppose it is only the burning of a Jew." "Yet," said he, "she was not wanting in humanity, yea, she was even tender and benevolent." But see the effect of persecution, education, and custom!

REV. BENJAMIN DAVIS, D. D.,

WAS originally tutor of the Dissenting Academy at Oswestry, where he had for one of his students Dr. Edward Williams, afterwards president of Rotherham College, and a writer of no little celebrity, especially in the Baptismal and Calvinistic controversies.

I was anxious to learn from him, whether this pupil of his, when under his care, had anything peculiar or superior about him, indicative of his future eminence. "Nothing," he said, "but more of a solitary disposition, a greater addiction to study, and a special seriousness of reflection."

Do constitutional propensities, or accidental circumstances, lead men into those departments of action and science in which they have mostly figured? In many instances, perhaps, this cannot be decided; in some, it is obvious, both unite and co-operate.

I remember eagerly perusing Dr. Williams' famous work on "Divine Equity and Sovereignty," but I found little satisfaction in reading it: perhaps I did not thoroughly comprehend it. I certainly did not feel, in consequence of it, more disposed for such investigations than before; and I had always had a full persuasion that there are depths in which the mind is swallowed up; and that Young's advice is wisdom here,—

> "Wait the great teacher, Death,
> And God adore!"

Did not Bacon say, "I am no metaphysician, for I am not an owl, I cannot see in the dark!" Do not some good men impose upon themselves and others? They feel and express great confidence and certainty as to the result of their own perceptions and discussions; but—

First: Are they not governed by terms and phrases of their own, hallowed and significant as to those who use them; but as to others, are they not words without knowledge, and which darken counsel rather than enlighten it? For what are they when they come to be explained? Or what satisfactory explanation are they capable of receiving?

Secondly: They imagine they have solved difficulties when they have only shifted them. They push them into holes and corners, but after awhile they are met with again by accidental approach, or revived research, to the awakening of their doubts, but seldom to the acknowledging of their mistakes.

Would it not be better for us to seize and improve the inviting and glorious truths of revelation, which are so plain and important, (and of which there are so many,) the experience of which we find useful to ourselves, and the communication of which we know to be useful to others? "The secret things belong unto the Lord our God; but those things that are revealed are for us and for our children."

And what a difference must a Christian and a minister feel, between the trammels of some systems of divinity and the advantage of Scripture freedom, the glorious liberty of the sons of God! The one is the horse standing in the street, in harness, feeding indeed, but on the contents of a bag tossed up and down; the other, the same animal in a large fine meadow, where he lies down in green pastures, and feeds beside the still waters.

But I remember hearing Mr. Owen (the Secretary to the Bible Society) say, after a long interview and discussion with Dr. Williams, that he never met with a systematic, who seemed to have so clear a view, and so ready a command of his system.

To return. Dr. Davis was afterwards, for some years, Theological Tutor of Homerton Academy; concerning which he often complained of the difficulties and trials of the situation and office, especially as they arose from the insubordination and manners of the young men, and which frequently induced him to exclaim, "Ye are too strong for me, ye men of Zeruiah."

He was also pastor of the church in Fetter Lane; but he was compelled to resign his public and pastoral labors, owing to an extraordinary pain in his head. After (in a remarkable manner) being relieved from this, he resided for a time at Reading, and preached often there. He then resided with his niece, who had married the Independent minister of Wells. There too he often preached, and was very useful. Lastly he came to Bath, and became a member of my church. Here he married again, and resided to the end of life.

He occasionally preached for me, and always with much acceptance; and it is remarkable that, though for many years he had always read his discourses, he latterly laid his notes aside; and never, as it might have been supposed, felt embarrassment. His preaching was of a more evangelical and experimental and simple order than that of some of his contemporaries in London; and he was one of the few of his stiffer, drier brethren who openly countenanced and commended Whitfield and his assistants.

He was a man of very considerable learning, of great theological knowledge, and of pre-eminent piety and spirituality.

I derived much benefit from him (I might have derived more) as a hearer, a companion, an admonisher, and an example.

He published but little. I had some of his manuscript sermons, and also his course of Theological Lectures, (exceedingly clear and good,) and a Treatise on Human Depravity and Regeneration; all of which are now in the possession of my grandson, the Rev. Cornelius Winter Bolton, a clergyman in the United States.

His reading towards the last was almost entirely of one kind; and his favorite authors were Leighton, Baxter, and Newton: Newton's Letters in particular he delighted to reperuse, for he observed, what an advantage he derived, (owing to the declension of his memory,) as the same works seemed again new to him.

When I informed him of the death of his distinguished pupil, Dr. Williams, he burst into a flood of tears, and said, "I am almost ashamed to be alive, and eighty years old, when so many good and great and useful men are taken away in the midst of their days."

He still lived considerably beyond this period, dying in a good old age, and gathered in like a shock of corn fully ripe in his season. His end was peace, but partaking more of trust than triumph. And I like best such modes of dying experience. Few can expect ecstasy and rapture, but many may die saying, "Let me not be ashamed of my hope;"—

"A guilty, weak, and helpless worm,
On thy kind arms I fall;
Be thou my strength and righteousness,
My Jesus and my all!"

REV. THOMAS HAWEIS, M.D.

DR. HAWEIS, in various respects, was a character well known in the religious world. He was for a time contemporary with the founders of Methodism, though he was not a student at Oxford till Wesley and Whitfield had left that University. I have heard him mention that, during his residence at the College, he sometimes went over on the Sabbath to Weston-Favel, to hear the celebrated James Hervey; and observing (what I had heard also especially from Mr. Newton and others, viz.) the dull aspect of his congregation, and the difference there was between the liveliness of his writings, and the unimpressiveness of his preaching. This rather strange result may excite wonder; but it furnishes matter for a twofold remark.

First:—How divided and individual, endowments and excellences are! and,

Secondly:—How the sovereignty of God appears, not only in his choice of instruments, but the way and work in which he employs them! And herein the Lord does not often conform to the judgment, or gratify the wishes of his servants themselves. They prefer a particular place or line of operation; but they find themselves unexpectedly in other situations and engagements; and though the providence may be trying at first, after awhile grace produces acquiescence, and enables the man to be thankful if in *any* mode or degree he is honored to be useful.

I enter not into the case of Dr. Haweis' obtaining the Living of Aldwinkle; concerning which there was a great difference of opinion, and several pamphlets published. The late Dr. Bridges and my father-in-law, the Rev. Edward Davies, also a beneficed clergyman, always defended him; and this was probably the case with others. I understood from Mr. Winter that Mr. Whitfield indeed much wished him to resign the living; and Lady Huntingdon advanced a very considerable sum to satisfy or silence the complainant. I have more than once heard the Doctor say, that he offered to do anything for the complainant, if he would accept it as a *distressed* man, and not as an *injured* man; but as he demanded remuneration as a *right*, he could do nothing without condemning himself.

The Doctor himself always avowed that the living was put into his hands after he had clearly and fully and repeatedly stated the only way in which he ought and only could consent to receive it, without an act of simony. But it made an impression generally against him; especially among those who judge not according to the rectitude of the case, but the usages of church-jobbing. Some, not wanting in impartiality, asked, Was it the avoiding the (perhaps) appearance of evil? and, Was it lovely and of good report?

The Doctor may, perhaps, be considered the first man in the South Sea Mission. Some years before the London Missionary Society was established, from the accounts published by Captain Bligh and some other navigators, HE was induced to choose, and bear the expense of preparing, two young men to go as missionaries to Otaheite, but who, as soon as they were educated, ignobly and deceitfully preferred staying at home. This exceedingly disappointed and distressed him; but he now drew off his attention and desire from the project and the place. When, therefore, this great and successful institution was formed, he rejoiced, and early attached himself to it. He preached the first sermon, at the first meeting at Spa Fields Chapel, on its behalf; and as the Directors and Managers were at a loss where to begin, he naturally and promptly directed their view to scenes of labor which had become familiar to his mind by much thinking and some effort and expense. And these were Otaheite and Tongataboo, the most central and advantageous stations for communication and extension.

As an author, he published a volume of sermons and several single discourses, with some essays and tracts. But his principal works were an Exposition of the whole Bible, in three volumes folio; and a Church History, in three volumes octavo. The former of these has often been supposed to be an abridgment of Henry, but it was not so designed, and is in reality a Commentary of his own, possessing no little value. The latter has been considered as a very hasty and superficial performance; but it has the recommendation of always nobly and simply looking after real and vital Christianity; and of frequently finding it and showing it where lying ecclesiastics have overlooked it, or anathematized it. It always breathes a most liberal spirit towards his brethren among the Dissenters and Methodists. He animadverts freely and judiciously with regard to Constantine, and the consequences of his conversion to the Christian Church, while his arguments against Milner, with regard to penal enactments in an Establishment, are unanswerable.

He had a peculiar confidence in himself, and a readiness of address which never failed him. But this rather injured him as a preacher, (and where has not this envied talent injured the owner?) so that leaning on his facility, he neglected retirement and study; and commonly had company on the evenings of his preaching, from which he seldom withdrew, till the clerk arriving with the robes and three-bushel wig reminded him the time was up. Hence, though able to do so much better, his sermons not only wanted method and consecutiveness, but were commonplace and unctionless.

It is a bad thing when a man has acquired the knack of preaching, and can talk on for an hour in the pulpit without effort and without effect. In proportion as the truths and doctrines we preach are well known and familiar, so much the more necessary is it to retire and meditate them much, that our own minds may he affected by them, and that we may render them impressive and interesting to those that hear us.

It is well for a young minister to feel difficulties; and if these induce him to retirement, study, and prayer, he will in time surpass, at least in efficiency and usefulness, many who proudly towered above him at the beginning. This is one of the cases in which the first shall be last, and the last shall be first. To whom was the admonition addressed,—"Meditate upon these things, give thyself wholly to them, that thy profiting may appear unto all"? Yet young men, who are not

Timothys, talk of the time when they finished their studies!

As before the Gospel was preached in the churches in Bath, Lady Huntingdon's chapel was a place of fashionable resort, and as many careless creatures attended, especially on the Lord's-day evenings, the Doctor's style of address was too invariably terrific; and derived from such texts as these: "It is a fearful thing to fall into the hands of the living God;" "Who among us can dwell with everlasting burnings?" "Depart, ye cursed," &c. But was this the more excellent way? Is there not danger that such tremendous expressions will lose their force by constant repetition? Is such horrifying declamation preaching the Gospel, and bringing good tidings of great joy? It would be well to endeavor to ascertain what is the legitimate employment of terror in an evangelical ministry. The use of it should not be a preacher's *pleasure*, but *pain;* and, as an old writer says, "he should always utter a Divine threatening as a judge would pronounce sentence of death upon his son." Our subject is "the faithful saying and worthy of all acceptation, that Jesus Christ came into the world to save sinners;" and the value of terror only is as an auxiliary or motive to enforce the reception of our message of pardon and peace. So the apostles employed it: "Knowing the terror of the Lord, we persuade men" to accept the mercy and grace we hold forth. He hath "committed to us the ministry of *reconciliation.* Now then we are ambassadors for Christ, as though God did beseech you by us, we pray you in Christ's stead, be ye reconciled to God."

The Doctor's manner also was high, and not sufficiently courteous to the common people. Hence, after preaching long in Bath, the dissatisfied congregation induced him to decline his ministry among them, and also his attendance at the chapel. From this time he constantly worshipped with us, till his death. I attended him in his last illness, if it deserved the name, for, as he had no fears, so he had no pains, so entirely was his end peace.

One thing he desired, and it was in character with his love of the missionary enterprise. On the very day of his death, one of the first class of missionaries to Otaheite was expected in Bath. It is hardly possible to express the earnestness with which he wished to see him before he breathed his last. He sent again and again to my house, begging that if he called upon me first I would instantly bring him to his dying bed. He came—he called upon me; and, without asking him to sit down, I hurried and introduced him. We found Dr. Haweis, like the expiring Simeon, saying, with tears, "Now, Lord, lettest thou thy servant depart in peace."

He left a large diary, which would have thrown much light on the earlier periods and events of the revival of religion in our own country; but the son, a clergyman, very opposite to his father's views, prevented the use which I wished to have made of it.

By the way, how was it when Evangelism was so persecuted in the nation, and our bishops were so averse to its doctrines, that so many of the obnoxious clergy were suffered to act so irregularly as to preach for weeks and months together in places unconsecrated and unlicensed, retaining their livings; which was the case with Berridge, Venn, Penticross, Glascot, Haweis?

Dr. Haweis, speaking one day of Whitfield's wonderful voice, and of its force as well as sweetness and variety of tone, said, he believed on a serene evening it might be distinctly heard for very near a mile. Was this possible?

PART IV.

SELECTIONS FROM THE CORRESPONDENCE

OF THE

REV. WILLIAM JAY.

SELECTIONS FROM CORRESPONDENCE.

Mr. Jay to Miss Davies, afterwards Mrs. Jay.

My dearest Love,—I always used to have a disinclination to preach at Bath, but I now think it long to Sunday week. You know the reason. May we have a happy and sanctified interview! I find the longer I stay here the more I like the situation, and the harder it will be to dissolve the connection. But I wish to live having my conversation in heaven, and then every place will be in some measure indifferent. Yes, my love, let us determine to live as strangers and pilgrims here, and plainly declare by our profession and conduct that we seek a better country, that is a heavenly. Not when we shall be incapable of pursuing this world, and when our gust for early pleasure shall be abated by old age; but now, while our affections are so warm, and when so many are carried away by the vanity of the world and the pride of life, let us unreservedly dedicate ourselves to God, and present ourselves as a living sacrifice, holy and acceptable to God, which is our reasonable service. Nothing but real religion can make us holy and happy in any situation or relation. In proportion as it prevails we shall find heaven begun below. If you should come to Bath Saturday, should be glad. Let us, if possible, visit Prior one day. Best respects to Mr. and Mrs. D., to Mrs. Hall, if yet with you, and Miss Isabella. The Lord bless you and help you, and

Yours, most affectionately,

W. JAY.

CLIFTON, Feb. 2, 1789.

If you write, should be glad to know how dear Mr. Tuppen is, and whether I may apprise Prior of our coming.

Rev. Cornelius Winter to Mr. Jay

PANSWICK, Jan. 22, 1790.

MY VERY DEAR BILLY,—It is enough to have a pretext of necessity to write to you, and my pen moves freely; you have awakened all my tender sensations by your late visit, and given me occasion to prove that I cannot say to you as a great man once said to me at the close of a family connection—"I cast you off, now sink or swim." No, my dear friend, to carry on the idea, I believe if you were to sink, I should attempt to dive for you; but blessed be God you swim: may you always keep your head above water, till you set your feet on the shore of that wealthy place where you shall find an everlasting abode. I hope you got safe and comfortable to Hope Chapel on Saturday, and found all well. Take proper care of your health, and employ it for Him who hath loved you and given himself for you.

I have employed some thought about Paul and Saul, and find Beza and Dr. Doddridge very candid. Doddridge adopts Beza's criticism on Acts 13, 9. * * * * * While writing this yours came to hand, and is a conviction to me of our attachment being mutual. Friendship well grounded cannot be easily alienated. Through various interruptions I have been prevented from proceeding with my letter from the day I received yours till now. To be sure the sermon is in the press, and the advertisement which precedes it not to be altered or improved.

I wish it may not appear too consequential, if not trifling. I repent that I have not spoken of you by an epithet expressive of the affection of my heart, for the world should know that you are dear to me. There is a delicacy in the use of terms, and they sometimes excite envy. My desire is that, in us, Cicero's remark on Friends may be exemplified: "Absentes adsunt, et egentes abundant, et imbecilles valent, et quod difficilius dictu est, mortui vivunt."

Yesterday se'n-night Mr. Surman gave a call and preached a sermon to us. I declare I was surprised to hear him, and wonder not that he was invited to Plymouth. What cannot the Lord do? May He condescend to give me a further proof of his power in my present family. They all unite in love to you with myself and Mrs. Winter. Mr. Griffin is under inoculation, and I trust will be brought abroad again. Recollect the hint I gave you about your parents, and when you write to or see them, give my love to them. I have a disposition to fill up the sheet, but I cannot. I therefore only add, come and see us when you can, and thereby add to the pleasure of my, very dear Billy,

Ever yours affectionately in our dear Lord Jesus,

CORNELIUS WINTER.

I saw Mr. Ashburn the morning you left me, who dropped a hint expressive of his approbation of what he heard the night before.

Mr. Jay to Mr. Withers.

LONDON, 1793.

MY DEAR FRIEND,—Having a leisure half-hour, I said to myself I'll embrace this opportunity to write to Mr. Withers. No sooner said than done, or at least begun. I thank you for your letter, but not for your apologies, as to your manner of writing, &c., &c. These I put amongst Mrs. Withers' kind ceremonies and cares when I am at your house. They are all bad things belonging to good persons; otherwise I should be more severe with them. You may depend upon it that I shall be always glad to see you and hear from you, but you must treat me with less compliment. I do not desire it, and I know I do not deserve it. I must be under strange infatuation indeed to think highly of myself. I have much to humble me. I am every thing that 's bad. "In me dwelleth no good thing." Whatever distinguishes me from others is the undeserved gift of God; and if, in any degree, I am useful to my fellow creatures, 'tis "not I, but the grace of God which is with me."

What fine weather we have had for the ingathering

of the fruits of the earth. How has our blessed God crowned the year with his goodness, and how lamentable is it that our world, so full of his mercy, should be so empty of his praise! Our fears were awakened, but they have been more than disappointed, and may we not hope that the same God will crown plenty with peace. Though the prospect is not favorable, all things are possible to Him. All creatures are under his control. The hearts of kings are in his hands. This is all the comfort I have as to present affairs.

I had a blessed time last Sabbath-day morning in preaching from these words: "Casting all your care upon him; for he careth for you," 1 Peter, 5, 7. I could not help wishing that a certain friend of mine who resides under your roof had been with us. Well, if Providence spares us to meet again, she may probably hear it second hand. Mrs. Jay unites with me in kind respects to her; thanking you all for your very great kindness towards our dear boy, to whom, through you, we transmit a few kisses, and a promise not only of a horse but a whip too. We have spent half of our visit here, and shall be glad, after four more Sabbaths, to return *home*. O why do I not long equally to leave this bustling world to go to my heavenly and everlasting *home*? Why do I not long to depart to be with Christ, which is far better? I have sometimes such views of this world and the next, that, if they were realized in experience, I think I should be in some measure what I ought to be, but alas, I have much more religion in my head than in my heart; and, with all my fine notions, I feel myself prone to cleave to the dust, and to neglect my Saviour. But my paper reminds me of the propriety of drawing to a close. Has Hymen yoked Mr. James yet? Tell him he must inform me if he expect anything like an Epithalamium. I love both of them, and hope God will bless them. I know he will if my prayers are answered. I have not seen your daughter since I wrote last. Desire her, when you write to her, to call upon us again, and as often as she pleases. We know not where to direct for her. You see I sometimes write to yourself, and sometimes to Mrs. Withers, but I always mean both. You are, I trust, not only one in the common sense of the term, but one in Christ Jesus. May your union, begun upon earth, continue in heaven.—I am, dear Sir, Yours, &c.

Mr. Jay to Mrs. Jay.

My dearest Love,—Last night I preached for the Sunday morning Lecture, and in honor of the accession of this family to the throne. Dr. Hunter prayed. The congregation was large; and just as I was concluding the sermon there was a general consternation and outcry. All was confusion—and people treading on one another, &c. It was rather dark, and the pulpit candles only were lighted. I saw something moving up the aisle towards the vestry. It was a bull! we presume driven in by pick-pockets, or persons who wished to disturb us. We were talking on the affairs of the nation, and John Bull very seasonably came in. But imagine what followed:—the bull could not be made to go backwards, nor could he be turned round: five or six persons, therefore, held him by the horns;

while the clerk, as if bewitched, gave out, in order to appease the noise,—

> "Praise God, from whom *all* blessings flow,
> Praise him *all creatures* here below," etc.

O that the bull could but have roared here in compliance with the exhortation! I looked down from the pulpit, and seeing the gentlemen who held him singing with their faces lifted up, as if returning thanks for this unexpected blessing, I was obliged to put my hand before my face while I dismissed the congregation. This I think is enough for once. I long to receive a line from you to tell me all your plans. Love to the dear children.

Yours, &c.

The same to the same.

My dearest Love,—You may imagine that I am always full of matter, but I assure you I have been sitting a considerable time with my pen in hand not knowing what to say. Love indeed would dictate a thousand fond things, but I am not certain that they would be most acceptable; and I hope they are not necessary. I would love, not in word only. I wish to make my whole conduct a proof of my affection and esteeem. Tuesday evening I preached upon family religion, and as an inference from the importance of it, I exhorted young people to beware how they formed connections:—"How can two walk together except they be agreed?" Here I hope we are agreed, and I trust we shall always "walk together as heirs of the grace of eternal life, that our prayers be not hindered." But I have been thinking that, notwithstanding there is no disagreement between us, in our sentiments and dispositions respecting religious exercises in the family, as is the case with many, we may be more useful to each other in our relation than we have been; and watch over, pray for, rebuke, exhort, teach, and comfort each other more than we have done. I know not indeed why I should class you with myself herein. But I am conscious of deficiency. I am to blame;—nor in this instance only. I seem all wrong. I have not half religion enough in my own soul to make me useful to others or happy in myself: I frequently doubt the truths I preach to others. I frequently fear lest, having been useful to save others, I myself should be a castaway: the conviction of my judgment goes far beyond the experience of my heart. You cannot conceive in what an inferior light all sublunary objects frequently appear to me; and still I am looking to and depending upon creatures. I might enlarge. In the midst of all this there is some relief. O 'tis well to have light enough to see our darkness, and softness enough to feel our hardness; 'tis well that Jesus Christ saves sinners; that unworthiness is no bar; and that he provides *strong consolation for those who have fled for refuge.* O examine this character of the righteous; when, O my soul, thou canst not derive comfort from any other, '*Hast thou not fled for refuge?*'

* * * * *

Yours, &c.

ON THE DEATH OF TWO CHILDREN.

To Mr. Newall, who was for upwards of fifty years a member of Mr. Jay's Church, and for many years deacon and treasurer.

Dated about September, 1805.

MY DEAR FRIEND,—By a letter Mrs. Jay has this morning received from Mrs. Lockyer, I am informed of the very severe trial with which the Lord has been exercising you. Had I been at home I would have hastened to comfort you at your dwelling, and have mingled my tears with yours at the mouth of the grave, under the loss of two dear children,—lovely children, removed almost at a stroke! But I hope that though a poor worm has been absent, He has been present, who has promised to be with us in trouble, whose property it is to comfort them that are cast down; and who while he *chastens* can *teach* us out of his law. Intervening objects are often removed that He may be seen, and even death commands silence that He may be heard. And the *blessed* sufferer, the *sanctified* sufferer, is the *humble supplicant*, who wipes his eyes and says,—"Speak, Lord, for thy servant heareth." "Lord, what wilt thou have me to do?" In our judgments we readily acknowledge His right to us and ours; but when he comes to take his own, how hard do we find it to say practically, "The will of the Lord be done." But I am persuaded this is your disposition—this has been your prayer; this will be your experience. He who knows our frame *means* us to feel. He who designs our profit by our pain, *requires* us to feel. But he expects that we should qualify and regulate the feelings of the creature by the grace of the Christian. And why? Because he has provided for all our wants, knows that His grace is sufficient for us, and that if we ask, we *shall* have. My prayers shall attend you through all this gloomy scene, and if they are answered you will never be afraid of trouble again. You will soon perceive reason to say,—"It is good for me that I have been afflicted." In the multitude of your thoughts within you, *His comforts* will delight your souls. You will be enabled to say,—"Well, my darling infants are not lost, but provided for. The shepherd has gathered my lambs with His arms, and now carries them in His bosom. I shall find them again in yonder happy world. I shall embrace them all perfect and immortal."

> "Our journey is a thorny maze,
> But we march upwards still,
> Forget the troubles of the ways,
> And rest at Zion's hill."

I cannot do justice to your affliction or my own feelings; but I have snatched a few moments from company and engagements, to show you that I sympathize with you, and am, my dear Friend, yours to serve in the Gospel of our dear Lord Jesus,

WILLIAM JAY.

To his daughter Statira when very young, and while he was absent in London.

[We give the following as a beautiful specimen both of his condescension to the capacity of a child, and of the tender and pious affection with which he watched over his children.]

My very dear Statira,—I assure you I intended writing when I left home, and before I knew you had desired your mamma to ask me to do it, but I was much pleased to learn that you wished it. It shows that you value my notice, and proofs of this notice you shall never want, while you continue to act as you have done. * * * Oh, if children did but consider the satisfaction they give their parents by being good, they would never be naughty. But their good conduct is not only attended with pleasure to their parents, but with peace and comfort to their own minds. It gains them the approbation of all around them; yea, it pleases God, who gives us all we enjoy, and on whose favor and blessing all our happiness depends. I do not know anything so lovely as a little girl of your size when she is good-natured, and not selfish, fond of reading and improvement, obedient to her mamma, and when she loves the Scriptures, and the Sabbath, and God's house; and often prays,

> "Make me to walk in thy commands,
> 'Tis a delightful road;
> Nor let my head or heart or hands
> Offend against my God."

and such, I have a full persuasion, I shall always find my dear and last-born child. I promise myself much pleasure for years to come in endeavoring to train you up in the nurture and admonition of the Lord, and in making you an amiable and useful member of society. But you, my dear Statira, may die, or papa may die, or mamma may die, and no more feel the kisses of their darling upon their cheeks morning and evening, but be laid in the cold grave; yea, we must all die, and so part sooner or later; and, therefore, we must so live here as not to be parted hereafter, but indulge the pleasing hope of living together forever in heaven.

I hope you feel much obliged to Mr. Bolton for his attentions. Tell him I thank him much on your behalf, and shall be glad to repay him in any way in my power, in addition to my having given him (I hope she is) a good wife. * * * * * *

I long to see Percy Place again, and one of the principal reasons is to see and embrace again my dear Statira, and to prove by more than a hasty and imperfect letter, that

I am, my darling girl, your affectionate and devoted father,

WM. JAY.

LONDON, October 30, 1812.

To the same.

MY DEAR SWEET PEA,—How I long for the time when I shall see thy image and thyself once more in my garden! But "to everything there is a season;" and we must learn to deny ourselves and wait. Neither should I object to view some other flowers in my little Eden, or even one or two birds. O when will that spring or summer arrive? But I must not sin against the rule I have just laid down; and, therefore, instead of giving way to impatience, I will try to write on. I hope you will find this journey useful and improving. It is in your power to render it so by keeping your attention awake, and suffering nothing to pass unobserved. Listen to what is said by persons of any talent in company, especially when they speak upon those subjects with which they are most familiar; and they who have no general information may be well versed in their own line, and commonly talk well concerning it. I some time ago overtook a little sweep. I did not suppose he could criticise Milton nor Locke, but there was one thing he understood better than I did; and before we separated, I knew how to climb a chimney. Not that I mean to set up in this calling. I am too big, too old, and fully occupied with some other things; but I love to learn, and I meet with few but are able to teach. Search your head all over, and if you find two ears, and only one tongue, be always more ready to hear and slow to speak; and when you speak, speak with diffidence and modesty. A forward, bold, decisive tone is never agreeable in a man; in a youth it is always offensive, but in a girl it is intolerable. You know how Miss —— was disliked and neglected after her father's death, for the freedom with which, in every circle, she delivered her opinion of men and things. Always say little of characters, and let this little as much as possible be in a way of commendation. Be less disposed to remark blemishes than excellences; and let it appear that you can discern and acknowledge merit of any kind with pleasure. Gain some little addition every day to your mental stores, and remember the axiom, "To him that hath shall be given;" that is, diligence and use increase what is good, both by their natural tendency, and the Divine blessing upon our endeavors. Be fond of composition; accustom yourself to write down, with as much accuracy and clearness as you can, every interesting occurrence, or any train of thought. I wish you to have a resource of pleasure through life, not only in reading, but in writing. I am glad you go on with your French. When you come home you must teach me to pronounce and speak it. I should be glad to receive a letter from you in this language. I am sure you are able to write it, especially under the eye of Mr. Bolton. How would it surprise Bella and mamma, and sharpen their curiosity when they opened it, as they always do so greedily every letter from Liverpool. How dependent will they feel, and come and beg of me the contents! I hope you rise early and take proper exercise. I hope also you *walk* well and *sit* well; for I know a few weeks back, some considerable improvement was required in both. Some attention to each of these is the more necessary as you seem determined to be tall; and the want of gracefulness is more observed in a tall figure than in a short. Mrs. William Evill is rapidly declining, and funeral rites will early follow nuptial solemnities. At present she seems to decline seeing any one; but I hope she is becoming sensible of her condition, though this flattering disorder may well be called, "a slow sudden death," and that by-and-bye I shall have some improving intercourse with her. In the space of four days I attended no less than four funerals. I endeavored to improve them all in a sermon from 2 Corinthians, v. 1,—"For we know that if our earthly house of this tabernacle were dissolved," &c., in which I observed, we have—

1. An object contemplated—"the earthly house of this tabernacle."

2. An event supposed—the destruction of it—"if it be dissolved."

3. A privilege apprehended—"a building of God, a house not made with hands, eternal in the heavens."

4. A confidence expressed—"we know" that we have this—a confidence of belief—a confidence of hope—a confidence of possession—not we *shall* have, but we *have*, &c.

When I mentioned Mr. ——, I said, "He was unknown to many of you; but he was well known in the world of sport and dissipation. He formerly distinguished himself on the turf, and obtained a subsistence by horse-racing. But this course of life for many years back he had abandoned; and reviewed it with that godly sorrow that worketh repentance unto life, not to be repented of. The revival of early instruction from pious parents, by the death of a beloved and only son, brought him to religious reflection. He was a man of a most warm and generous disposition, and delighted to do good, especially in visiting the fatherless and the widows in their afflictions, and attending the bed of pain and sickness;" and when I added, "in the afternoon he passed my house,—in the evening ordered his nephew to read the 6th chapter of St. John,—prayed with his family,—retired comfortably to rest,—awoke at eleven,—complained of a pain in his stomach,—said, 'Come, Lord Jesus,'—and in the twinkling of an eye expired,"—there was a half-fetched involuntary groan through the audience, that made it very solemn. What I said of ——, was this:—"She was an interesting infant; a sufferer from the hour of her birth; her early and continued affliction she endured with a patience above her years, and often spoke of

God and heaven in language very unusual for one under five years of age. This is an event of congratulation rather than of condolence. At the grave of a child we always feel a peculiar satisfaction, arising from the persuasion that they are disposed of infinitely to their advantage. Under the protracted illness of this little martyr, the Saviour said to the parents—'Suffer this little child to come unto me, and forbid her not, for of such is the kingdom of heaven.' The Shepherd has gathered this lamb with his arms, and now carries it in his bosom." Of Mrs. —— I said:—"She was for many years a member of our church, and walked consistently with her profession. She was a plain, inoffensive, upright character. There was nothing distinguishing in her life, and her dying experience was the same. Through her lengthened disease, she was patient and submissive, often complained of herself, and felt alternately the prevalence of fear and hope; and I am persuaded that HE who does not 'break a bruised reed nor quench the smoking flax' has received her."

"Mr. J——," I said, "many of you were acquainted with. I see several of his companions in iniquity here this evening. O that your former associate could now address you. We have reason to hope and believe that he saw and deplored the errors of his conduct, and has obtained the mercy for which he so earnestly prayed. His language was penitential. His concern to warn and admonish others was striking, and he drew whatever relief he felt from the Friend of sinners. But O, ye bereaved neighbors, friends, and relations, my business lies not with the dead, but with the living. *They* have done with all below. Their state is now fixed, and their happiness or misery cannot be affected by your opinions or my representations, were I disposed to condemn or eulogize. They are beyond the reach of the Gospel, but you are yet in the land of the living, and have another opportunity to hear the merciful admonition—'Seek the Lord while he may be found, and call upon him while he is near.' What is your duty but to retire, and, falling upon your knees, pray with Moses, 'So teach us to number our days that we may apply our hearts unto wisdom.' And what is wisdom? What is that wise part creatures circumstanced as you are ought to act? Is it not to prefer your souls to your bodies, and the realities of eternity to the vanities of time? Is it not to seek without delay pardon and renovation? a title to heaven, and a meetness for it? You talk of happiness, uncertain as you are of life. I defy you to be happy without a hope beyond the grave. He—he only is happy who can look forward with humble confidence and say—'We know that we have a building of God, a house not made with hands,' &c."

You complain of inability to fill *your sheet.* Look at the size of my paper, and see *my* lines, not wide apart like the hedges of a London road; nor the whole begun two or three inches down from the top. But how am I to fill up the remainder of this folio? I have no other *news* to communicate, except, indeed, a subject that is always *new*, and which I hope you love, the love of Jesus—the love of Him who, though he was rich, for our sakes became poor, and died that we might live. You have often heard me repeat his encouraging assurance: "Him that cometh unto me I will in no wise cast out," and you know (O what a privilege!) that to come to him is to believe his word, and call upon his name. But while he rejects none, he peculiarly regards some. "Feed," says he, "feed my *lambs.*" "I love them that love me, and they that seek me early shall find me;" that is, find him as others never *will*, never *can.* And the case speaks for itself; for if religion can preserve us from snares and embarrassments; if it can make us amiable and useful; if it be profitable unto all things; if it yields the truest pleasure, the sooner it is possessed in the same proportion, the more are we privileged, and, next to the reality of their conversion, I am persuaded the people of God daily bless him for the *earliness* of it, if they have been thus favored; and the greater part of them are called long before they are advanced in years. O, my dear Statira, what a season is youth: of the day of life it is the morning; of the year it is the spring. And how much depends upon seizing the one, and improving the other! How desirable is it to sanctify the present in every kind of preparation for the future; and before the journey is begun, such a journey as we have before us, to secure a guide, a guard, a friend who will never leave us nor forsake us. I trust, my dear child, that you are placing yourself under his conduct, and saying—"I will go forth in the strength of the Lord."

My time of going to London is now fixed. My visit commences the last Sabbath in May, and takes in the three first in June. Either in my way thither or back, I am to preach a sermon at Newport Pagnell, in favor of Mr. Bull's Academy there; and I am also requested, at the same time, to preach before the Bedfordshire Union, at Bedford, along with Mr. Hall.

Your affectionate and devoted father, &c.

To the Same.

BATH, May 23, 1816.

MY DEAR SWEET PEA,—Though the last blown, yet not the least loved of all my flowers. I wish I had more time to write; but my preparation for the approaching journey to London leaves me very little. But the length of my last must atone for the brevity of the present; and remember you have to boast of receiving the longest letter papa ever wrote. I suppose by this time Mr. Spear and his daughters, who accompanied him to Broomsgrove, are returned, and you are probably thinking of returning to Liverpool. But you must not suffer the little nephew or niece to make you impatient. If you should feel it to be a self-denial to be absent from them, you must exercise it. This virtue is indeed of such constant and universal utility, that we cannot begin to cultivate it too soon. We cannot expect to have everything according to our mind as we pass through a world like this: it is not fit we should, and, therefore, we must learn to bear disappointment, and be able easily and gracefully to accommodate ourselves to every changing scene. Hitherto your way has been smooth, the lines have fallen to you in pleasant places; your wishes have been generally, if not invariably, gratified.

> "All without thy care and payment,
> All thy wants are well supplied."

But you cannot reckon upon a perpetual exemption from inconvenience and trial. "Truly the light is sweet, and a pleasant thing it is for the eyes to behold the sun; but if a man live many years, and rejoice in them all; yet let him remember the days of darkness; for they shall be many. All that cometh is vanity." I would not by future forebodings prevent your enjoying the kindnesses which Providence affords you at this pleasing period of life, but I know youth is sanguine, its hopes are too glaring, and require to be sobered by that prudence which results from experience and observation. You ought ever to be thankful for the comforts and indulgences of your condition. But do you not feel your need of something better? Is there not an emptiness in the midst of all? Yes, and the world will never fill it; but He can who mercifully cries—"Seek ye *me*, and ye shall live." And those dissatisfactions which attend all creature-good are the inspirations of the Almighty to give us understanding, and to make us wise unto salvation. I hope, my precious girl, that you are listening to his voice, and dedicating yourself to his service, which they who have tried know to be perfect freedom. Having given yourself unto the Lord, I trust I shall have the pleasure, after your return, to witness your "giving yourself also to his Church, by the will of God." In Dr. Doddridge's little volume of Sermons to Young People, there is a discourse on the subject of "Early Communion," which I wish you to read. I dare say Mr. Spear has it. I hope, wherever you are, that you not only devote some time to private devotion and reading the Scripture, but that you look over the books you meet with in the house where you visit, and read as much as possible of those you have not seen before. Of course I do not mean that you should shut yourself up from enjoying the prospects of nature at this season, and the society of your friends; but there are many moments to be seized which carelessness overlooks. It is by making use of these, and by early rising, that I have obtained much of the little I possess. Like the *bee*, be always extracting materials for honey. Yesterday morning, I was invited to breakfast at Mr. Hallet's, and to give the new-wedded pair my advice and blessing. But how changeable and chequered is every earthly scene! No sooner had the party returned from church, than Mr. Griffith, sen., was called out of the room to be informed that his only brother at Frome was just killed by leaping from a *sociable*, the horses of which had taken fright. This damped the joy of the season. But he was a very holy man, an occasional preacher in Mr. Wesley's connection, and at the time of the accident—so people call it, I should rather say *appointment*—he was returning from preaching in a village. He was a widower, and has left no child, but the poor will exceedingly miss him, for he was a father to them, and a fine image of Him who went about doing good.

On Saturday morning we set off for London. Miss Shepherd goes with us far as Hammersmith. We are all longing for the time when we hope, under the smiles of a gracious Providence, to "meet and mingle into bliss," to kiss, and cry tears of joy.

Your affectionate and devoted father, &c.

To his son Edward, at Wymondly College.

BATH, March 2, 1816.

*　　*　　*　　*　　*

I urge you be sparing in your remarks on character. They who hear them may report them inaccurately, and with exaggeration; and as the consequence you will, when charged with them, be tempted to deny, or perplexed to explain and qualify. But I wish to deter you by a better principle, the command of Him who has said, "Speak evil of no man." "Be swift to hear, and slow to speak." "Love every one and every one will love you." "Who is he that will harm you if you be a follower of that which is good?" While you talk little (especially concerning persons) *observe* much. Be continually adding a little to your mental stores. Accustom yourself to composition; put down your thoughts on paper with as much accuracy and clearness and celerity as you can be master of—I long for you to be able to *sermonize*. Whenever a text strikes you turn it over in your mind, and endeavor to divide it. If you cannot satisfy yourself the effort will do you good—exertion will prepare for exertion; and thought will produce thought. While you attempt much you must not be discouraged, if at first the result be little. The infant bird practices his wings, as he stands up in the nest: then gets upon the edges of it: then upon the neighboring boughs: and then takes short excursions, before he flies his more daring lengths; and "to him that hath shall be given," as the natural consequence of use and improvement, and as also the effect of the Divine blessing. You cannot begin so low as I did; but I felt a love to study bordering on enthusiasm; and despaired of nothing; not from a high opinion of my capacity, but an apprehension that diligence, with the Divine assistance, (which he had graciously disposed my heart to seek,) would do wonders. I was placed indeed in a situation peculiarly suited to the cast of my mind, and never wanted for excitations and encouragements. And you, my dear boy, have great advantages at present, and the prospect of every future help and direction. Trials you would have in any line of life; but in the sacred calling to which you are looking forward, you will be sheltered much from a stormy and wicked world; you will have opportunity for intellectual and pious improvement; you will enjoy the pleasure of being useful, and of doing good; and if you act from principle, when the chief Shepherd shall appear, you shall receive a crown of glory that fadeth not away. Let me know whether you are able to read my writing. I shall feel a pleasure in corresponding with you. Write when you have an opportunity, and write with freedom. All join in love.

Your very affectionate Father, &c.

To the same.

BATH, March 2, 1818.

I WRITE according to my promise, but I believe I must in future alter my epistolary day, and make it Tuesday instead of Monday; as of late I feel so enervated by the anxieties and labors of the Sabbath, that on the Monday I *exist* rather than live. I wish also not only to please you by a few lines monthly, but to render my letters instructive and useful; and when I feel as I do to-day I can scarcely command a thought, and every effort fatigues. I believe, should my days be prolonged, that I shall be a very premature old man. I began early. I was emulous to advance. I labored under a thousand disadvantages from which you are free; and being, from the first, thrown into popular and trying situations which had great claims upon me, I applied myself with more unrelaxing tension of mind than my frame (never remarkably strong) could bear; and I now begin to feel peculiarly the effect of it. This I think I may say without vanity regarding myself or ill-nature towards others. This is not the common failing of the students and younger ministers of the present day. I wish to perceive in them a habit of greater application and diligence, a greater sense of the value of time, and the importance of their work—as also more of an humble and devotional spirit. I can make allowance for some things in young ministers which I could not tolerate in older: but still, as the apostle says, "A bishop must be grave,"—a general sedateness of speech and behavior is so becoming in him, that, whatever be his talents, he will never inspire respect without it. It was to *young* Timothy Paul said, "Let no man despise thy youth;" but for his purpose, "Be thou an example of the believers, in word, in conversation, in charity, in spirit, in faith, in purity. Give attendance to reading, to exhortation, to doctrine. Neglect not the gift that is in thee. Meditate upon these things; give thyself wholly to them, that thy profiting may appear unto all. Take heed unto *thyself*, and unto thy doctrine, *continue* in them; for in doing this, thou shalt both save thyself and them that hear thee." It is a great thing in all our private and social intercourse to be cheerful without being light; and serious without being sad, or appearing sanctimonious. Some few ministers, even in earlier life, have attained this excellency. Let *them* be your models, rather than pulpit flirts and fiddles, and your story-telling parsons, whose sole ambition in company seems to be to make mirth; and who generally succeed so well, that they are not only laughed *with*, but laughed *at*. Nothing is more lovely in a student and a minister than a freedom from everything dictatorial and dogmatical in his manner of address. It becomes him rather to listen than to speak,—to inquire than to controvert. Not that he is obliged to believe everything that he hears, even from a senior, or to admit without evidence; but he must dissent with seeming reluctance, propose his doubts with modesty, and appear to distrust his own judgment rather than depreciate that of another. Speak with warmth (and let it come from the heart) as much as you can in commendation and praise of others;—but—"speak evil of no man;"—"Love all and all will love you." "Who is he that will harm you if you are a follower of that which is good?"—and though spiritual religion can never be relished by depraved minds, yet "he that in these things serveth Christ is acceptable to God and approved of men."

I have been a Sabbath at Marlborough, where the prospect is delightful. Mr. Williams of Shrewsbury (now Sir J. B. Williams) is publishing memoirs from the diary of Mrs. Savage, daughter of Philip, and sister of Mathew, Henry, for which I have written a pretty long preface at his desire, &c.

To the same.

BATH, May 9, 1819.

* * * I AM sorry for the interruption your studies will again sustain in your long absence from

Wymondley. The plan of attending lectures in London, too, does not strike me as of much importance; as however it is appointed, and seems a privilege shown a few of you for good conduct, you must avail yourself of it; and you may turn it to advantage. It is a great recommendation to be able to *read* and *pronounce* well; but then it must appear to be natural; primness and affectation always displeases more than *simple* and *earnest vulgarity*. The great thing is to forget *one's-self*, and to speak with *seriousness* and *affectionate feeling*. Feeling is always eloquent; and if the preacher be obviously affected, and appears concerned to do good, and not to gain applause, he will always be felt, and always approved. Nothing also is more becoming, in a young minister especially, than an apparent consciousness of the importance and difficulty of his work; an *un*forwardness to engage; a diffidence and modesty; in a word, the very reverse of what we see in many of the assuming, pert, bold, fearless, self-sufficient, and self-admiring academies of the day. Keep this to yourself. I take care how I reflect upon the sprigs of divinity before others, as there is too much readiness to censure young ministers among modern hearers already; and I am thankful to see that all are not alike, and I can reprove when I do not wish to condemn. I hope tutors will be increasingly attentive to the *spirit* and *manner* of students, both in the pulpit and in the parlor. Let me beseech you, my dear son, to keep your eye upon the best models, and pray for grace to conform to them. With regard to what is exceptionable in others, keep as far from it as you can, but never talk about it. It can do no good, and may be easily ascribed (before a man's character is highly established) to ill-nature or envy; and one of the worst features of many of the students and young preachers of the day, is an unbounded license in speaking of others, especially their brethren. Speak evil therefore of no one, but let the law of innocence and kindness dwell upon your tongue. But to mark the improprieties of others for your own improvement—that is, in order to avoid them—this is a different thing; and while you keep your mouth shut, you must keep your eyes and ears open.

* * * * *

Your devoted father, &c.

To Sir J. B. Williams.

On the very sudden death of John Lee, Esq., the Gentleman to whom several of Mr. Winter's Letters, introduced into Mr. Jay's Life of Winter, were addressed.

BATH, October 9th, 1818.

MY DEAR SIR,—You will doubtless wonder that I have not noticed your very affecting letter earlier; but I was from home when it arrived, and I have been again from home on pressing business; and while having more to do than usual I have been very unwell, first in my head, and then in my bowels, so that I have dragged on heavily and been fit for nothing. But be assured your communication was not received without producing that interest which a sincere and warm friendship requires. I wept with those that weep, and I prayed with those that pray. Tell the bereaved family how much I sympathize with them, and what a persuasion I have that the God of my departed friend will be "the Father of the fatherless, and the husband of the widow in his holy habitation," and in their own. How surprising was the event! How well he seemed when I shook hands with him, alas! for the last time, at the coach-door! I knew the year before he sometimes complained, but was not aware that the least danger of such an issue was attached to the complaint. Well, nothing has occurred by chance; a sparrow falls not to the ground without our heavenly Father, and the very hairs of our head are all numbered. And be it remembered ever, that while He does all things, he does all things well. His dispensations are not only sovereign, but wise, righteous, and kind—kind even when they seem to be severe. We may be unable to explain them at present; but "we know that the Messias cometh, which is called Christ, and when he is come he will tell us all things." Till then, let us walk by faith, and give him a full credit for the goodness of his designs, and the manner in which they are accomplished. This is the way—the only way—to reach rest in a world like this. "Thou wilt keep him in perfect peace whose mind is stayed upon thee, because he trusteth in thee." Though we must not dictate, but leave it to God to determine by what death we shall glorify him, such a dismission as our lovely friend was favored with has always appeared to me very enviable. The partings,

> "The pains, the groans, the dying strife
> Fright our approaching souls away," &c.

Here all this was prevented; and we can say over his grave,

"A soul prepared needs no delays,
The summons comes, the saint obeys,
Swift was his flight and short the road,
He closed his eyes, and woke with God."

I felt, too, for the shock your good wife must have felt in her delicate situation; and hope she is now disburdened, and has forgotten her anguish for joy that a man is born into this world. Remember me to her; and to all the dear afflicted house, where I was so cordially entertained. I do bear, and I will bear them all upon my mind at the throne of grace—that refuge, that resource of benevolence and friendship. I had three funeral services to perform last week only. What a dying world!

Yours to esteem and serve, &c.

To Miss Harman.

LYMOUTH, August 11, 1830.

MY DEAR MISS HARMAN,—Your very acceptable parcel arrived just before we set off from Bath. I am much obliged by both the works, but you should not have had them bound so expensively. Baxter's "Life" we took with us, with some other mental and spiritual provender; but when we got out of the coach at Bridgewater, we left the parcel in the boat, and as there was no direction upon it, we did not recover it till two days ago. Though generally acquainted with Baxter and his works, I find much that is new and interesting in the "Life," for you must know I have nearly devoured it already, and even the charms of this God-made spot could not draw me off from the perusal. Your lamented friend and pastor* has, I think, done much justice to this extraordinary man; to his *character*, and to his *publications*—to the excellences and infirmities of the one, and the orthodoxy and errors of the other; and I hope the book will be largely circulated. Henry says it is impossible to read the book of Psalms and not be inflamed or ashamed by the perusal. I say the same of this work. But I fear I shall be more shamed than fired. What piety! what diligence! what sufferings! what patience and submission! Well, by the grace of God he was what he was; and the God of all grace remains the same, and is within our reach in all that we call upon him for.

Instead of growing tired of this Swiss village, we admire it more than ever. Mr. and Mrs. Kingsbury have been here four days with us; and though they have travelled much over our country, they prefer this to everything they have seen. They occupied the room *you* would have slept in, could I have had power enough to overcome your good father's objections. Give my kindest love to him notwithstanding, for we are bound to *forgive;* nor forget your dear mother, who, I believe, pleaded for us. We all lament your absence; and Mrs. Jay and Miss Protheroe send their most lovingest regards. I wish I could give a better account of my most dear wife; but she is very poorly, and can hardly enjoy any of the pleasures of the place. This is a sad deduction. "Full bliss is bliss Divine." The weather, too, at present is much against her. To supply your place imperfectly, a young pious lady, and an old acquaintance, Miss Browning, from Ilfra-

* Rev. W. Orme, of Camberwell.

combe, has come over to take lodgings near us, and we find others are coming. But I wish not for more. I wish to be entirely disengaged; not, however, to be idle, but to be at liberty to use my pen,—and I do use it daily, as much as comports with the design of the excursion. What a work is this in France! I trust no violence and excess will mar it; yet I could wish that the wretched family of the Bourbons was entirely excluded. I always felt a persuasion that Providence would destroy it. Much yet remains to be done in the Popish countries. Adieu, my dear Miss Harman. The Lord bless thee and keep thee.

Yours, &c.

To his son Edward.

LONDON, June, 1832.

I FULLY intended returning home to-morrow, but circumstances have determined us to go round by Henley, as Mr. Bolton is not very well. I cannot, therefore, be at home before Thursday evening; and, therefore, it will be necessary to engage some one to preach. We shall be taken up at Reading by the new company's coach. I have secured our places. Anne comes by the same coach to-morrow; let her be looked out for, and see that her parcels be safe. Your precious mother is pretty well upon the whole; but she has been too much excited, and I long to get her home. We have been much crowded. Last Friday I dined at the Lord Mayor's, and met a very agreeable and interesting company, the *lion* of which was His Highness the Rajah Rammohun Roy. You cannot imagine what a full-minded, and clever, and agreeable man he is; always more than a match for any one who disputed with him, especially the Tories—and we had several of them. As it was known that he was to hear me at Surrey Chapel last evening, we were not only full, but hundreds went away. He came in his carriage, ten minutes before six, with Dr. Henry and Archdeacon Stockport, and was conducted to a good place for seeing and hearing. His fine figure, and his rich and elegant costume, attracted every eye. He was observed to give great attention, and frequently jogged his companions without taking off his eye from the pulpit. I preached an hour and a quarter, raised above the fear of man by previous retirement. When it was over, he said, loud enough to be heard by many, "I must have this sermon, and publish it." He came into the house, with immense difficulty pressing through the crowd in the yard, all waiting to see him. The house also, in both rooms, was full. The pleasure he expressed from hearing the sermon, before all the people present, was really affecting. It so completely met with his sentiments, he said, that he hoped I would not deny him the sermon to publish himself, and circulate among his friends. I tried to decline, till delicacy would permit it no longer; and so I have committed myself, and must write it out as soon as I come back, for he is going to the Continent in a few weeks. Dr. Henry and the archdeacon were especially delighted; and when I said to the former, "Doctor, I fear you have suffered from the crowd and the heat," he replied, "Sir, I felt nothing but the sermon." You see, my dear boy, I keep back nothing from you; but I could not say all this to others. Garfit does not seem amended. I have just walked with him to the

Mansion House. The Lord Mayor could not attend yesterday, but the Lady Mayoress was present with a very splendid carriage. Kindest regards to Mrs. Burton; and kiss Margaret for me, if you do not object to it.

Your affectionate father, &c.

To the Rajah Rammohun Roy.

SIR,—I herewith transmit the manuscript of the sermon you so candidly heard, and, so unexpectedly to the preacher, wished to see and to circulate. I could not send it earlier, owing to my travelling, and the numerous engagements and interruptions I met with immediately on my return. Your Highness will observe that I had not written the sermon previously, but delivered it from short notes only; and, therefore, I should have had more difficulty in recalling the language as well as the sentiments, had not a friend furnished me with a short-hand copy. In consequence of this the discourse will be found more than *substantially* the same with what was spoken from the pulpit. In the very *trifling alterations* I have made, I did not attempt to reduce the *free and popular* mode of address I assumed, and which was so requisite in so very large and mixed a multitude of hearers. For want of this many preachers preach inefficiently, or sacrifice impression on the mass to the gratification of the few. The manner of the Great Teacher sent from God may be inferred from the reproach, which was yet an eulogium,—"the common people heard him gladly."

It is presumed that there may be some few things in

the discourse in which your Highness may not entirely coincide; but it afforded me pleasure to conclude from your request that, upon the whole, and as having some useful bearings, it has met your Highness' approbation. I commend it to the Divine influence; and, imploring the blessing of God upon your Highness, permit me to subscribe myself,

Your Highness' obliged and humble servant,

WILLIAM JAY.

BATH, June 29, 1832.

To his Son Edward.

WEYMOUTH, August 22, 1832.

I DROP you a line to say we received the basket of fruit safe and sound. * * * * So your precious mother instantly made up a nice little present for Lord and Lady W——, who were at the Royal Hotel, in their way back from Guernsey to Sidmouth, and who, hearing of us, called, and said, if I preached on the Sunday they would stay over the day. They did so; and this gave me an opportunity of several interviews. I like them both much, as far as I have conversed with them. She knows the truth, and I really believe feels the power of it; and is resisting all the fanaticism that rages in the West of England, and all around Sidmouth. He seems very amiable and promising, and is exceedingly attached to his wife. He is a thorough Whig; says he was a member for one of his father's rotten boroughs, but was bound hand and foot, and obliged to vote on the wrong side, and would not endure the farce any longer. He says he reads my

"Exercises" every day, and uses my "Prayers." They much wish to come and live in the near neighborhood of Bath. * * * * Give my best regards to our elders and friends, and let them be immediately informed of my return. They will see that I have not encroached upon their kindness, taking in part but two Sabbaths, for the other pertained to my month of privilege. But where love actuates, we do not need restraints and rules. I love home, and never preach with so much pleasure as in Argyle Chapel, where I have employed for God the flower, yea, the far larger part, of my whole life. And, blessed be His name, He has not withholden tokens of his approbation. I refer not only to my own church, but to strangers also who occasionally attend there. A lady who lives in a neighboring village called in her carriage the other morning, and said that eighteen years ago she was at Bath with her gay companions, but felt an inclination one evening to leave them and go to Argyle. I preached, she said, from—"Is not this a brand plucked out of the fire?" From that time she left the world, and has been ever since not only blessed, but a blessing. She came to hear me on Sabbath morning, and I have been to her house.

Tell Mrs. Hallet and Mr. and Mrs. Griffiths, with my kindest respects, that Mrs. Chamberlaine is to be married very soon to a gentleman, a local Wesleyan preacher at Colne. I had this from herself. Mrs. Parsons also is not without hope, though she lost her admirer here some time ago: another is coming forward with only seven children! Well done, little Cupid! All join in dearest love to all, with, &c.

To Miss Harman.

June 29, 1832.

MY DEAR MISS HARMAN,—You know how I admire that precious little text, "By love serve one another." Could it be brought into general operation, it would soon turn our wretched earth into "a garden of the Lord." I believe I know *you* have no objection to it, for we have long put it to the test. But I am never very prolix in my introductions. This, therefore, is to say that, coming to London, and returning from it, we had some coffee at Thatcham after dinner; *we* think it the best we ever drank; and Miss Fromont told us she bought it of Mr. North, near the Bridewell Hospital, Blackfriars. Will you, therefore, when you go by, call there, and purchase for us four pounds, and send it by the new company's coach? I here pledge myself to repay you—not, however, I suppose, when you come down at the end of the month, to go with us to Ilfracombe. We got home safe and well. My precious invalid was very little tired. She now, in very strange language, (for I know her meaning,) begs to be remembered to you, and says, it is very hard the *woman* won't let *him* come. Amidst many engagements and interruptions, always multiplied on returning home, I have just finished my transcript for the Rajah, and am now (it is Friday evening) preparing for the Sabbath. Preaching is trying work this weather; so you say is hearing, unless the pastor makes us lie down in green pastures, and feedeth us beside the still waters. How delightful the five points would be now treated in the jargon of the school-theology! O my charming Bible, how I love thy simplicity, and grandeur, and grace! Prov., vi. 21, 22.

One of my best members died the day after my return. She was "an old disciple," whose life was goodness and whose end was peace. With best respects to your good father and mother, I have but just time to subscribe myself,

Yours, &c.

Lord Barham to Mr. Jay.

LONDON, December 31, 1834.

MY DEAR MR. JAY,—You will be glad to hear that we arrived safely in town, though the fog was so thick on Saturday evening as we approached London, that we were in some danger of an overturn by driving up a bank. Parliament, you see, is at last dissolved. Some Tories I have seen, think that this is a very unwise measure for their own interests. They have now nothing to fall back upon, which they would have had if they had first endeavored to meet the now late Parliament. May the Lord direct the ensuing election as shall best promote the nation's good!

We were very sorry not to see you the morning we left Bath. We hope dear Mrs. Jay continues pretty well. We beg our most kind regards to her. Will you accept our little offering for the rich gratification and edification we have enjoyed from our late attendance upon your much-valued instruction? And believe me, my dear Mr. Jay,

With much respect and affection,

Your obliged friend,

BARHAM.

Mr. Jay to Lord Barham.

BATH, July 11, 1835.

MY DEAR LORD BARHAM,—I was out when your letter arrived, and I have been since engaged, even to engrossment. As your Lordship says nothing of your own, or Lady Barham's health, I hope you are both in the enjoyment of that greatest of all temporal blessings. My dear Mrs. Jay has not been so well for the last month as usual, and seems to grow weaker. Of course my trial is increased, and I live in constant alarm and anxiety. But He, whose we are and whom we serve, knows what we need, and has engaged to make our strength equal to our day.

Did your Lordship see, in the "Christian Observer" about three months ago, an extract from the "Reminiscences of Dr. Valpy" concerning Mrs. More, and the account which he says *she* gave him of her communing once in Argyle Chapel? Never was there such a tissue of misrepresentation; and, could I believe that Mrs. More had been capable of uttering it, I should never feel respect for her memory, or read her works with pleasure again. But she had a mind too good and honorable to express what, as coming from her, would have been no less than falsehood, to serve the purpose of what she hated, *bigotry*. I was urged to write to the editor, but I declined. All these things will get rectified and known in due time; and *then* some illiberals may feel a little mortification, though it is almost unreasonable to expect a thorough-paced ecclesiastic to blush.

I hardly know what to say to your Lordship's question. I have always considered high Churchism and low Popery as nearly the same; or the difference between them as the difference between the tadpole and the toad. None of our passions so readily assume the mask of rectitude and religion as *anger;* but "the wrath of man worketh not the righteousness of God." Many, I fear, "know not what manner of spirit they are of;" or forget that it is said of our Example as well as Saviour, "He shall not strive nor cry, nor cause his voice to be heard in the streets; a bruised reed shall he not break, and the smoking flax shall he not quench." If "the servant of the Lord must not strive, but be gentle towards all men," violence, and defiance, and scorn, and insult, are not the weapons of *our* warfare. "He that winneth souls is wise;"—and the best way to convert men, or at least to induce them to attend to what we advocate, is to convince them that we love them, and desire to do them good. Between ourselves, I have always thought that these Reformation Meetings would do more hurt than good; and I am persuaded they have already increased Popery, by awakening zeal and courage in its defence; and flattering its adherents (for they must feel delight in such announcements) as amazingly multiplying, and endangering Protestantism and the Church. But if the Church be in danger, it is not the Church of Christ; or He was mistaken when He said, "On this rock I will build *my* church, and the gates of hell shall not prevail against *it*." "Secret things belong to the Lord," but we must act according to his will, and do justly, and do unto others as we would have others do unto us. I cannot, therefore, but believe we have done what God approves, in "loosening every yoke and letting the oppressed go free." I was, therefore, a friend, and I am still a friend, to the Catholic Emancipation. Everything like persecution is hateful to the meek and lowly religion of the Lamb of God; as we see in his rebuke to James and John, with regard to the Samaritans who had not received him, "The Son of Man is not come to destroy men's lives, but to save them." I should be ashamed to take a liberty to think and act for myself in religion which I was unwilling to grant. Neither am I afraid of Popery—neither do I believe in its increase, but as papists increase relatively with other parts of our population, or in some few and particular places by occasional influxes of Irish. But why are not *some* individuals ashamed to let out what they believe to be a fact—"Popery increasing, amazingly increasing," without the encouragement of the State! without an Establishment! against an Establishment! and a richly-endowed Church doing nothing! Yea, retrograding and in danger of coming to naught! What! has this pure and Apostolical institution been tried so long in Ireland, and found wanting? And while we abhor Popery, we must be candid enough not to *wonder* that upwards of six millions, brought up in the religion of their forefathers, should *feel* an Establishment over them, consisting of so small a minority; for how small is it when all the other Protestant parties are deducted? Was there ever such a state of things in any other country under heaven? With regard to some of the wretched and alarming tenets of Popery, (though these are seldom war-whooped by *many* churchmen, till some movement seems to threaten the loaves and fishes,) we may ask, how would some other parties appear, if some of their former and abstracter principles were to be published among them now? Take Knox's pleading for destroying papists as idolaters; and the Church of Scotland's confession of the duty of exterminating prelacy; and Dr. Dopping's Sermon (Bishop of Meath) that no faith should be kept with papists, &c., and trumpet this at Exeter Hall, and run down those who are regarded as brethren!

Besides, if Popery is the same, the times, the state of society, and public opinion are not the same. Papists, however disposed, could not put a heretic to death, or imprison him in any country, even where it prevails. Neither will it be ever able to do it again; the power is gone forever. Look at Germany—look at Switzerland, where some cantons are popish and some protestant; and some consisting of both intermingled; and exercising alternately the same places of worship. See America. Is Popery, civilly and politically, more dreaded than any other denomination? The reason is, they are all tolerated, and none exclusively favored. How true is your Lordship's remark, that "political opinion tinges all information." But let us judge as well as we can for ourselves. Let us be zealous in doing our Lord's work while it is day; but let us do it in his own spirit. I am no croaker. I am persuaded real religion is advancing; and I know that "the knowledge of the Lord shall cover the earth," &c., "for the mouth of the Lord hath spoken it." How glad I should be to talk over many of these things with your Lordship, but I have not time to enlarge this letter.

We all unite in best regards to your much esteemed Lady Barham.

And believe me, &c.

[*Note by the Editors.*]

THE reader of this letter must not fail to observe its date, and to remember that it was written nearly twenty years ago; a circumstance which, if in the perusal he felt any surprise at the tone in which Mr. Jay speaks of Popery, will tend considerably to explain the tone used, and abate the surprise of the reader. The movements on behalf of Protestantism at that day were of a totally different character from those of our own. Had Mr. Jay been alive, and required to express his opinion on the subject of Roman Catholic claims and emancipation now, especially in view of Dr. Wiseman's elevation to the Cardinalate, and the creation of an ecclesiastical hierarchy, based on, and designed to enforce, the infamous Canon Law of Rome, we believe he would have somewhat modified his language and opinion. He might not, any more than ourselves, have changed his opinion on the expediency of admitting Roman Catholics to equal civil and political privileges; but he would certainly have expressed his indignation, disgust, and alarm at the turbulent, encroaching, and intolerant spirit of the papacy, and its abettors in Ireland, which, instead of remaining satisfied, as it was understood it would be, with the concessions of the Relief Bill, has used it only as a vantage-ground, from which to urge further demands, till it has become too apparent that it aspires at nothing less than a political and ecclesiastical supremacy. Nor would Mr. Jay, had he written upon the subject at the present time, have expressed himself so confidently of the safety of concession, after what has taken place in

Tuscany, and even in Ireland. An intolerant religion is always and everywhere an enemy, and even the greatest of enemies, to the well-being of states. Those who execrate liberty of conscience, and would extirpate heretics by the secular sword, ought to be indulged with only a limited power, but never entrusted with the liberties of England, while they declare that their object is to introduce the *Canon Law*, which is thoroughly intolerant, and bitterly persecuting against subjects, as well as treasonable against royalty. In contemplation of such facts, Mr. Jay could have viewed the whole Roman hierarchy as merely an organized conspiracy against the liberties of the world. Their view of liberty is a freedom granted to ecclesiastics to sustain the laity; while they deem themselves persecuted if they are restrained from persecuting others.

We wish also to offer a remark upon Mr. Jay's views of the Irish Church. As nonconformists ourselves, we cannot but coincide generally with his remarks on this subject; and yet we are not forgetful that a more devoted and laborious ministry does not exist than may be found in many of the parishes of the Established Church in Ireland. Their successful efforts for the conversion and emancipation of the miserable slaves of Roman Catholic superstition and tyranny, as set forth in the statements of the Society for Irish Church Missions, entitle them to the highest praise; while the pitiless persecution endured by their agents and converts should call forth the sympathy of the Protestant world, and at the same time convince it, that Popery, either at home or abroad, is the inexorable enemy of all liberty, whether civil or religious, though the loudest clamorers for both, when it is deprived of the means of encroaching on the liberty of others.

Lady Barham to Mr. Jay.

1838.

Dear Mr. Jay,—You will have seen by the papers the loss my dear husband has sustained in his father, who died last Wednesday, leaving behind him many pleasing instances of his heart having been renewed; and to us the delightful hope of his having entered into glory—entered upon that endless life of bliss. I shall indeed be very happy to present your "Morning and Evening Portion" to the Queen. I think it would be well to write a note *with them*, expressing your humble hope that Her Majesty will condescend to accept of your book, which has already had the honor to have been graciously received at the court of Petersburg, &c.

I have written this to you to give you an idea (as you wished) of the manner in which Her Majesty generally is addressed; and then you will of course write what you like, only after this fashion. I think it would be better not to write the Queen's name in the books. Perhaps mentioning where they had been received would be an additional inducement to her to read them.

Will you give my kind and Christian love to dear Mrs. Jay, in which Lord Barham joins, and also in best remembrance to yourself? When I see Mrs. Wilman I can deliver your message to her. She is now staying at Eston.

Believe me, dear Mr. Jay,

Yours respectfully and sincerely,

F. BARHAM.

CATMORE LODGE, Feb. 26, 1838.

TO THE QUEEN,

On presenting to Her Majesty a copy of the "Morning and Evening Exercises."

BATH, March, 1838.

MADAM,—Will your Majesty pardon the freedom of one of your loyal subjects, and graciously condescend to accept this humble offering at his hand?

The Author has long been honored with the intimacy of Lord Barham, and his excellent lady has kindly and readily offered to present the work to your Majesty.

The publication is designed to furnish the reader with a text of Scripture for every morning and evening in the year, accompanied with very brief reflections; the better suited to those who have multiplied engagements, and yet are concerned to feel their dependence upon God, and not lose his approbation in the discharge of them.

Though the writer is very sensible of the imperfections of his work, yet he is not a little encouraged by hearing of its continued circulation; the reception it has met with in some of the higher walks of life; the approbation of it expressed by Her Majesty the Empress of Russia; the notice it has obtained from several of your Majesty's illustrious House; and, above all, the blessing of God, which has honored it with many tokens of usefulness.

Though he will be unknown to your Majesty, there is not one in all your applauding empire who more sincerely and earnestly prays for your Majesty's safety and happiness, than,

May it please your Majesty,

Your Majesty's most humble servant and dutiful subject,

THE AUTHOR.

To Miss Head.

BATH, March 8, 1838.

* * * * YOU see from her information (*from America*), and she is not querulous, that religion is not in such a state as we could wish; and that the preaching is defective, because the preachers *there* (as too often *here*) wish to appear to be learned and intellectual, and so the common people, who heard our dear Lord gladly, and understood and felt him, "look up and are not fed." What can the mass of an audience do with nice distinctions, and abstruse reasonings, and long argumentative paragraphs? A preacher may as well take a fiddle into the pulpit, and better too, especially if he could make the people dance; this bodily exercise would profit a little. "The *words* of the wise are as goads and as nails." Let ministers read Bunyan, and Leighton, and Henry, and Flavel, and many more, under whose ministry "the poor had the Gospel preached unto them." However well composed (according to a certain standard) *I* could not sit

patiently under many an American and many an English preacher, though I should not do as I knew a man (for *I* can vouch, and many more now living, for the truth of the fact) at Avebury some years ago. He, one Sunday afternoon, after listening for some time to a sermon, correct enough, but perfectly dry and uninteresting, rushed up from the aisle, and pulled the man —the Rev. Mr. G—— by the collar out of the pulpit, and then with his iron-tipped shoes kicked the pulpit in pieces, for which he was confined five months in Fisherton gaol, but for which he ought to have had a statue erected to his memory. Poor fellow, I well remember him. The last time I saw him, after *mowing* all day, he had walked six miles, and had the same distance to return, to get something to *affect his poor heart*, and which he could think of when whetting his scythe, or eating his crust upon the new-mown swath. Our old divines and the Methodist preachers, when they just sprung up, had something to *rend* or *melt*, to *strike* and *stick*—to lead their hearers to think of again and again when alone, and to talk of again and again when in company. But what is the recommendation of many of the moderns? Oh, they *glitter*—they do —but, as Foster says, with *frost*. You know my fondness (amounting almost to idolatry) of dear *John*. What a pretty sentiment is this which I recently met with from one of his pilgrims! I give it the more readily because I am sure my dear friend can make it her *own*. "I always loved to hear of my Lord, and wherever I saw the print of his shoe, I wished to put my foot." There—is not that as good as some sermons? Do you think there was ever such another tinker in all the world? When I was last week with your friend, the blind clergyman, (his sister-in-law now comes to our Monday evening meeting,) I was speaking of Bunyan's "Holy War." This he had never read. I long to hear how he liked it. I was going foolishly to say, I wish *I* had never read it, but had the *entire* pleasure to *come*. How I should like to read it through to your uncle and aunt, and weep over parts of it together! Though the image of war is not so agreeable as that of a pilgrimage, and though, as a whole, the "Holy War" is not equal to its predecessor, yet I am surprised that it is not more read, and I cannot but think some parts of it are peculiarly affecting —witness the sending of the letter to Immanuel by *Mr. Weteyes;* the *difficulty of destroying the doubters*, &c. I cannot endure transcription, and therefore I send you (preserve it, for I have no copy) a passage which Mr. Bedford had just found in, and translated from, Milton's Second Defence, in Latin, of the people of England in putting Charles to death. He felt it, dear man; it came home to his own affliction; and I observed he was not a little moved when his daughter read it for him. * * * * * * * *

I am, &c.

To Miss Head.

BATH, NOV. 27, 1838.

Now for a little news for maiden ladies—and even good and pious maiden ladies like a bit, let them say what they will; and why, in the name of wonder, should they not? *First.* We had a series of glorious services at our Missionary Meeting; and how pleasing and satisfactory is it that the spirit of these benevolent convocations keeps up! *Secondly.* We have had four deaths in our congregation since I saw you—Mr. Slowcome, an attorney, perfectly sudden; Mrs. Widcombe, a poor woman whom I think you knew, chargeable with considerable faults, yet of Quixotic kindness and liberality; Miss Peacock, a precious soul, and without any of that bird's vanity and pride; and Mr. Smith, who has left a widow and four children. You remember her sufferings two years ago, when she lost three lovely children almost together, at the time her husband was in prison, but not for crime. *Thirdly.* I have just received an imperial green-gage plum-tree from Worthing, the sight of which brought, O what vivid recollections of the dear company and delightful hours enjoyed *there!!* *Fourthly.* Last week Bella wrote, inquiring after your welfare, and begging her love "to dear Miss Head." They were transported, she said, with the prospect of coming to Bath, before which *then* seven Sabbaths were to intervene, *now six.* *Fifthly.* I put down things as they occur; as friendship is free and open, I must inform you that Mr. W—— has left me £200, free of legacy duty; but it is after his wife's death. Whether all he has left is in the same way, I cannot tell; but I believe he has left more than £10,000 to various institutions. Mrs. Jay feels and talks of his death very much. He was a great favorite with her; and we have known him intimately for fifty years nearly. *Sixthly.* To-day we had a letter from Lord ——, who is on a visit to the Queen at Windsor. He says, "he thought dear Mrs. Jay would like to have a line from *thence*, and learn how well our amiable and excellent Queen is, and also

Lady ——." He laments the bigotry of Wilberforce's life; and says, "I have just seen Miss ——, who says, 'Mr. Wilberforce said to me, a few weeks only before his death,' 'my sons are sad high churchmen—all trumpery and nonsense.'" *Seventhly.* Sunday: I was again in Bristol, and preached at New Brunswick Chapel, to immense congregations, for the Sunday-school. I called on the Dean, Dr. Lamb, but he and his wife are now at Cambridge. I dined with Mr. and Mrs. Hare, who will not be satisfied till you and Mrs. Jay have paid them a visit.

I only add that I love a laugh when it leaves no sting in the conscience, or stain upon the mind; and that such a laugh cannot be disagreeable to your uncle in his long solitudes, and (I love to hear him laugh, he does it so heartily) tell him, therefore, I lately heard of an Irishman who was very ill, and who, when the physician told him he must prescribe an emetic for him, answered, "Indeed, doctor, an emetic will never do me no good, for I have taken several, and could never keep one of them upon my stomach." Walter Scott says, "When in Ireland a poor man did something for me, and having no change, I gave him a shilling instead of a sixpence, saying, 'Now, Paddy, remember you owe me sixpence.' 'God bless your honor,' said he, 'and may you live till I pay it.'"

"I walked," says a gentleman, "into one of their fields, and to try him, I said to one of the haymakers, 'Well, Pat, if the devil was to come and fetch one of us, which would he take first?' 'O surely,' said he, 'myself.' 'Why so?' 'Because he 's sure enough of your honor at any time.'"

Mrs. Jay joins in all loving kindness with, &c.

To Miss Harman.

BATH, January 7, '24.

UPON the reception of your letter with a second sorrowful announcement, I thought I would not write to you again for some days, till you would have gone through a fresh painful service, and be a little more composed, and be able to receive an epistolary visit. But after our long and endeared friendship, I cannot refrain from breaking in upon you immediately, lest you should think we do not sympathize with you, so much as I am sure we really do. I say *we*, for my precious invalid, to whom your letter was addressed, deeply feels for you, as well as myself, under these sudden and closely successive losses of a father and a mother. May He whose property it is to comfort those who are cast down be a very present help in this time of trouble. I know your judgment will immediately acquiesce in this trying dispensation, because He has done it; and if your feelings are not so easily ruled, and nature now and then seems ready to repine, do not condemn yourself as destitute of submission, while your desire is to the Lord, for He knows your frame, and looks to the heart. You have too, and these must not be overlooked, many alleviations and comforts to mingle in your affliction, especially that the dear departed are disposed of infinitely to their advantage, and after being continued to you so long, while you have a good hope through grace that, in due time, you will be received by them into everlasting habitations. Were I near, how gladly would I call and weep with you; but Mrs. Jay and myself do hope that you will relieve the scene as soon as possible by a change, and let us have the great pleasure of welcoming you under our roof for a season. The travelling is now nothing, and the old, I will not call it an *excuse*, for I am sure it was not, but *prevention*, is removed. You shall interpret my dear wife's language, which you can do better than any other, and ride out with her in the carriage; and I will give you as much of my company as I can afford, and you shall detect me if I preach old sermons, &c. Mrs. Ashton is now with us, as her husband, through business, was obliged to return before her, and will return, I expect, to-morrow week. But should you be able to journey before she goes, we have plenty of accommodation, and she will be delighted to see you here. She joins with her dear mother and myself in every kind and tender regard.

My dear wife says you must come, and you know her husband seldom differs from her.—In haste, &c.

Rev. T. Grinfield to Mr. Jay.

CLIFTON, February 6, 1841.

DEAR SIR,—I am sure the well-known kindness of your nature will pardon the freedom I take (as an unknown stranger) in sending a transcript of some lines which appear in the "*Bristol Journal*" of this morning. They were almost an irrepressible effusion of feeling on the occasion mentioned. And, having just perused the beautiful account, in the same journal, of the jubilee proceedings of Tuesday last, I cannot refrain from begging your acceptance of my mite among so many worthier offerings. Born at Bath, about two years before the commencement of your ministry, I well remember having often heard a beloved mother speak with pleasure of your early popularity and usefulness. And though I have enjoyed but four or five opportunities (few and far between) of hearing you, (once years ago at Bridge-street, for the Moravian Missions, once at Broadmead, on "grace and truth" coming by Christ, once at Lady Huntingdon's, on the fine analogy between the influence of the *Rain and Snow* and that of God's Word,) I have retained a most pleasing impression of your preaching, and congratulate those who could statedly enjoy it; while I cannot wonder at their zeal in expressing their regard for one who had so well secured it. Excuse this trespass upon your time and attention, and permit me to subscribe myself, with every sentiment of respect and esteem,

Yours sincerely, THOMAS GRINFIELD.

P.S. I rather think you remember my school-fellow at Mr. Simons', of Paul's Cray, Kent—Cornelius Neale, who used to see you at his father's, and to speak of you to myself as early as 1804. Your "Christian Contemplated" I read with admiring delight.

Lines

Occasioned by the perusal of the very interesting Sermon delivered on Sunday, January 31st, 1841, in Argyle Chapel, Bath, by the Rev. William Jay, on the completion of the Fiftieth Year of his ministry in that Chapel.

Dear venerable Pastor! whose career
Of laboring zeal hath closed its fiftieth year
Within those favored walls, where once thy youth,
Where still thine age, hath taught celestial truth;
Well did thy flock, with grateful love, agree
To celebrate thy Pastoral Jubilee;

Honoring their friend, their father, honoring Heaven,
Who such a father, friend, so long had given.
Oh! in this changeful world, how few like thee,
Have trained *one* church through half a century;
With undeclining constancy like thine,
Alone, unaided,—save by strength Divine!
How well in thee was piety combined
With kindly converse, and a master mind;
How well thy natural eloquence impress'd
Wisdom, devotion, on the listening breast!
A spreading throng caught manna from thy lips,
Thy popularity knew no eclipse;—
The wise, the good, still hail'd thy faithful course,
And with thy foremost friends, the sweet-soul'd Wilberforce.
Happy like him in enviable age!
With Canaan opening on thy pilgrimage!
Oh! golden sunset of a beauteous day!
Soon in the clime of glory, thou too, Jay,
Midst the bright host shalt shine, a star of loveliest ray!

THOMAS GRINFIELD.

To Miss Harman.

BATH, December, 1841.

WHAT a blunderer am I! I read in your extract "Home" for "Rome." This puzzled me, and under the perplexity I instantly wrote to prevent hinderance! In future, I will (if anything perplexes me) read a letter a second time before I answer it.

But now, in reply to your proposal. It does strike me that your brother's offer should be readily accepted. Your motive would not be unjustifiable were it only rational gratification; but it may be useful to your health and spirits. You will also turn many things (with your mind) to moral and pious account, while you will yield satisfaction to a worthy youth whose relations in America and in Bath will thank God for the providence. As far, therefore, as the decision depends upon me, I say go, and the Lord be with thee. You *will* not, you *cannot*, suppose that I wish you at a greater distance than London, (*that* being too far away,) and nothing will be dearer to me than your return. But I see no one objection of weight, especially as you will meet with Mrs. E. Jay, and her brother and sister; and your expenses will be defrayed by one whom I long to thank on your behalf. But O, to think how you will glory over us when you come back, and "once more mingle with us meaner things!" But to prevent your despising us too much, you must remember who maketh you to differ, and that some of us have not had the same opportunity or means. Let this be an answer to Jay's note. As I presume you cannot set off before the beginning of the week, could you not see Bella, who comes up on Monday? If so, appoint her by a line a place of interview; but if you can set off sooner, do not delay; but let me have a line as soon as you have arranged things, and blow me a salutation in it. Shall the books be still sent? Have you seen the engraving? I heard from Bartlet last evening that Jay dislikes it. How sad, should it not answer. You must not forget to correspond with me, and I will do my goodest in return. Regards to Mrs. Dore, &c. My respects to the Pope, but do not kiss his toe. Get Paul's old lodgings if you can, Acts, xxviii. 30. And the "goodwill of Him that dwelt in the bush" be with you in going out and coming in.

Ever yours truly, &c.

I think you know Mark Wilks at Paris, otherwise get a line from Mr. Burnet.

To Miss Harman.

BATH, December 21, 1841.

I HAVE just received your kind letters to my wife and to her husband. They are like your whole self, or at least, like all you have exhibited towards us, ever since we were indulged with your friendship. I was a little anxious whether you would have made up your mind so easily and so soon, till I heard again from you, notwithstanding your obliging deference to my opinion; as, in such cases, after all, we must judge for ourselves. But I cannot conceal my satisfaction at your decision; and not entirely on a kind of selfish account, but hoping that one so dear to us as you are will derive pleasure and profit from so interesting a prospect. O, that I could be your companion and your chaplain; and be able by-and-bye to say as you will,—"I have seen Rome!" But the providence which approves of your going requires me to "sit still." But spirits like bodies are not fettered, and I shall think of you much, and follow you much, and shall expect a visit from you as soon as ever you return, to tell us about it; and to hold up your head above us all while doing it. As you write short-hand, it will be inexcusable not to keep a kind of journal; and if you should wish to publish, who knows but I may write a preface, and so our names be blended together before the world. Be attentive to your health, and brace up your mind by some daily retirement for meditation and prayer. Idle away none of the short time you will be there; and be sure to see and hear what you cannot see after your return. Especially observe whatever is connected with the sacred volumes; and neglect not to go "as far as Apii-forum and the Three Taverns;" and for any expense you may incur there *I* will be answerable. Whether any one at Rome ever prayed for me before, I know not; but I shall prize your remembrance of me much more than his Holiness's,—yet if you can get him to frank your letters to a heretic, you will induce him to do one good thing in his Pontificate. To induce him to do this, or to enclose them with any of his missives, please him by telling him how favorably things are going on in the Church of England; and how many are longing to return home from their Reformation wanderings.

What a feeling I have to see you both before your departure; and I assure you I have been trying to arrange things so as to allow of the pleasure; but I find it is not practicable. So I embrace you at a distance, and commend you to the God of our mercy. Read this to-day with my love and concern,—and believe me,

Yours most truly, &c.

To Miss Head.

WORTHING, August 21st, 1842.

I AWOKE this morning with the words upon my mind, "I was in the Spirit on the Lord's day." "The Lord's day," as you well know, means the day of our Saviour's resurrection; and is so called because it was dedicated and observed to the glory of his name, and the service of his people. John's being "in the

Spirit" on this day, *immediately* intends a state of inspiration; and this was abundantly exemplified in the visions he received and reported. But we do well to use the phrase (as we do in our prayers) to mean a peculiar frame of mind under the ordinary agency of the Spirit; and what is a Lord's day without this? Yet it struck me that there are two mistakes to which we are liable concerning it. *First*—We are not to think we are not in the Spirit because we are not in a *lively and comfortable frame.* Such a frame is not to be undervalued; but it may be overvalued, and it is so, when we make it exclusive. For we want many things besides consolation; and we shall be "in the Spirit" if we feel much of His enlightening, or convincing, or humbling influences, and are more empty of self at the end of the Sabbath, than at the beginning of it.

And *Secondly*:—We must not suppose that such a Lord's day is impossible, unless we are favored *with the usual, and social, and public means of* grace. John was away from all these in the mines of Patmos; yet he never had such a Sabbath before; and the Lord, who always teaches his children to love the temple, will show them that he is not confined to it. Not that we are to expect his presence when we *can* repair to his sanctuary; but if we are *his prisoners*, he will not despise or forget us; but will render the house of mourning or the chamber of sickness "none other but the house of God and the gate of heaven." I know not whether your present duty deprives you of the whole, or a part only, of your sanctuary privileges; but in either case, apply to yourself, my beloved friend, the remarks I have made; and be sure to apply them also to your precious sufferer under every secret, silent, sightless Sabbath she may be called to endure. I trust her confidence, and calmness, and comfort continue, and that as her day, so is her strength.

I did not, however, mean to preach, but only to call upon you in a letter for a few moments, and to exchange a few words; though I forget that you always in these written visits leave all the talk to myself—but is this quite fair? "Bell's Daily Advertiser" will doubtless inform you of all that may be called *news.* We all go on much the same; only by the goodness of God, I feel much better, and seem to hope that I may become, not a young man again, but what I was before my several late indispositions; and should this be the case, I trust I shall improve the blessing, by doing more than I have done for some time past. O what a privilege is health and strength, when we not only *enjoy* but *employ* them!

My reading has been various since I have been here; my present engagement is with the life of "Billy Dawson," the celebrated Wesleyan preacher. It is not well written, but it contains interesting and profitable matter. He was truly a great man; not equal to our divine Bunyan, without learning, or at least without academical preparation for the ministry.

* * * * *

I have just received a letter of three sheets from my spiritual daughter, Miss Harris, at Caen in France. Had I a private hand I would send it for your perusal; as it would afford you pleasure to see how much decision and yet gentleness and prudence she displays; and how useful, in a land of barrenness, she is likely to be. I wish you had known her when she was in

Bath. Should she come there again, I must bring *her*, or fetch *you;* and you will soon be like two drops of water on a table when they touch and run into one.

I am, &c.

To Mr. Rice Hopkins.

BATH, Dec. 10, 1849.

MY DEAR SIR,—I duly received your kind letter, and also the pamphlet. In addition to all your former kindnesses, I am much obliged by your remembering my wish, and taking pains to gratify it. If the publishers (Jackson and Walford) would have no objection to inform you of the author, I should be glad to be informed. But whoever was the writer, the work is masterly, and cannot be easily answered. It falls in with my views, which have never altered upon that subject.*

I am glad you are in prospect of settlement with a pastor, and pray for a blessing upon the approaching union; but I must decline your application, for my attending at the reopening of your chapel. I do not

* The work here honored by the notice and commendation of Mr. Jay, is entitled, "Objections to the Doctrine of Israel's Future Restoration to Palestine, National Pre-eminence, &c. In Twelve Letters to a Friend, with an Appendix. 1828." Mr. Jay's strong language, used so late as the year 1849, informs us of his matured opinion upon a subject which has long divided the judgment of the Christian Church, and upon which it will probably remain divided so long as the two opposite modes of interpreting prophecy are followed—the figurative and the literal; or till the decisions of history shall supersede the comments of opinion. Mr. Swaine's Work has received the commendation of many other eminent divines besides Mr. Jay.

like to refuse in anything such peculiarly kind friends as Mr. and Mrs. Hopkins,—but Mr. and Mrs. Ashton will be here at the time, and &c., &c.—

My dear Mrs. Jay is sitting by, and begs to join in everything that is kind and loving to Mrs. Hopkins and yourself, with,

My dear Sir, yours most truly,
WILLIAM JAY.

To the same.

BATH, Jan. 7, 1850.

MY DEAR SIR,—I believe I thanked you for the discovery and present of the letters I so much wished to see, and I ought to have thanked you last week for tracing out the clever author. The work is well written, and the point well argued. Some things perhaps may be added, and would require to be so, as the subject has excited so much attention *since* the publication. The works, however, I have not read; but when in Cambridge I met with Professor Lee, who is very strong on Mr. Swaine's side, and has lately published a work on prophecy, in which there is much which I should like him to see. So also is there, I am told, in Professor Stuart's work on the Revelations. I should be glad to see a new edition of the Letters, and would do what I could *orally* to notice and recommend them in private and public; but some rules which I have laid down, and some fears of being at my time of life drawn into controversial publicity, forbid my *writing* a Preface. Give my best respects to Mr. Swaine, though personally unknown, and hope he will accept not my excuse but reason.

The Ashtons are now with us, and with Mrs. Jay join in best regards to Mrs. Hopkins and her husband, with, my dear Sir,

Yours truly, &c.

To Lady Ducie.

BATH, Dec. 29, 1846.

MY DEAR LADY DUCIE,—I thought I heard a jingle, and examined the floor, but, finding nothing, I concluded it was a *lapsus auris.* But does such honesty grow everywhere? Certainly wherever it is found it ought to be rewarded. But to whom am I indebted? As Lady Mary Wortley Montague says—"In all my travels I never met with but two kinds of people—men and women," so the finder must be, I presume, male or female; and as your ladyship *can* decide this, will you present to *him* or *her* the little publication I have enclosed—"Clarke's Memoirs." I would have inscribed it, but, again, I know not the name. Should I have the pleasure of a future visit to Tortworth, and the servant be still with you, I will then do it.

Along with the "Short Discourses for the Use of Families," which I begged your ladyship to accept, I have put into the parcel the "Charge to a Minister's Wife," and the sermon to a bad husband, not for you to keep, but just if you like to throw your eye over them, and then dispose of them where you think they are most called for.

By the way, when I spoke to your ladyship of my having *delivered* and *written* out a course of lectures on Scripture Female Biography, and that my plan would be completed by four lectures more—two on Hannah, and two on the Mother of our Lord,—I intended to ask whether (if I should have health and leisure to finish the series) your ladyship would allow me the honor and favor of dedicating them to *yourself?* Should you be disposed to yield this request, your ladyship may be assured I would not offend by dedicatory fulsomeness. "I know not (with Elihu) to give flattering titles to any; for in so doing my Maker would take me away;" yet I wish to bear my witness to goodness and excellence, and to remember the words of Solomon—"a gracious woman retaineth honor."

I was sorry I was too tired to give you words of exposition, and to leave your kind roof without a *devotional and social* benediction; but I did not forget the family in my chamber; and if my prayer be heard, Lord Ducie's health will be restored and established and perpetuated; and he will be a growing and public blessing in his day and generation; and will much, and long walk together with his estimable companion, both "as heirs of the grace of life;" and see their fine and lovely children "as plants growing up in their youth, and as corner-stones polished after the similitude of a palace." Amen and amen.

My best respects await Lord Ducie (not forgetting Mr. Watts, if yet with you).

I am, my dear Lady Ducie,

Yours to esteem and serve, &c.

I got home safe a quarter after 10. My wife (one of the best women God ever made) begs her most esteemed regards.

To Lady Ducie.

BATH, Feb. 3, 1847.

MY DEAR LADY DUCIE,—I ought to have written earlier to thank you for your very kind present, every article of which proved very good; and as, being a teetotaler, I could not *drink* your ladyship's health (unless in an element which all do not value as I do, and as Samson did) I *ate* it, heartily wishing your ladyship much of that blessing (and the Earl too) which is the salt that seasons, and the honey that sweetens every temporal comfort; praying also in a better exercise, that bodily health may be accompanied with every kind of spiritual welfare. This sentence would be almost long enough for Dr. Chalmers.

"By love serve one another." What a beautiful little text is this! the practice of which would turn this vale of tears into a paradise; and as your ladyship, I know, does not consider it an interpolation or wrongly translated, I venture to give you a little trouble. The Dean and Mrs. Lamb would be much obliged, if your ladyship could say "whether you could recommend a governess who once lived with you of the name of ——; as to her character, accomplishments, piety, and good temper." The wish has been transmitted through my daughter, Mrs. Ashton, from Cambridge, where the Dean now is. A line to her, or him, or myself, will suffice.

Is the Mr. Wyat, near Stroud, mentioned in the papers as dead, the very pleasant and amiable gentleman I met at your house so recently? I presume it is; and, if so, the circumstance is affecting. Ah! if we had all foreknown it then, would not our intercourse and conversation (I am blaming nothing) have been more specifically religious, and bearing upon his (and indeed our own) spiritual welfare? Should we not meet and part more as mortals and immortals; and would this injure the allowed sociabilities of life?

What awful accounts still from Ireland and Scotland! I pleaded for them successfully on Sunday. My text was, "A cloak of covetousness;" and I. I described the evil—*covetousness.* II. Proved that its folly, baseness, and sin, by common feeling, needed a covering. III. I showed some of the cloaks it was accustomed to wear. Here I led them into the devil's wardrobe, where they would see a fine assortment of articles to suit any purchaser—cloaks of every color and shape, and size and price. Here a scarlet one, fringed with fur; there a velvet one, lined with silk; here a shorter, and there one reaching quite to the ground; there new ones, and here some only a little injured by wear; some a little soiled and mended, but then cheaper. That was introduced by Lady ——; and this is now much admired by ——, &c. I then passed from irony (justified by the sacred writers) to seriousness, and from figure to fact, and exposed four of these excuses and disguises, which I have not time on paper to do justice to. IV. I inquired how far these cloaks would conceal the things? and answered, 1st. They cannot always conceal it from the wearer *himself.* 2dly. They cannot *commonly* conceal it from *others.* 3dly. They can *never* conceal it from *God.* I then concluded—1st. By calling upon them to take heed and beware of covetousness. 2dly. Admonishing them to seek the true riches, in which there could be no excess in their desires, or failure in their hopes, &c.

As I am not sure whether you are in the country or town, I direct this to Tortworth House, supposing, if I am mistaken, it will be immediately forwarded on. I trust Lord Ducie is quite convalescent. Please to present to him my best regards. Earl Gainsborough and the Countess are here. He has had a severe attack since they came. God bless you, my dear lady.

And believe me, &c.

The Jay's *love*
To the *Dove*.

To Lady Ducie.

BATH, Jan. 8, 1848.

MY DEAR LADY DUCIE,—We duly received your very kind present of game, and return many and very sincere thanks. They would have been transmitted earlier, but I only returned this evening after a week's absence from home, and during which I have had an attack of the very common complaint. It has not indeed been severe, but sufficient to lay me by for some days, and to qualify me to sympathize with much greater sufferers. As ministers we frequently escape what others endure, not because we do not deserve or need personally the same trials with others; but because of the duties we owe to others; for if physicians were to experience all the ailments of their patients, they could have neither time nor strength to practice; and, as our exemptions are often relative to others, so also are our inflictions. Ezekiel heard the knell—"Son of man, behold, I take away the desire of thine eyes with a stroke;" not because of any offence of his, for which God would chastise him, but that he might be "a sign unto the people." It is the doctrine of Paul, 2 Cor. i. 6. Indeed this will, in some measure, apply to Christians as well as ministers: we are all parts of some little whole, more or less affected and influenced by us. "None of us liveth to himself, and no man dieth to himself."

For some good while back I could not make out where your ladyship and the Earl were. Some said you were at home—some at Malta—some in Syria. But, though I knew not how to follow you locally in my prayers, I could address One who saw where you were, and could afford you whatever blessing you needed from Him as the God of providence and of grace. If the excursion has been in search of health, (the salt that seasons and the honey that sweetens every temporal blessing,) I trust it has not been sought in vain, and that the Earl has returned with renewed strength, and growing disposition to walk before the Lord in the land of the living.

Neither do I now know whether the family is in the country or in town; but I venture the present direction, knowing this thanksgiving will surely reach persons so well known, wherever they are.

It is rather late to send the congratulations of the season. But another year is gone, and by far the most important we ever passed through, because it is the nearest to our "long home," and the bar of God; and we have entered on a new period of our time, not knowing what a day may bring forth; but, as Cowper sings, if we give up ourselves to him,

"It can bring nothing with it,
But it will bear us through."

My text last Sunday morning, in reference to the season, was, "These days should be remembered." What days? Days of unregeneracy—days of conversion—days of persecutions—days of bereavement—days of providential interposition—days of particular speciality, viz., birth-days—nuptial days—new-year-days.

I beg my best regards to Earl Ducie with my prayers for his entire welfare. I presume he approves of the Bill for the Removal of the Jewish Civil Disabilities; and condemns the conduct of those who have opposed Lord John in one of his noblest actions. Many are not aware as yet how much the spirit of popery has prevailed of late years in the Church of England (for we have nothing of it among all other parties). May it be detected and *thoroughly* encountered before it be too late. Mrs. Jay begs to join in best thanks and regards, with,

My dear Lady Ducie, Yours, &c.

To Lord Ducie

My dear Lord Ducie,—Yesterday Mr. Bidwell called upon me. The interview was very agreeable in itself, but particularly so as I learned from it that Lady Ducie was well, and your lordship so much improved in health, and, as usual, active in doing good. And how much obliged am I to your lordship for the beautiful present, and for such a kind proof of remembrance, and that out of sight is not always out of mind: I hope I can also say that I sometimes thought of your lordship in your absence and distance, and—where I think your lordship would most value my remembrance—at the throne of grace. I had but just begun this letter before the hare and the birds came, requiring another qualified acknowledgment.

Another year is rapidly closing; and what an eventful year has it been! Among its most remarkable (and I am persuaded influential) events in our own country, has been Mr. Noel's secession and his Essay on the Union of Church and State. The book, in many respects, is one of the most extraordinary I ever read. It is written with great ability, and with much Christian spirit. It must make a great impression in favor of our free churches. Will it lead to any improvements in the Establishment? yet, if something be not done there, I think that church is in danger.

I am sorry that, by several little indispositions, and also by engagements and interruptions, my visit into Gloucestershire has been prevented; and for some time longer now it must be postponed, as my daughter and her husband from Cambridge are soon coming to see us.

Soon after this reaches Tortworth we shall enter on a new period of time, not knowing what a day may bring forth; but under the care of Him who sees the end from the beginning and has said, "I will never leave thee nor forsake thee." Allow me to send (in which Mrs. Jay joins me) the congratulations of the season to Lady Ducie and your lordship, with our prayers that all grace may abound towards the whole family.

I am, &c.

To Lady Ducie.

BATH, October 22, 1849.

MY DEAR LADY DUCIE,—You will think it strange and probably blame-worthy that I have not answered your letter earlier; but I was from home when it arrived, and I have been variously absent nearly ever since,—not for my pleasure, but on my great and good Master's business, doing a little, and wishing to do more; but I find the old man rapidly coming on, and the infirmities of eighty keeping me from doing the things that I would. One of my excursions was to Kingswood, occasioned by the death of my old friend Mrs. Long. I much wished to have gone over to Tortworth; but I was hurried for time, and the weather was wet, and I heard that the Earl was suffering confinement. I long to hear that his lordship is released, and able as he is willing to be well-doing. I was thankful to be informed of your ladyship's fresh deliverance; and pray that the life spared and the life given may be precious in the Lord's sight, and sacred to his service and praise. "Lo, children," says David, "are an heritage of the Lord;" and some have a much larger portion than others. But, says Henry, "Children are certain cares, and uncertain comforts, and possible crosses." In these matters, however, we are not left to our own choice; but are under the management of Him "who performeth all things for us," and "doeth all things well." But there is a part belonging to us, and if we discharge it in dependence upon Him, we are entitled to expect the exemplification of the *proverb*, if not the *promise*,—"Train up a child in the way that he should go, and when he is old be will not depart from it."

At Budleigh Salterton, where I spent a month, I met with good Dr. ——, of America, who spoke with pleasure of his visits to Tortworth. I heard him preach (*i. e.* read) several times, and was *pleased;* but when I hear I love to be *rent* or *melted.* I do not like for preacher's mouth to be lined with velvet. When will ministers remember what the mass of every congregation consists of; and learn to preach *ad populum?* By whom was He heard "gladly" who spake as never man spake? The words of the wise are as goads and as nails, they pierce and remain. What are fine smooth periods that slip off from the conscience like water from a duck's back? What evaporates in the mere article of hearing can do little good; but that which is carried away to be again and again thought of alone, and talked of in company. "Let the word of Christ dwell in you."

Mrs. Jay and myself are tolerably well. I wish we could see you in Bath. With best regards to Earl Ducie, believe me, &c.

To Lady Ducie.

BATH, December, 1851.

DEAR LADY DUCIE,—How kind and good you were to think of us, and furnish our table with such fine game; the last of which we have only recently despatched, and during our partaking of which I more than once drank your ladyship's health in a bumper of the purest water the neighborhood affords. By the way, the American ambassador (Mr. Stephenson) told me that when he dined with the Queen, he made her smile by drinking her Majesty's health, as a teetotaller, in the same beverage.

I ought to have written earlier,—but this morning, I said, with a blush, "I will write to Tortworth." No sooner said than done, or at least begun. But now, whether I shall finish as I wish, depends much upon "Satan," who often interrupts and hinders, by favoring me with calls of indefinite length from persons senseless of the value of time, and who, having nothing to do, discharge some of their idleness and curiosity under a cover of business.

But now, after our acknowledgment and thanksgiving, what can I write about? There is, indeed, one subject of supreme importance which is always at hand, and on which we should be always ready in our thoughts and communications. It is the Name above every Name. But with this your ladyship is graciously acquainted, though in a rank of life in which He is so little known and honored;—otherwise how could I speak of Him both from office and experience as "fairer than the children of men;"—as "altogether lovely;" as having "giving himself for us an offering and a sacrifice to God for a sweet smelling savor;"—as "remembering us now he is come into his kingdom;—as "ever living to make intercession for us;"—as "the Lord our righteousness and strength; all our salvation and all our desire, our glory and our joy."

"Such Jesus is, and such his grace,
O may He shine on you;
And tell him when you see his face
I long to see him too."

I was delighted to see Lord Ducie's letter to the chairman of the Protestant Alliance. It did him much honor, both as showing his aversion to the "mother of harlots and abominations of the earth," and also nobleness of mind in being willing publicly to retract an opinion. A very learned man has said,—"The three hardest words to pronounce in the English language are, '*I was mistaken;*'" and when Frederick the Great wrote his letter to the Senate,—"I have just lost a great battle, and it was entirely my own fault," —Goldsmith says, "This confession displayed more greatness than all his victories."

I should much like to hear his Lordship's opinion with regard to the new Revolution in France. He must, I think, dislike the character of the usurper; though, perhaps, one tyrant is better than twenty agreed in nothing but mutual opposition for selfish ends. If he succeeds, as is most probable, the effect I fear will be favorable to Popery; yet, if he allies himself to a cause doomed to perish, he will place himself in the way of God's judgments, and be easily brought down. Our comfort is, that "the Lord God omnipotent reigneth;" and that "He will overturn, overturn, overturn, until he comes whose right it is, and it shall be given him."

You were, my dear Lady, misinformed as to my objection to the Liturgy. I even like much to hear it occasionally, though I certainly should like it better were it curtailed, and stripped of its repetitions. That I am not an enemy to all forms of devotion is obvious from my volume of Prayers for the Use of Families; and for the publication of which I have great reason to bless God. Nor, though a firm Dissenter, am I unfriendly to the Established Church. My connections have been very much among its members and ministers, as you will see from my Reminiscences, which will be published at my death. But I do *hate* all exclusiveness; and I *lament* that a church should be less tolerant and liberal *now* than when it first left Rome, and could be excused some mother-marks upon it. But *then* it did not unchurch other churches, nor invalidate other ordinations, but even allowed preferments to some who only had had on their heads "*the hands of the presbytery.*" But see the mess the good Archbishop of C—— gets himself into! O that he had *avowed* and *gloried* in what he conceded to his deceiver! But instead of *this candor*, he applies what he said *only to these foreigners;* and not to any here, though standing on the very same terms. The fact is, the wretched notion of Apostolical Succession so far *unites* the *Church of England to the Church of Rome, and dissociates it from all other churches*, however orthodox or useful. Some must break through, and lead in a better way. I, therefore, rejoice, and thousands beside, that Lord Ducie and a few more are serving the Lord Christ in a mode which will please God, and draw down his blessing, whoever may censure or condemn. Bolton speaks of your visiting Bath. Is it so? I wish it may be, and that we may be favored with a little of your company. Mrs. Jay unites in kind regards to yourself and Lord Ducie. I am, &c.

To the same.

O Lady Ducie,—You have made me break through a rule I have never violated yet, in communicating my text beforehand. From one of these five (D.V.) I hope to preach to-morrow morning:—"Take it by the tail." —"It was always so."—"Amen, the Lord God say so too."—"In that day a man shall nourish a young cow and two sheep."—"The people that know their God shall be strong and do exploits." I do not mention the chapters and verses, as this may employ Lady Alice to find out. I forgot to ask her to tell me at what time Joseph dined? (Gen. xliii. 16.) And why a covetous man was like a medlar?

I feel very weak and poorly, and expect to feel difficulty to-morrow. I wonder which of the texts you will be led to wish for and choose. Well, all will be known in *due* time. I hope his Lordship is still mending. We never forget him in our prayers. What a scrawl to a lady of quality! Pray forgive, and believe me, &c.

To the same.

BRADFORD, June 10, 1853.

DEAR LADY DUCIE,—

"If thou shouldst stay, e'en as thou art,
  All cold and all serene,
I still might press thy silent heart,
  And where thy smiles have been:
While e'en thy chill-loved corpse I *have*
  Thou seemest still mine *own;*
But *there,*—I *lay* thee in the grave—
  And now *I am alone!*"

Such was the language of Wolfe, who wrote the fine monody of the death of Sir John Moore. In more instances than one I have felt the truth and force of the tender and touching sentiment. While the remains of the dear departed are only in the coffin, and not in the grave, and we can yet go and look, and gaze, and weep, we seem to possess him still; but when we have laid him in the tomb, and return to the lonely house in which we have taken sweet counsel together, and walked to the house of God in company; ah, then we feel its emptiness and know what real *solitude* is. I, therefore, would not write during the engagements and distractions of funeral preparations, but resolved to wait upon you with a few lines when you would be saying—"And *now* I am *alone*."

And yet in another and more important sense, your Ladyship will not be alone, because the Father will be with you; for He has said, and the Scripture cannot be broken, "I will be with thee in trouble." And surely you are now entitled to claim and plead that promise. But you must not expect it to be miraculously fulfilled, or in a way that will raise you above the sense of the greatness of your loss. There is no patience in bearing what we do not feel, or resignation in giving up what we do not value. But you may expect from it support under the affliction, however great; and that you shall be able to say (or endeavor to say—and the Lord looketh to the heart), "It is the Lord; let him do what seemeth him good:" "The Lord gave and the Lord hath taken away, and blessed be the name of the Lord." What a state was David in when he came to Ziklag? All was gone! and, hero as he was, he lifted up his voice and wept. "But David encouraged himself in the Lord his God." *He* was left—and never left *him;* and after every distress enabled him to say, "Come unto me, all ye that fear God, and I will declare what he hath done for my soul."

You also will prove a witness for God, and be able to acknowledge that it is good for you that you have been afflicted. Great as your trial is, remember, my dear Madam, how much greater it might have been. Only consider what the God of all grace has done for the deceased, whom we all loved, and all will miss. I confess the late development of experience did not surprise me. I entertained from the time I knew him a good hope through grace; and latterly I felt a deep and constant impression which ever excited my prayer on his behalf. Well, his pains are now over; and the days of his mourning are ended; and though he was not permitted to enter his exquisite earthly mansion, he is now in a house not made with hands, but eternal in the heavens. Your loss, therefore, is his infinite gain; and under this loss may you know that God is the husband of the widow in his holy habitation and in her own, and also the Father of the fatherless! May the affliction be sanctified to them! and may they prove that "it is good for a man to bear the yoke in his youth;" and from this time cry unto *Him*, "My Father, thou art the guide of my youth!"

I hope that none of the religious resources of such a family will be dried up; or any of its useful institutions, and exertions, and influences cease, or be impaired.

Thus, while you have attended the entombment of the dear Earl, I have communed with you in spirit, in writing these few lines. Believe me, my dear Lady Ducie, &c.

Mrs. Jay joins in all this. I long to know Lord and Lady Moreton; and will not cease to pray for them.

My state is much the same, as to health and strength, as when I was at Stone. I am able to do but little; but the spirit is willing though the flesh is weak. "Let her alone, she hath done what she could."

To Dr. Bowie.

PERCY PLACE, January 24, 1853.

MY DEAR DOCTOR,—Uncertain whether I should see you this afternoon, I write a few lines, and they must be few, as I find writing, like every other exertion, a trying task. You know not only my sense of obligation for all your kindness, but the confidence I have in your judgment, and what a submissive patient I have been. But I am now venturing a step of my own accord, and hope if you reprove you will strike gently. I have felt the last few days worse, *i. e.* lower in my strength, and more painful in my complaint. I am, therefore, going, if possible, to Bradford to-morrow morning, thinking whether the change may not probably affect me. My stay, I presume, will not be long; and if anything peculiar arise, I or Mrs. Jay can inform you.

But I forget not the nature and character of the ensuing Sabbath, when sixty-three years ago I was ordained over the people of Argyle Chapel, after occasionally laboring among them full twelve months before. On the next Sabbath this long, happy, and endeared connection terminates; and pastor and people have to look *backward and forward* under awful responsibilities.

Should Mr. Dyer see fit to have any reference to the event, I wish him to inform the Church and Congregation how much I have all along hoped to have been able to address them on the occasion; but the Lord has prevented it, as I could not undertake any public service, much more a service which would rend me to pieces!

He may also assure them that, though my pastoral relation has ceased, I shall be delighted if a degree of ability shall enable me occasionally to address them again from my old chair and pulpit.

I am much concerned for their proper settlement, and pray that the Lord may direct them to the choice of a pastor after his own heart; and that peace and prosperity may ever be within their lovely borders. They may be assured that, in proportion as the people of his late and long charge are satisfied and edified, *he* will approve and rejoice, who, in finishing his ministry, can say—

"Ere since by faith I saw the stream
Thy dying wounds supply,
Redeeming love has been my theme,
And shall be till I die."

I wish I could write more and better, but I am as weak as I am willing.

Believe me, my dear and beloved physician,

Yours, &c.

PART V.

THE LITERARY REMAINS

OF THE

REV. WILLIAM JAY.

LITERARY REMAINS.

LINES ON THE DEATH OF HIS DAUGHTER STATIRA.

Oh! had I known, when we embraced,
That parting kiss would prove the last,
I surely should have held thee fast,
Statira!

One week elapsed, and home I fled,
From Devon's hills, in musings dread,
And breathless sought thy mortal bed,
Statira!

"Know'st thou," I said, in accents mild,
"Thy father's voice, my darling child?"
But thy dear lips nor spake, nor smiled,
Statira!

Bereft of hope, yet hoping too,
Led by thy mother, I withdrew;
For well the worth of prayer we knew,
Statira!

We kneel'd, and, by each other's side,
In tears, not words, to heaven we cried:
Could tears avail, thou hadst not died,
Statira!

I feel it still—that dying look,
Mine eye to briny gushings took,
While every nerve with anguish shook,
Statira!

I see it still—that lovely face,
Illumed with wisdom and with grace,
O'er which no clouds of passion pass'd,
Statira!

I see thee clasp thy mother's neck,
And print thy kisses on her cheek:
In vain will she thy equal seek,
Statira!

The canvas did thy taste confess:
Thy beauteous landscapes I caress;
E'en Ruben's tints would please me less,
Statira!

Thy pen's remains I prize the more
Than would the learn'd, the letter'd lore,
From Persian bards, or Attic shore,
Statira!

Thy conduct, still above thy age,
Each opening virtue did presage,
And every heart and lip engage,
Statira!

Oh! how I loved that temper'd tongue,
On which the law of kindness hung,
From which no ill or folly sprung,
Statira!

Each Sabbath saw thee with delight
Within my house the babes unite,
Whom thou didst teach to read and write,
Statira!

The power of grace I joy'd to see,
From guile and affectation free,
Take up its young abode in thee,
Statira!

Thy heart well loved the holy place,
The queen of days, the throne of grace,
The Saviour's words, and works, and ways,
Statira!

A violet was thy piety,
Retired in charms of modesty,
And most betray'd by fragrancy,
Statira!

I feel thy loss in every part;
I mourn, I bleed beneath the smart,
Yet kiss the hand that breaks my heart,
Statira.

Thou hast, in all thy early bloom,
First tenanted thy father's tomb,
And made him willing there to come,
Statira!

Ah! were this all of nineteen years
The end of all our loves and cares,
What hand could then e'er wipe our tears,
Statira!

But no, we 've rear'd thee for the skies;
Thy soul is now in Paradise,
But thy dear flesh again shall rise,
Statira!

LINES WRITTEN ON SEEING MY PORTRAIT BY MR. ETTY, DESIGNED FOR MR. AND MRS. BOLTON, AT LIVERPOOL. SEPT. 13TH, 1817.

Etty, 'tis done! The very man breathes now;
I feel the likeness, and my friends avow.
Yes, here—or much I err—thou surely hast
(What none beside could do) thyself surpass'd.
And still, thou child of nature and of art,
Thy mind all taste, and ardor all thy heart,
Let each success to higher fame beguile
And rise the Reynolds of our peerless isle.

Now go, my shade, and let my children see
Their absent father present still in thee.
Look on them well,—yet not in sullen mood
To chill their freedoms, and their joys exclude:
On nothing frown, but reason would condemn;
Nor what is past to *me*, forbid to *them*.

Say,—"Love each other; love all human-kind,
And spread the mercy which you hope to find.
In nothing e'er the voice within despise,
Nor slight the Book that beckons to the skies.
No word, no action, let his God displease,
And, in a sire's inspection, feel at ease."

Yet should—as danger e'en the good surround,
And they are ambush'd most who most *abound*—
Should e'er forgetfulness a blame incur,
Then rise, my type, and prove the *monitor*.
Yet still with meekness chide, and melting mien,
And from a fault, with kind caressings, win.

And when, in days to come, in silence laid,
Low sleeps the form that skill has here portray'd,

Some stranger asks, who ne'er the living knew,
If strong the likeness, and the features true?
"O yes," my first-born cries, "my father dear—
'Tis what he was, his very self is there;
The way in which he *sat;* the *air* he wore;
His *look* benign, yet tinged with frowning o'er;
His *aspect* varying, yet the general view—
Easy, though anxious; pleased, yet plaintive too.
His *eye* retired and close, which yet confess'd
A mind in action, but a heart at rest;
The *mouth* his own, whose kindness oft was found,
And half a smile would lurk his lips around.

"Such was the man from whom my breath I drew,
Whose love to me no ebbing ever knew:
That *transversed knee* was long my favor'd seat;
That *hand inclined* oft led my infant feet;
That *hand unseen* ne'er waked a moment's fear,
The plum was seen, but not the rod was there;
And be *my boast* in her *confession* known—
She never gave *me* pain but by her *own.*"

LINES SUPPOSED TO BE SPOKEN BY MRS. BOLTON, ON THE RECEIPT OF HER MOTHER'S LIKENESS, SENT HER BY MR. ASHTON.

My Mother! 'tis your own dear face
Here meets my eager view.
Yes, at each glance, again I cry,
"My Mother, it is *you!*"

But how my spirits flow and sink,
What mingled thoughts arise,
As o'er this welcome shade I throw
My joyful, weeping eyes!

Backwards I rush to those first hours
  When round thy neck I hung,
And thou didst guide my tottering feet,
  And bless my prattling tongue.

Thy counsels, and example fair,
  In love's soft bondage led,
And taught me how to rise *above*,
  And how *earth's* paths to tread.

But how time flies! since thee I left,
  What varied scenes I've traced!
What changes, trials, blessings, known!
  And here I'm fixed at last;

Away from Albion's soil—my friends—
  My father's house so dear;
And far from thee, whose sadden'd age
  'Twould be my heaven to cheer!

O what were life without the aid
  Of faith's supporting power?
Ah! but for this my heart had died
  In many a trembling hour.

More worn with days and sighings oft
  Thou seem'st, than when I took
(The sacred spot remembered well,)
  That last, that lingering look.

O could I once again behold
  That placid, plaintive mien,
And but embrace the lovely wreck
  Of what thou long hast been!

And is the sight forever barr'd?
  Are we no more to meet?
O happy brevity of life
  That will our bliss complete!

Then, freed from all thy present griefs,
  Thy raptur'd child shall see,
And tell thee, dearest Mother, how,
  How much she owes to *thee.*

APRIL 15, 1838.

TO MISS BROWNE, ON HER PRESENTING HIM WITH A PAIR OF GLASSES.

So you, my friend, with kindness prompt
  Long known and often tried,
Have thus, to aid your pastor's sight,
  The need of art supplied.

And he, not senseless of thy care,
  Would wish the boon repaid;
And hopes, by instrument Divine,
  To yield thee kindred aid;—

By *faith*, a glass of sovereign use,
  That brings the distant near,
Enlarges sense and reason's bounds,
  And makes the doubtful clear.

He 'd gladly help thine eye to read
  The record God has given,
With brighter gaze thy Jesus see,
  And view thy right to heaven.

"Father of lights," from whom proceed
Whatever gifts we own,
Various the mediums may be found,
But Thou the source, alone!

To Thee, our being and our weal,
Each power and bliss we owe;
All *nature's* treasures flow from thee,
And *art's* improvements flow.

Nor let us ever little deem
What so our good befriends,
That lengthens out our visual ray,
And all its joys extend:

That aids us still the pencil's tint
In glowing charms to ken,
And read, alone, the letter dear
From Friendship's absent pen:

That helps us still the page to scan
Of authors grave or gay;
Theirs, who our pleasure but consult,
And theirs who teach to pray:

That guides us to the Tree of Life,
The Book of heavenly grace;
To *see* and *gather* from the boughs
The fruits of joy and peace.

But ah! my friend, a present such
A solemn voice assumes:
"See how of life the noon is gone,
And how the evening comes!"

The leaves that fade and fall foretell
The year's last setting sun,
And Autumn is but Winter seen
Approaching and begun.

Not sudden shuts the eve of life,
Nor without warnings due;
Deaf grows the ear, and dim the eye,
To preach, "Thy days are few."

And shall we dream of years to come,
Nor note our frame's decay?
Waken, O Lord, our sleepful souls
And bid us live—*to-day*.

JULY 29, 1819.

TO MISS BROWNE, ON PRESENTING HIM WITH SEVERAL BANDS MADE OUT OF HER GRANDFATHER'S ARCHIEPISCOPAL SLEEVES.

A MIND to observation turn'd
May well with wonder glow,
To see the changes human things
Are doomed to undergo.
A vesture that a palace graced
May serve a meeting-house at last!

"What impious profanation this,"
So D—b—ny would speak;
"To take a robe a Bishop wore
And bind it round the neck,
Design'd a sacred badge to be
Of schism and of heresy!"

But he who now assumes the lawn,
Oh! let it well be known,
Ne'er stole a pair of crosier'd sleeves,
Or wished such sleeves his own;
Nor thought e'en such a bit to win
As now depends beneath his chin.

Yet such a present he esteems,
Peculiar in its kind,
And which, whene'er he puts it on,
The giver brings to mind,
Whose brains the plan unique conceived,
And whose own hands the work achieved.

WITH THE PRESENT OF A BIBLE, WRITTEN AND PRESENTED TO HIS VERY DEAR DAUGHTER, MRS. ROBERT BOLTON, THE MORNING OF HER MARRIAGE.

This Book, whose aim and Author are Divine,
This best of books, my much-lov'd Anne, be thine!
This early bless'd thee with an influence mild,
It charm'd the infant, and it form'd the child.
This, when a daughter, sweetly ruled thy life,
And now demands thy duty as a Wife.
O daily read; and in this Volume trace
Thy Sovereign's pleasure and thy Saviour's grace.
These rules will keep thee in a world of snares,
These comforts cheer thee in a vale of tears.
In every scene to this dear Book be just,
Each counsel follow and each promise trust.
Be this thy study; this thy glory be;
And let thy Mother be renew'd in thee.

TO MRS. GILL, ON HER DESIRING FROM HIM A LETTER OF HIS OWN WRITING TO BE KEPT FOR HIS SAKE.

January 22, 1823.

So you, dear Madam, ask a line,
And how can I deny you?
That you may keep, in my own hand,
A brief memorial by you.

Well, here it is, when I am gone
To tell, whoe'er may note it,
How long I knew, and much I prized,
The Friend for whom I wrote it.

To tell how warm, and changeless too,
The kindness of her heart;
And how in all my joys and tears
She bore a feeling part.

To tell that none at wisdom's gate
More constantly was found,
Or with more joy, when call'd, e'er trod
The temple's holy ground.

To tell how she, not free from fear,
A lively hope possessed,
While all her walk and spirit show'd
The Gospel she profess'd.

So spake her pastor while below;
Nor can his hope be vain,
That she will prove his joy and crown
When they shall meet again.

LINES ON HIS FIFTY-FIFTH BIRTH-DAY, MAY 8, 1824.

WHAT, my soul, O, what emotion
Should I on this morning feel,
Shame, and *grief*, and new *devotion*,
Hope, and *gratitude*, and *zeal;*
These, if conscience be addressed,
These become my Birth-day best.

SHAME, that fruit so small, if any,
Should from such high culture spring;
GRIEF, that seasons rich and many
Should no longer profit bring.
O, how guilty life appears,
When compared with means and years!

PRAISE, that though, His counsels shining,
I' ve rebelled against the light,
He his love revealed each morning,
And his faithfulness each night.
If a tear my eye-lids knew,
Mercy shut and wiped it too.

HOPE, that He who ne'er denied me,
In my worth or in my woe,
Will each day with grace provide me,
And his strength in weakness show.
He, my Guardian, yet can shield,
Till I leave the conquer'd field.

ZEAL, for now the sun, descending,
Calls to mind the close of day;
And how soon, in life declining,
Will the seasons flee away.
I may then their loss deplore;
But they can return no more.

PRAYER;—alone I would not venture
  On a year of good or ill;
Saviour Jesus, with me enter,
  And afford thy presence still.
Let me live, or let me die,
Nought I want if thou art nigh.

LINES WRITTEN ON VISITING HIS NATIVE VILLAGE, IN 1800.

[Before these lines we place a brief extract from a letter written to a friend, after another visit to Tisbury, many years subsequent to that on which the lines were written:—"My visit was pleasant, but the Sunday was wet all day, yet we had many to hear. I felt more than usual, perhaps from the thought, how few more visits I was ever likely to pay the place. I found my parental cottage clean and neat, with many flowers before the door. I sent the occupants (distant relations) into the garden for awhile, in order to be alone; and so I 'went in and sat before the Lord, and said, What am I, and what is my father's house, that thou hast brought me hitherto?' I sat in the very same great arm-chair which I had always seen my father sit in; and all is still in tolerable condition. I was affected with the thought that seventy-four years ago, in this humble room, the peculiar child of Providence breathed his infancy and childhood—how unlikely to become what he has since been!"]

THE way by which a gracious God
  Has led me all my days,
Demands, on each review, a song
  Of wonder and of praise.

His care, attending every step,
  Was my perpetual guide;
His ear attentive heard my prayer;
  His hand my wants supplied.

The course through which my journey ran
Was winding and unknown;
His providence the scenes had plann'd,
And each appeared His own.

More now, since first I left this spot,
Than twice eight years have fled;
And many once who charm'd my youth
Are number'd with the dead.

'Twas here I drew my infant breath:
Here fled my youthful hours;
Here first I heard the Gospel sound,
And felt its heavenly powers.

When o'er my former walks I rove,
How fresh the scenes appear!
And *here* I pour'd an artless prayer,
And *there* indulged a tear.

Unknown to fortune and to fame,
My early years expired;
No science had enrich'd my mind,
No hope my bosom fired.

But Heaven a *Winter* thus addressed:
"This youth I charge on thee,
Go, take him—I the impulse gave—
And train him up for *Me*.

"Awaken thou each dormant power,
Chase every cloud away,
And on his understanding pour
An intellectual day.

"The tree that in a barren soil
Can no good produce bear,
Transposed, may flourish, and with fruit
Repay the dresser's care."

Winter,* I love to think on thee,
And those dear hours review,
When in thy house, and from thy lips,
I sacred wisdom drew.

Thy life, enforcing all thy rules,
Shed every grace abroad,
And thine example all alive
Portray'd the man of God.

Nor would I now the blessings lose
Which from thy care have flow'd,
For all that schools of fame have given,
Or colleges bestow'd.

* Mr. Jay says, in the Life of Winter, p. 272, concerning these lines, when transmitted to Mr. Winter, he wrote thus:—"It is impossible I can keep the little poem to myself; and yet I truly blush at being the subject of so much honor as it intends me. I pray God that in the judgment-day I may be found the consistent character such as I ought to be. From the many imperfections known to myself, I feel shame; while from my fellow-creatures I meet with applause, to which my dearest Jay contributes much. I sometimes tremble on this account. I know that I am not disposed to make an improper use of it, and am sure that it does not in the least divert me from the Saviour, whose name is all my trust. I need His mercy, and am in His service an unprofitable servant. If, like '*Charles*,' in Cowper, I have been desirous to please, and have made any effort to serve acceptably, it is because I love my Master; and wherein I can best serve him, I would be most willing." "I feel," says he, "as indifferent to everything above the supply of food and raiment administered in a decent manner, as a dead man does to the coffin in which his remains are confined."

Here, O my soul, the time recall
  When my commission came—
How bless'd when sixteen years had roll'd,
  To preach a Saviour's name.

Poor Ablington! among thy sons,
  The shepherds of the plain,
My first attempt to preach was made,
  Nor was it made in vain.

The cloudy pillar leading on,
  Its motions I pursued,
Till o'er the city famed for cures,
  The holy symbol stood.

"Here," cried the voice, "thy station fix,
  And here thy rovings end;
Here teach the words of endless life,
  And here my charge attend.

"Proclaim a Fountain nobler far
  Than this Bethesda knows;
'Tis always open, always free,
  And with salvation flows.

"The sons of pleasure here who come,
  Invite to endless bliss;
He who another life receives,
  Can only relish this.

"Here Satan's seat exalted stands,
  And vice in triumph reigns;
A crown for him who owns *Me* here,
  And all My truth maintains."

O Lord, evince the choice Thine own,
  Which placed me where I move;

And, while Thy people see Thy power,
May one a thousand prove!

Here I return, increased and bless'd
By all-indulgent Heaven;
My God, the joys of wedded life,
And children, too, has given.

Yonder appears, by Anna led,
My lovely train in view;
My cherubs, round your mother play,
The scene shall end with you.

To raise an Ebenezer *here*,
My God is surely just;
My motto, "*Praise* for all the past,
And for the future, *trust*."

In the Hymn Book used at Argyle Chapel, as a supplement to Dr. Watts's, Mr. Jay inserted about twenty, composed by himself. As these are not distinguished by any peculiar mark, we have thought it would be gratifying to his friends to have them pointed out. As far as we have been able to ascertain, they are the following:—79, 151, 161, 230, 270, 360, 370, 422, 441, 443, 446, 455, 458, 462, 465, 471, 483, 498, 501, 503.

ANECDOTE.

Conversion and subsequent History of Mrs. Ulph.

WHEN I knew the subject of this brief notice first, she was bar-maid at the White Hart Inn, Bath, then kept by Mr. and Mrs. Pickwick. My acquaintance with her commenced very incidentally. I was going to Chippenham. The London coach from Bath took me up at my own door. I found in it only one passenger. This was a young female, in whose countenance and manner of speech there was something very pleasing and interesting. I felt a wish to say something during our journey that might be useful, though she was an entire stranger; remembering the assertion and admonition of Solomon—"A word fitly spoken, how good is it! In the morning sow thy seed, and in the evening withhold not thy hand, for thou knowest not whether shall prosper either this or that, or whether they both shall be alike good." I had an opening for this without the impropriety of forcing religious reflection upon my fellow-traveller, as is often done, abruptly and offensively.

This arose from my mentioning the design of my journey, which was to preach a funeral sermon for a very good man, who had died in such a blessed manner as to exemplify the words of David—"Mark the perfect man, and behold the upright, for the end of that man is peace;" and which must have induced all who witnessed it, or heard of it, to exclaim "Let me die the death of the righteous, and let my last end be like his."

I noticed also something of the excellency of character with which such a decease well harmonized. I soon perceived that, instead of wishing this kind of discourse broken off, she encouraged its continuance. I therefore spoke on till I left the coach. I was glad to see she was going on alone, hoping solitariness would help impression, and that what had been spoken might be useful in days to come.

I was happy enough to learn afterwards that this was the case. In consequence of what she had heard, she was favorably disposed towards me; and finding that I was a minister, and preached in Bath, she resolved upon her return to go and hear me. She did so, and it was not in vain in the Lord. For one day, some months after, I received a note from Mrs. Pickwick, saying, that a young person whom she much valued was very ill, and was anxious to see me, and begging that I would visit her. I immediately went. As I approached what was supposed to be a dying bed, she wept much. When she had recovered herself, and I saw her face, "Why, surely," said I, "I have seen you before." "Sir," said she, "blessed be God, you have;" and then called to my remembrance our transient intercourse when we travelled together to Chippenham at such a time, and the benefit (she hoped she was not deceiving herself) she had derived from it.

The difficulties and hinderances we meet with in the things of God arise not so much from the subject as from ourselves; and when the heart is once opened and humbled, and we are brought to the foot of the cross, and to the foot of the throne, we are soon led forward in the right road. I found, therefore, the mind of the sufferer much advanced for the time in spiritual knowledge and experience; and knowing what I now learnt, had she then died, I should have had the fullest satisfaction concerning her eternal state; but she soon surprisingly recovered, was finally restored, and continued attending at Argyle Chapel.

Her opportunities of attendance were soon enlarged, in consequence of her having made it a condition of her remaining in her place, and which was readily conceded from a regard to the value of her services, rather than from any wish to favor the object of her desires. O how much may those who are in official situations accomplish by walking in wisdom towards those that are without! They may put to silence the ignorance of those who are ready to accuse them, remove their prejudices, and win them without the word. And who ever walked uprightly without walking surely? and when did God ever falsify his own word: "Them that honor me I will honor"?

Not long after these occurrences, a passenger through Bath stayed a few days at the White Hart Inn. He was a truly good man, possessed of landed property, and also carrying on a large business at St. Ives, near Cambridge. Being a Dissenter, and having heard of my name, he inquired of the bar-maid, on the Sunday morning, where Mr. Jay preached? She answered,—"I am just going to his chapel; and, if agreeable, I will show you the way." He accepted the offer. After the service, meeting her in the house, he thanked her for directing him, and spoke concerning the sermon; and again and again he noticed her.

And now another leaf in her book of providence was to be turned over without any thought of hers. Though she was very modest and retiring, (and indeed very much because she was so,) she much impressed him. Owing to this impression, he prolonged his stay; and the impression continually increasing, he offered her his hand, and she, after reflection and proper inquiry, saw no reason to refuse it.

She now, of course, removed to his residence at St. Ives, where, for many years, she exemplified the excellences of the wife, the mother, the mistress, the friend, and the neighbor—in the Christian. Her conversation was such as became the Gospel. She bore richly of the fruits of the Spirit, and adorned the doctrine of God her Saviour in all things. Having now the command of property, she added beneficence to benevolence; and, instead of only saying with many, "Depart in peace; be ye warmed and filled!" she gave them liberally such things as were needful; and, while not forgetful of the body, she showed herself still more concerned for the soul; and by her prayers, and influence, and example, the diligence and gentleness of her instructions and invitations, and the uniformity and loveliness of her character and conduct, she was always endeavoring to bring souls to the Saviour, and in some way or other to promote his cause.

Some years after her marriage, and at her earnest and repeated request, (her husband cordially joining in it,) I visited St. Ives. She was a good *trumpeter*, and had prepared the way for my coming. My preaching proved peculiarly acceptable, and I hope and believe good was done in various instances. To add to the effect of my public addresses, she pressed persons to come to her house to attend the domestic worship. But, as the number increased to the inconvenience and disordering of the family, and as the meeting-house was near, I proposed that, during the rest of my visit, I should perform the service there every morning. This I did, beginning at seven, and continuing then, and in all my after visits, a little more than half-an-hour, adding to the psalm and prayer a short exposition of Scripture. Though the exercise was early, the attendance commonly filled the place; and surely God was in the midst of us of a truth. The services were informal and simple, and the spirit of devotion was certainly felt. With what pleasure does the writer call back those delightful engagements, in which many joined in saying, "Lord, it is good for us to be here."

The pastor of the church at this time, instead of feeling jealousy or indifference, was himself most pleasingly excited, and did everything in his power to increase a brother's acceptance and success. He was the excellent Mr. Crisp, who is now, and has been for some years, the president of the Baptist College in Bristol; and his removal to that important station was one of the results of the writer's intercourse with St. Ives. Nor can he forbear mentioning another event originating from it, viz., the marriage of his second daughter to Garfit Ashton, Esq., an event very interesting to his feelings, and which has furnished one of the greatest satisfactions of his life. After a course, blameless, exemplary, and useful in no common degree, this follower of the Lamb finished her course in peace, and fell asleep in Jesus; and is had in applauding remembrance of all that were about her.

A minister should feel peculiarly honored and grateful when God gives him a convert that not only obtains good, but also perpetuates, multiplies, and diffuses it. We believe that none of the subjects of divine grace are entirely barren and unfruitful in the knowledge of our Lord and Saviour; but some of the good ground brings forth, not only thirty but sixty, and even a hundredfold.

N.B.—I shall here mention a little incident which I met with before I left St. Ives. One day I saw on a small under-shelf in the pulpit a volume of hymns and spiritual songs; it consisted of three books:—1st. On various subjects. 2dly. Adapted to the Lord's Supper. 3dly. In peculiar measures. It was designed as a Supplement to Dr. Watts. I had never seen it nor heard of it before. I took it to the house of my friend; and after examining it, I borrowed it; and finding it was not used in the worship, nor found in the congregation, I begged it. The compositions themselves betrayed much spirituality and evangelism, and no little degree of poetical excellence. A few of them I have inserted in my own appendix to Watts. As the book seems to be now unknown, and the author, one of the most extraordinary individuals that ever lived in our world, it may be interesting to mention a few facts concerning him. His name was Simon Brown, and he lies buried at Bridgewater. He first labored in Portsmouth, and afterwards preached somewhere in London. For many years before his death he fell into the strange notion, that God had for his sins annihilated his rational soul, and had left him only the soul of a brute. He never after this felt the least doubt to shake this conviction. Yet he wrote several works; one was a Defence of Christianity against the Deists; the dedication of which, as a most singular curiosity, is to be found, under his name, in the "Encyclopædia Britannica."

In some respects his case surpassed Cowper's; yet, under all his delusion, there was nothing exceptionable in all his productions; so that Mr. Toplady said of him—instead of having no soul, he wrote, and reasoned, and prayed as if he had *two*.

THE EVANGELICAL ALLIANCE.

Addressed to Mr. Charles Godwin.

UPON the formation of this Christian Association in Bath, Mr. Jay received an invitation to attend. He was unable to comply, owing to a previous engagement, but expressed his concurrence and approbation thus:—

I preached, indeed, last evening, but with difficulty, and at present I shrink back from any additional excitement or exertion.

This, however, is not the only reason of my non-attendance. I am this day seventy-and-seven years old, 2 Sam. vii. 18; the day is felt interesting to my family, and some more immediate connexions, and I had made engagements which I cannot now alter, and engaged those I cannot put off.

I was not brought up among the *Exclusives*, and I have served all religious parties, holding the Head, who have applied for my services. I have always held my own sentiments with firmness, and preached them without disguise; and I never found the sober and candid statement of these offensive to those who differed from me, as they saw I gave the liberty I took.

I have long been convinced that illiberality is not confined to any one denomination of Christians—we are all verily guilty; and that bigotry is not to be subdued by bigotry, but by an opposite spirit.

The attempt (*to form the Alliance*) commenced at Liverpool, was a noble one, and failure in such an endeavor would be far preferable to success in a thousand other causes; but no good effort, begun with such an aim, and carried on in such a spirit, and with God in the midst of it, ever was, ever will be, ever can be, in vain.

I shall be with you in spirit; and I have such confidence in the wisdom and goodness of my brethren, that, whatever they agree in, I shall unite in with them; that is, as far as to acquiesce, and countenance, and recommend, for I must give up positive agencies. It is too late for me to take part in initiative and executive proceedings; and, blessed be God, there are enough to be found of leisure and ability for such purposes. I have too much for my age upon my head and hands from the press and the pulpit; and I must draw in from other things; for which, too, I was always less fit."

May 3, 1846.

I wish the Evangelical Alliance met with more encouragement. I expect good from it. It must tend to liberalize and unite—which we so much want. May the Lord be in the midst of them as a spirit of judgment and a spirit of burning!

DR. JOHN OWEN.

I HAVE been dipping a little into dear Doctor Owen's book on the "Glory of Christ," which he wrote and published in his last illness, when he was above half way to heaven. O what a savor is there in every page, every line, every word! If other books lead us to religion, rouse us, and attach us to religion, this brings us into it. "The *true spouse* of Jesus Christ," he says, "is to *be known* by her always enjoying the company of her beloved, or *mourning* after it." This, I think, is one of those remarks that a Christian may easily apprehend and rejoice in. The Doctor observes, also, "That Christ in heaven does not live a life of mere *glory*, but of *office*." Yes, it was expedient for us that He went away. His exaltation has not banished us from his mind. He appears in the presence of God for us. O could we by faith see our High Priest in his complete administration—could we see him as John saw him, clothed with a garment down to the feet, and girt with a golden girdle—what a consolation would it infuse into our souls under painful apprehensions of our guilt and imperfections! What an energy would it communicate to all our exertions! What a fervor into all our devotional intercourse with God!

APOSTOLICAL SUCCESSION.

"LET me know," he said, writing to a friend, "when —— has *established* the Apostolical Succession, as I intend then, old as I am, to conform. Many of the clergy here begin to be shy of the notion, seeing the use the Puseyites make of it, and that it appears to be the main pillar of Popery. One of them (a rector too), conversing in my library some time ago, when a very foolish thing was said, exclaimed, "Really I know nothing so absurd, except our notion of Apostolical Succession!" Newton and Scott, &c., &c., knew nothing of this; nor the best of our evangelical clergy now. The lower ground for a Church-of-England man is the safest. A high churchman will never be able to contend successfully against a papist.

WORDSWORTH.

I WAS rather surprised at your admiration of Wordsworth. He is always beyond me. I can never understand him; and I have no notion of studying poetry, which is designed to please, and which, like a fine scene of nature, strikes and delights me at once. Do you remember (though I have not been influenced by them) how the Edinburgh Reviewers dealt with him some years ago? But it has become fashionable to extol him; and much of this has been owing to his Tory friends, in reward for his bigoted aristocratic feeling. I have here presented you with Cowper's Life and Works. Read, and eat, and drink him. He is *the* poet—all nature and all grace too; never in the fogs—never making his readers pause to ask what is the meaning of this? or if there is any? and is it just or not? is it interesting or not?

MORAL AND EVANGELICAL PREACHING.

THE difference between these is, not that one preaches good works, and not the other, for both preach them; but one expects motion without life, the other looks for life in order to motion; the one waters dead trees, and obtains no fruit; the other living trees, that bring forth abundantly.

INDWELLING SIN.

SAINT PAUL said, "I am sold under sin." But it is recorded of Ahab that he sold *himself* to work wickedness. There is a great difference between the man who sells himself and the poor negro who is kidnapped. "It is no more," says the Apostle, "I that do it, but sin that dwelleth in me."

THE RELATIVE MISERY OF SIN.

"That man perished not alone in his iniquity."—JOSHUA, xxii. 20.

THERE is no greater fallacy than is involved in the common phrase, "He is no man's enemy but his own." Every bad man is the enemy of his wife, his children, his family at large, his church, his country, and his kind; nor does any rank he may hold in society invalidate the truth of this remark, nor diminish the responsibility of the transgressor.

ORTON'S "LIFE OF DODDRIDGE."

MR. JAY said that Mr. Wilberforce considered Orton's "Life of Doddridge" one of the best pieces of biography in our language; and Mr. Cornelius Winter observed, that if ever he felt disposed to pride, he took down that work to read.

COMMON SENSE.

WHEN will the grace of God enthrone common sense in the minds of religious people?

FAITH.

MAN originally fell by losing his confidence in God, and can only be raised by the restoration of his confidence. In other words, unbelief was his ruin, and he now stands by faith.

FISHING FOR COMPLIMENTS.

SOME people angle for praise with the bait of humility. I hope you will never be caught by it. They condemn themselves, hoping that you will contradict them and commend them. Rather join in running them down. It is always better to err on the safe side.

THE SIN AGAINST THE HOLY GHOST.

It is most probable that the Almighty has chosen to veil the precise nature of this sin under more or less of obscurity, in order that we may keep at the utmost possible distance from it. If I wish to protect an enclosure from depredation, and for that purpose affix the usual notice, that traps or snares are set within, I do not at the same time advertise the public *where* they are placed, or I may be sure they will enter where they consider it safe.

TYPES AND SHADOWS.

The Jews, like children, had a picture placed above their lesson.

THE GREAT INTERCESSOR.

He who knows but the alphabet of prayer, and he who has been most experienced in its use, must alike take refuge in *Him* who ever liveth to make intercession for us.

ON LORD BYRON.

In a sermon preached in May, 1824, from 1 Pet. i. 24, 25: "For all flesh is as grass, and all the glory of man as the flower of grass. The grass withereth, and the flower thereof falleth away; but the word of the Lord endureth forever; and this is the Word which by the Gospel is preached unto you,"—in noticing the death of this illustrious individual, Mr. Jay delivered the following apostrophe, which was soon after inserted in the "Bath and Cheltenham Gazette":

"O Byron! Byron! thy death brought this text to my remembrance! O Byron! thy premature fall gave rise to these solemn reflections! Who can help lamenting the perverse and unhallowed use of thy stupendous powers! Who can think, unmoved, of the vigor of thy intellect—the riches of thy imagination—thy breathless sublimities of conception and expression! Who can think, unmoved, of the going down of such a sun at noon! of a genius, that might have ranked with a Milton, quenched forever; and leaving so much to admire—so much to deplore—so much to abhor! No knell of departed greatness has ever more solemnly sounded forth this sentiment: *All flesh is as grass, and all the glory of man as the flower of grass: the grass withereth, and the flower thereof falleth away.*"

SERMON I.

"He shall choose our inheritance for us."—Psalm xlvii. 4.

David said, "I rejoice at thy word as one that findeth great spoil." "The law of thy mouth is better unto me than thousands of gold and silver." The Scriptures abound with instructions, admonitions, and counsels; and he who studies and observes them will find that they are "profitable for doctrine, for reproof, for correction, for instruction in righteousness, that the man of God may be perfect, thoroughly furnished unto all good works," and may stand complete in all the will of God.

The Book of Psalms we have always considered as the treasury of religious experience: whether we are in sorrow or in joy, whether we pray or praise, whether we exercise confidence or resignation, here we always find "a word in season;" and O "how good is it!" "'Tis like apples of gold in pictures of silver." Such is the language of our text, "He shall choose our inheritance for us." May the God of all grace enable us to make this sentiment our own! In order to accomplish this purpose, let us make four inquiries; and, 1st, To what does the sentiment refer? 2dly, On what is the sentiment founded? 3dly, By what is the sentiment enforced? 4thly, How is the sentiment to be improved? "Consider what I say, and the Lord give you understanding in all things." FIRST, TO WHAT DOES THE SENTIMENT REFER—"our inheritance"? Now Canaan was the inheritance of the Jews, and God chose this for them. Thus they could say, "The lines have fallen to us in pleasant places, we have a goodly heritage," for it was the glory of all lands, and flowed with milk and honey. The Christian has another and a better inheritance, "an inheritance incorruptible, undefiled, and that fadeth not away, reserved in heaven for him;" and this God has chosen for him, and he cannot be satisfied without the possession of it. "As for me," says he, with David, "I will behold thy face in righteousness; I shall be satisfied when I awake in thy likeness;" for, be it remembered, his resignation to the choice of God with regard to his eternal destiny does not extend so far as some profess to extend it; he does not express himself with those deluded persons, and say (this is the language of one of them), "Lord, if thou send me to hell or to heaven, thy will be done; whether my portion is to be saved or to perish, I shall never cease to love or to praise thee." Why, a little experience of the misery of the lost would bring these poor creatures to their senses.

There are two things which we may observe. The one is, the thing of which they boast is *impossible*. You *cannot* love one that you are persuaded is an enemy to your eternal happiness. And, secondly, the thing implies also a contradiction, for God has commanded us to seek, above all things, "his kingdom and his righteousness." Therefore, he can never be pleased at our disregarding what he has enjoined, or with our willingness to sacrifice what he has promised. But a Christian can leave to his heavenly Father all the choice of his eternal inheritance (that is, when he can realize his interest in Christ), knowing that "in his Father's house are many mansions;" and as to the degree of glory he shall obtain, for "one star differeth from another star in glory;" and as to the employments in which he shall be engaged, for "his servants shall serve him" as well as see his face, and shall "serve him day and night in his temple." His grand concern is to gain the reality, and, as to the rest, in regard to all the appendages, he can say, "If by any means I may attain to the resurrection of the dead."

But the sentiment refers to *time* rather than to eternity, and to God's choice in the regulation of all our enjoyments on earth. Thus, therefore, the Christian can say, "The Lord shall choose my inheritance for me," *as to my abode.* He shall determine the bounds of my habitation, and the place of my residence. A change of situation, contrary to my disposition and inclination to a fixed abode, I find to be trying; but I know not what effects with regard to myself or others may result from it.

"To me remains nor place nor time,
My country is in every clime;
I can be calm, and free from care,
On any shore, since God is there.

At home, abroad, what sweets they prove,
Whose souls are fired with sacred love;
In heaven, on earth, or on the sea,
Where'er they dwell, they dwell with Thee.

While place we seek, or place we shun,
The soul finds happiness in none;
But if Thy smiles attend our way,
'Tis equal joy to go or stay.

Could I be cast where Thou art not,
That were indeed a dreadful lot;
But regions none remote I call,
Secure of finding Thee in all."

"He shall choose my inheritance for me" *as to occupation.* He shall determine the nature of my profession and calling. He has servants in all vocations, and they are all equally respectable when appointed by Him, and all are "sanctified by the word of God and prayer." "He shall choose my inheritance for me" *as to condition.* He shall determine whether my plans shall flourish or fail; whether I am to be known or to be obscure; whether I am to be affluent or poor. "He shall choose my inheritance for me" *as to connection.* He shall determine whether I am to serve Him individually or relatively, whether I shall preside over a family or be written childless in the earth, whether I shall have friends, or whether I am to feel the want of them. "He shall choose my inheritance for me" *as to health.* He shall determine whether I am to serve Him actively or passively, whether my strength shall be equal to my day of labor, and my hands be sufficient for me, or whether I shall be made to possess months of vanity, or have wearisome nights appointed unto me. "He shall choose my inheritance for me" *as to life itself.* He shall determine how long or how short shall be its continuance; and the time and place, the mode and the means, of my removal, I leave with Him in whose hands my breath is, and whose are all my ways. Thus, all that alarms my fears, all that excites my hopes, all that engages my expectations, I commit to Him in compliance with his merciful admonitions and injunctions, "Cast thy burden on the Lord, and he shall sustain thee." "Commit thy way unto the Lord, trust also in him, and he shall bring it to pass." "Casting all your care upon him, for he careth for you."

"My cares, I give you to the wind,
And shake you off like dust;
Well may we trust our all with Him,
With whom our *souls* we trust."

Let us inquire,

SECONDLY, ON WHAT THIS SENTIMENT IS FOUNDED. It is founded, my brethren, on the belief of God's supreme agency in all our affairs. Now, as to *the fact itself.* There is such a thing as a Divine providence. He who made the world has not abandoned it. "In him we live and move," as well as "have our being."

And He does not govern all by mechanical laws, as a man who may form a machine that can go without his inspection, and which he may therefore leave, for a season at least, to another, while he attends to something else. For here, were God to suspend *his* attention for one moment, all would run into confusion and disorder. Nor does he govern all by general laws, as if he regarded whole systems and whole worlds, or a series of worlds, while he overlooks individuals and minute concerns. This notion, half philosophical and half infidel, some in our day have embraced, as if, forsooth, it were beneath God. What! can it be beneath him to manage what it was not beneath him to create? Or, as if they would save him trouble and perplexity arising from a multiplicity of cares. But surely Infinite Wisdom and Power can never be in perplexity. He "fainteth not, neither is weary; there is no searching of his understanding." There are those who cavil at the notion of a *particular* providence; but we should remember that universal providence necessarily implies a particular one, as the whole is necessarily made up of various parts. Let us, therefore, come and hear Him, into whose lips grace was poured, and who spake as never man spake. Let us hear Him, who maketh his sun to shine on the evil and on the good, and sendeth rain on the just and on the unjust,—Him, who wings an angel, and teaches the spider to weave his web—who numbers the hair of our heads, remembering it is said, "A sparrow falleth not to the ground without your Heavenly Father." Look, said our Lord to his disciples, Look at the fowls of the air, which neither have storehouse nor barn, yet they are provided for; though when they drop from their perches in the morning they know not where they shall find one grain of food. "And why take ye thought for raiment? Consider the lilies of the field, how they grow; they toil not, neither do they spin;" but yet he clothes them, and "Solomon in all his glory was not arrayed like one of these. Wherefore, if God so clothe the grass of the field, which to-day is, and to-morrow is cast into the oven, shall he not much more clothe you, O ye of little faith?" When we speak of little things, we often know not what we are saying, for how can we determine what is little? There are many things which are very small in themselves, yet, by their connection and by their results, what are they? How often do we see events of the greatest importance hanging upon apparently trifling circumstances! When Joseph was sent to inquire after his brethren in Dothan, how little did he think that he should go by a way by which he should never return, and that his successes would furnish matter for entertainment and instruction to the end of time! We should always bear in mind, when we go forth in the morning, that something may overtake us before evening, which may give a complexion to the whole of our future days. The providence of God extends not only to our minute affairs, but to what we call casual concerns; for we are expressly told, that "the lot is cast into the lap, but the whole disposing thereof is of the Lord." And what is accidental with regard to us is not so with regard to God. "He worketh all things according to the counsel of his own will;" and "of him, and from him, and to him are all things; to whom be glory forever and ever. Amen."

Now, my brethren, you will observe this is a fact,

whether you hear, or whether you forbear; but he who uses this language realizes it, and brings it home to his own bosom; he is persuaded though God is high, yet that he condescends to manage his minute affairs, and, therefore, says he, "I will cry unto God most high, unto God that performeth all things for me." While unbelief keeps God at a distance faith brings him near, and with his presence fills what otherwise would be a gloomy and aching void. When I am enabled to realize this principle and say, "He shall choose my inheritance for me," then can I exercise confidence in him, and then I feel fresh motives for my praise and gratitude. When I sink in deep waters where there is no standing, this principle raises me up, "sets my feet upon a rock, and establishes my goings, and puts a new song into my mouth, even praise unto the Lord." Now, I go on my way rejoicing;—now, he who was once afar off is made nigh, and my God sustains me;—now, I have a God who has succeeded me in my endeavors, who is doing all things for me, and doing all things well.

The doctrine, my brethren, of a particular providence puts the Christian and all his concerns on board a vessel, and then gives God the supreme command; so the Christian feels supreme satisfaction when he is persuaded that all the Divine arrangements are made with reference to his providence. I am well aware that this notion may be carried to excess. We have all some secret tendency in us to enthusiasm and fanaticism; and we sometimes meet with persons who seem to think that they are the very centre of God's designs, as if God had nothing to do but to attend to them. Yet it is true, he does act and care for the

Christian *individually*, for there are circumstances in the life of every Christian that will not allow of his questioning it. *When he looks back* he can say,—

> "Many days have pass'd since then,
> Many changes I have seen,
> Yet have been upheld till now;
> Who could hold me up but Thou?"

Then, as to the present,—"Thou tellest all my wanderings; thou puttest my tears into thy bottle; are they not in thy book?" And it is, my brethren, a truth, that while all creatures are the *subjects* of providence, his own people are the *end.* Therefore it is said, "The eyes of the Lord run to and fro throughout the whole earth, to show himself strong on the behalf of them whose heart is perfect toward him."

Let us now ask, and endeavor to answer, a third question, viz:—

THIRDLY, BY WHAT IS THIS SENTIMENT ENFORCED? We will mention only one particular. Nothing can be more reasonable than this confidence; and, whatever the people of the world may think, "wisdom" as our Lord says, "is justified of all her children;" and they are able to give a reason of their prospects, as well of their hope. Let us, therefore, consider *five* things by way of argument. God has a *right* to choose for us, and we have *not* a right. God is qualified to choose for us, and we are not qualified to choose for ourselves. God has *already* chosen well, and is willing still to choose for us—why should we resign Him? and you never will feel so peaceful and so comfortable as when you know all is under his care and direction, that he has undertaken the charge in answer to your resolution, "The Lord shall chose our inheritance for us."

First. He *has a right to choose* for us. A right much greater than a tutor over his pupils, or a father over his child—a right derived from absolute sovereignty; for, has He not a right to do what he will with his own? Suppose He were to say to any creature, "Go thy way—take that that is thine own;" what would he be able to take away? Would he be able to take away himself? Why, his being would immediately relapse into its original nothingness. He has a propriety in us—we never can say, He takes away from us what does not belong to Him.

"The dear delights we here enjoy,
 And fondly call our own,
Are but short favors, borrow'd now,
 To be repaid anon."

But what right now have *you* to choose? Produce it if you can; justify it if you can. Have you made yourself? Have you redeemed yourself? Have you sustained yourself? From whose wardrobe have you been clothed? At whose table have you been fed? Who is it that draws your curtain at night around you, and tells creation to be quiet while you slumber and sleep? Whose mercies are new every morning? A gardener may admire a beautiful flower, and may wish to preserve what he has raised with so much care, in the parterre. He comes into the garden, and finds it gathered. But he is disposed to be angry, and asks, "Who has gathered it?" "Oh," says a fellow-servant, "It was our master. He came here this morning, and gathered it." What is the consequence? Why then the gardener is still, and opens not his mouth, because the owner has done it. And shall it not be much more the case with regard to us, with regard to our losses and bereavements? Then you will observe,

Secondly, *God is qualified* to choose for us;—as the right belongs to Him, so the *ability* belongs to Him; and His judgment is always according to truth. He can never be mistaken, therefore,

"Since all the downward tracks of time
God's watchful eyes surveys,
Oh! who so wise to choose our lot,
Or regulate our ways?"

He knoweth your frame. He can distinguish between your wants and your wishes. He knows what will be good for you, forty years hence, if you live so long. He knows perfectly how you will feel in *any* condition in which you can be placed. He knows well how to refuse you, and when to indulge you.

Are you qualified to choose—"to have your own desire"? "The way of man is not in himself. It is not in man that walketh to direct his steps." Alphonso, king of Spain, was addicted to the study of astronomy, when that sublime science was less known than at present; and having, in his ignorance, observed, as he thought, some irregularities in the heavenly bodies, he said, "If I had been by the side of the Maker when he put these in motion, I could have given him some good advice." Now you shudder at such an expression, but have you not done this with regard to the providence of God? Have you not often thought that you could "direct the Lord," and "be his counsellor"? Everything unfits us to choose our inheritance for ourselves. We are too *ignorant* to choose for ourselves. We may choose that which may issue in our mischief and misery. We see only a small portion of the whole—but a few parts only; nor do we see their connection with others; nor do we see their final results. We know what we feel in our present situations and conditions; but we cannot know how we should feel in new and untried ones. Observe the case of Hazael, when the man of God wept, and Hazael said, "Why weepest thou, my lord? And he answered, Because I know the evil that thou wilt do unto the children of Israel, their strongholds shalt thou set on fire, and their young men wilt thou slay with the sword, and wilt dash their children, and rip up their women with child." What, said he, am I a dog that I should do this? He was then sincere in his detestation. But said the prophet, the Lord hath showed me that thou shalt be king over Syria. So he came to the throne—put off humanity—put on tyranny, and became all that the prophet predicted. And though he had said, "Is thy servant a dog that he should do this great thing?" Yet, as an old writer observes, "*The dog* DID *do it.*"

Then we are too *sensual* to choose our inheritance for ourselves. We may desire dainty meat, when perhaps we need medicine. We are anxious to gather fruit while it is green, whereas it must be most nutritious when it comes to maturity. So Lot desired the plains of Sodom because he saw they were well watered and fertile; but little did he reflect upon the neighbors and the intercourse he might have there. He therefore had soon occasion to lament his choice; and "his righteous soul was vexed from day to day with the filthy conversation of the wicked;" then he was burnt out of house and home; then his wife became a pillar of salt, and his character became tarnished and disgraced—and all this from his choosing his own inheritance.

Then we should be too *impatient* to choose it. We should prefer what is near to what is remote, what is present to that which is future. We should be disposed to reap as soon as we have sown, not reflecting that the months of winter must come between the seed-time and the harvest; and there must be long patience until we have the early and latter rain. Then,

Thirdly. Let us remember that *He has chosen already for us:* why, then, should we abandon Him now, that He has chosen for us well, and that He has proved himself worthy of our confidence? And seeing we are incapable of judging for ourselves, why do we not now approve of His designs? Do we not now see wisdom in what once appeared irregular and confused? Do we not now see kindness in what once appeared to be severe? "O generation, saith the Lord, have I been a wilderness unto Israel? a land of darkness?" —"O my people, what have I done unto thee, and wherein have I wearied thee? testify against me!" Have I taken advantage of thy dependance to injure thee? Have I not made all things work together for good? But if I have done this, why do you decline me as to your *future* confidence? What narrow escapes have some of you had! When questioning your inability to judge for yourselves, had I allowed you for awhile to steer your little bark across the ocean of time, you would soon have stranded or struck against a rock, if I had not interposed on your behalf.

Fourthly. God is willing to choose for you still. Yes, this is wonderful, but it is true. If you had been placed under the direction of any creature, even of any angel, he would have long ago abandoned you; but God has borne with your manners and with your faithlessness in the wilderness. He hath said, "I am the Lord—I change not; therefore ye sons of Jacob are not consumed." This leaves you without excuse. You might otherwise have said, "God hath forsaken me, and I must manage as well as I can for myself." But this is not the case. But God is ready still to hear your prayer. You may, therefore, cry unto Him, "O Lord, I am oppressed; undertake for me." Place your reliance upon Him, and he will lead you and guide you in the way you should go. Repose a childlike trust and confidence in Him.

Then, *finally*, and to close the argument,—You will never feel *peace and comfort* till you feel assured that all is under the guidance and direction of your Heavenly Father—that he has undertaken the charge of all, in answer to your resolution, "The Lord shall chose my inheritance for me." The only way in which you can obtain your desires is, always to commit them to God. He will guide you by his counsel. The only way to happiness in a world like this, so full of changes, is, to trust in Him—to "trust in the Lord forever, for in the Lord Jehovah is everlasting strength." Therefore He hath said, "Thou wilt keep him in perfect peace, whose mind is stayed on Thee, because he trusteth in Thee." Solomon has this fine passage, "Commit thy works unto the Lord, and thy thoughts shall be established." And do you commit your thoughts unto the Lord? Our thoughts create anxieties, they produce tremulousness and vexations of mind, according to Solomon. And what is to be done in the multitude of our thoughts arising from our various concerns? What can *calm* them? Why, *confidence* in God. Commit thy works unto the Lord, and thy thoughts that may arise from them, however they may be multiplied, shall be established.

The heathens acknowledged that care was a cross and a malady, and they prescribed for the malady; but all their prescriptions proved ineffectual in removing the complaint. But the apostle prescribes an effectual remedy, in his Epistle to the Philippians, where he says, "Be careful for nothing, but in everything, by prayer and supplication, with thanksgiving, let your requests be made known unto God." And, Christians, what a load of care would be removed, what relief, what serenity would you feel, were you able to realize this! But let us hasten to consider once more.

FOURTHLY, IN WHAT THIS SENTIMENT IS TO BE IMPROVED? And, my brethren, we may improve it *in a way of concession.* We acknowledge this cause is difficult. It implies the mortification of pride and vanity—the sacrifice of self-will, of self-conceit, and self-sufficiency—it implies a willingness to be deprived of our possessions—to have our inclinations crossed, and our fond hopes destroyed. And you may feel assured of this, that the man is a stranger to the thing who is a stranger to such an attainment. No, it is the consequence of hard striving, of much observance of the misery of others, of much of the experience of those evils to which we have found ourselves exposed, when, instead of trusting in the Lord with all our heart, we have leaned to our own understanding. And, after all, there are some remains of this wretched leaven still left in the believer in our Lord Jesus. But they are hallowed, heavenly hours in which the Christian, with a holy heroism, can relinquish all, and say, falling upon his knees, "The Lord, He shall choose my inheritance for me."

Then we may improve it by remarking, that it is *so rare.* We cannot look for this state of mind except among Christians. The generality of mankind are "living without God, and without hope in the world;" and, though surrounded by so many proofs of his goodness, God is not in all their thoughts. They don't wish to be considered as atheists, and would perhaps be offended if we did not consider them as possessors of Christianity. But what are they?—Practical atheists. They have no abiding impression of God upon their minds—they don't refer to his glory in their pursuits—they use no means to ascertain his will, nor endeavor to secure his approbation.

We may improve it in a way *of inquiry.* Is the text your language? And is it the expression of the heart? for while man looketh on the outward appearance, the Lord looketh at the heart. There is much that is speculative in many professors of religion. But it would be absurd to suppose that such a sentiment was sincere and not operative. Surely the creed will guide the conduct; and we judge of the reality of your possessing godliness by the influence it will have upon you. You will not be urging after what God has denied, or quarrelling with him for what he has bestowed; but you would rather say with David, "Surely I have behaved and quieted myself as a child that is weaned of his mother; my soul is as a weaned child."

Let us also improve it *in a way of admonition.* Now have any of you an important movement in view? Learn to wait much upon God, seeking his direction. Move not but as you see the pillar of cloud or pillar of fire move, unless you would have God left behind you. There may be some difficulty; but in such cases never engage in anything without a conviction of its being right; if conscious of this, God will spare you, and peace shall be with you; but otherwise, what can be your peace?

You must wait *for* God, you see, as well as wait *upon* God. There are some, James tells us, who *will* be rich, whether God will have it so or not—they *will;* but says the Apostle Paul, "They that will be rich, fall into temptation and a snare, and into many foolish and hurtful lusts, which drown men in perdition and destruction." Alas! how much we see of this! And hear again the language of James: "Go to now, ye that say, To-day or to-morrow we will go into such a city, and continue there a year, and buy, and sell, and get gain; whereas ye know not what shall be on the morrow. For what is your life? It is even a vapor that appeareth for a little time, and then vanisheth away. For that ye ought to say, If the Lord will, we shall live, and do this or that." Now, here we have an unsanctified tradesman. He carries on business to great advantage: he seems to have no desire to monopolize, or to run down others: his aim seems to be to use it only in a lawful way of business. What, now, is there in this at all reprehensible? seeing it is the hand of the diligent that maketh rich, and if any provide not for his own, and especially for those of his own house, he hath denied the faith, and is worse than an infidel. But, perhaps you say he is avaricious—he is ambitious—and that it is not a substance he wants, but an abundance—not a competency, but splendor, and to be carried away by the pride of life. But, however this may be, God is not present to his mind. He never prayed before his undertaking. He never sought Divine direction, or said, "He shall choose my inheritance for me." He has been regardless of Him upon whom everything depends. He never said, "If the Lord will I shall live to do this or that." But he is to succeed; he is to live another year, regardless of vicissitudes and accidents, and he is to gain, notwithstanding faithless servants and heartless friends, and all those changes to which mortals are exposed while here.

Then it is the only way of *usefulness*. The Christian being blessed, becomes a blessing to others.

It is also the only way of *happiness*. God has given the dearest and highest enjoyment here in the place of our pilgrimage. The source of our highest happiness and dearest blessedness consists in our triumphs over sin, over self, and usefulness to others.

All without, and all about me, tells me I am a sinner. The Bible tells me what I must do to be saved. I must repent of sin, and believe in the name of the only-begotten Son of God.

O my hearers, may this not be a lost opportunity, or the means of your greater condemnation. Remember that "now is the accepted time, now is the day of salvation."

In conclusion—Though I wish it not to be exclusively regarded as an address to the young, yet I wish to impress these words, and press the sentiment upon you, my dear young friends. Your knowledge is small. You are destitute of that kind of information, the most valuable, derived from experience. Your feelings are easily and powerfully wrought upon. How much importance attaches to your conduct in the futurities of life, and upon any step you may take! A wrong step may produce a thousand bitter remorses, and cause repentance to be quartered upon you for life. Where is your safety? I tremble for you when I see you entering upon, and having to pass through, such a world as this. Where, I ask again, is your safety? Will you not from this time cry unto God, "My Father, thou shalt be the guide of my youth"? It is a mercy that some of you have wise and good parents to counsel and direct you. These, however, are not a substitute for God—but God can be a substitute for them to you, if you should be deprived of them; and if father and mother should be called to forsake you, the Lord will take you up. O that you may see the importance, and be influenced to make a surrender of yourselves to Him! And you know who hath said, "I love them that love me, and those that seek me early shall find me."

SERMON II.

"I will bring the blind by a way that they knew not; I will lead them in paths that they have not known; I will make darkness light before them, and crooked things straight. These things will I do unto them, and not forsake them."—Isaiah, xlii. 16.

The sky is not more beautifully spangled with stars than the Bible is filled with promises. It is to remind us of the greatness of these assurances, that the Apostle Peter tells us there are given "exceeding great and precious promises;" but this would only have prepared the way for disappointment, by raising our expectations high, unless they could be absolutely depended upon; and, therefore, the Apostle Paul says, "all the promises of God are yea and amen in Christ Jesus." Now, thus recommended, you cannot be too well acquainted with them; you cannot too frequently review them; nothing can be more pleasing, nothing more profitable, than to place them opposite all your exigencies; to seek from them relief for all that is trying in creatures around you; and to compare them with their accomplishment in others and in ourselves. "I will bring the blind by a way that they knew not; I will lead them in paths that they have not known; I will make darkness light before them, and crooked things straight. These things will I do unto them, and not forsake them."

These words have been completely accomplished in those who have reached Immanuel's land, and in whose number we now reckon so many of our own beloved friends and relations who are waiting to receive us into everlasting habitations. I say they are completely accomplished in them. As soon as ever they had taken possession of the inheritance of the saints in light, some Joshua said to them, "Ye know in all your hearts that not one thing has failed of all the good things which the Lord your God spake concerning you; all are come to pass unto you, and not one thing hath failed thereof." But, Christians, you are not yet come to the rest of the Lord, but you are journeying towards it; so far He has been your helper, and because He has been your helper it becomes you to say, with David, "Therefore under the shadow of thy wings will I put my trust." And to aid you a little in your gratitude in the reflection of the past, and in your confidence in prospect of the future, let us in this brief and familiar exercise examine God's engagements, and see the advantages we are to derive from them.

First. As a Leader.

Secondly. As an Interpreter.

Thirdly. As a never-failing Friend.

My brethren, it is our mercy that though we cannot know God perfectly we can know Him savingly: though we know not what He is in himself, we see what He is to us. He is held forth in His Word as our *Leader.* "I will bring the blind by a way that they know not; I will *lead* them in paths that they have not known." What could we do without such a guide? What would be the condition of man without God with him in the world? He is a wanderer on the dark mountains, exposed to every destroyer, and by a miserable time working out a more miserable eternity. You may go to hell without God, but you will never go to heaven but under His conduct; and yet men naturally are not sensible of their need of such a guide. There is nothing men are so proud of as their knowledge; they would generally rather be considered knaves than fools; of everything that pertains to them they are pleased with nothing but their understandings; they have not enough of anything else, but here they are completely satisfied; in any kind of contention or reasoning you will always find them preferring their own modicum of sense to that of others, and this, too, just in proportion to their ignorance, and deficiency, and want of judgment; and so vain man would be wise, though man be born like a wild ass's colt. "We go astray from the womb," says David. We are "alienated from God by wicked works," says Paul. If ever you have sincerely reflected on your condition; if ever you have been in earnest to reach eternal glory; if ever you have been duly sensible of your own guilt and weakness, and the difficulties and dangers of the passage,—this has been from that hour your prayer, "Lead me in thy truth, and teach me. Teach me to do thy will, for thou art my God." And does He disregard such a prayer? He always pays attention to it; He takes us under his guidance; and every believer may therefore say, with David, "He restoreth my soul; he leadeth me in the paths of righteousness for his name's sake." And hence the church exults and exclaims, "This God is our God forever and ever; He will be our guide, even unto death." Well may we rejoice, if we are under the care of such a Being in our way to heaven; one so almighty to defend us, so condescending to converse with us, so kind to indulge us, so patient to bear with us, and so wise to choose our inheritance for us. But the persons whom He thus leads are called *blind*. How is this? Are they not in Scripture always represented as children of the day? Does not the apostle say to them, "Ye *were* darkness, but *now* are ye light in the Lord"? In the 9th of John you read that the Pharisees said unto the *blind* man;—he was not blind *then*, but he *had been* blind, and they called him by the old name. So it is here. They are called from what they once were; and what they are indeed now partially. Let us, therefore, now see for a few moments how, and where, He leads them. "I will lead them in paths they have not known." This is true.

1. *In their spiritual concerns.*—What, Christian, did you formerly know of things you now see the beauty and feel the importance of? What did you once know of conviction of sin? You now see its evil and guilt as well as its danger; you see its pollution, and how it excludes you righteously from the presence of a holy God; you now not only fear it, but you hate it; and you now not only leave it, but you loathe it. What did you once know of faith in Christ? Now you claim him as your foundation and your refuge; now you rejoice in him with joy unspeakable, and full of glory. But did you go this way heretofore? What did you then know of a throne of grace? You heard of prayer —you said yours, perhaps, very regularly; or, if not, when any danger or distress excited you: but now you hunger and thirst after righteousness; now you come unto God by Him; now you have boldness and access with confidence, by the faith of Him; now you can say, "It is good for me to draw near unto God." But did you go this way heretofore? No. He hath brought the blind by a way that they knew not. If now you are Christians, you were not born such; you

were made such. He has made you to differ, and the difference arises from His having called you "out of darkness into his marvellous light;" the conversion, which you have been made the subject of, is, therefore, in Scripture, said to be your "walking in newness of life;"—observe this,—in *newness of life.* There is always a leaning in people to antiquity, and there is some reason for it; it is not a mere prejudice; and the reason is this, because truth was before error; for error is the perversion of truth, and a thing must exist before it can be perverted or abused. Now people know this; and, therefore, when the "truth as it is in Jesus" comes into a neighborhood, the common language is, that it is a novel thing. But nothing can be more false than this accusation. The Gospel was preached to the Jews—The Gospel was preached to Abraham 430 years before the giving of the law—yea, the Gospel was preached in Paradise to Adam and Eve in the first promise. What do we say? An infidel has entitled a book "Christianity as old as the Creation," and we accept the charge in one view. As old as the Creation! It is much older. "We hope," says the apostle, "in eternal life, which God, that cannot lie, promised before the world began." But though the charge of novelty be false in this respect, it is true in another. There is a newness in these things as to their perception. Though you have heard of them —read of them—before, yet, when you are called by grace, you have other views of them, and other feelings than before: you seem to have entered a new world. Thus would it be if some of you went to Italy;—it would not be a new country, but it would be new to you. If a man were born blind, and restored to sight,—why, he would not see a new sun, but it would be new to him; and thus it is that the Lord leads us in paths that we have not known.

It is equally true with regard to Christians,

2. *In their temporal concerns;* for here, what do you know as to future scenes? what with regard to nations, families, individuals? what with regard to yourselves? Why, you know not what a day may bring forth. And when you look back on life, all that is very important in it you had not once been led to expect; the places in which you have resided, your friendships, your employments, your enterprises, your disappointments, your successes,—all these would formerly, had they been presented to you, have appeared strange; and, had they been foretold, would have led you to say, with the unbelieving nobleman, "If the Lord should make windows in heaven, might such things be!" Now this is peculiarly the case with regard to some men. In their lives there has been such an opposition between obscurity and splendor, that there seems to be between them a gulf which could not have been passed; but it has been passed under the leadings of Him "who is wonderful in counsel and excellent in working."

When the Jews returned from Babylon, and, instead of being peeled and stripped, were even enriched;—"when," said they, "the Lord turned our captivity, we were like them that dreamed." When the Jews were in the wilderness, they never knew where they should fix their next station; and this was not often a straightforward motion, but, as Moses remarks, "he led them *about;*" and yet the psalmist makes this remark upon it, "he led them by a *right* way." So

Abraham went forth, not knowing whither he went, but he knew with whom; and as Job said, "Behold I go forward, but He is not there, and backward, but I cannot perceive Him; but He knoweth the way that I take."

Having viewed God as our leader, let us

Secondly. See Him as our Interpreter.—The knowledge he imparts to his people is always gradual, like the dawn that shineth more and more unto the perfect day. "I will make darkness light before them, and crooked things straight." Let us see how this may be exemplified in five cases or instances.

"He makes darkness light, and crooked things straight."

1. *As to Doctrine.*—It is not for us to determine with how much ignorance in the mind, and error in judgment, grace may be associated in the heart; but we read in the Gospel of a blind man, on whose eyes our Saviour put his fingers, and said to him, Look, and he looked up, and said, "I see men as trees walking." But he was under the operation of Christ; and when He put his hand a second time to the work, and said, Look up, he said, "Now I see all things clearly." So it is here, it is precisely the case with persons; for some have very defective, obscure views of some of the leading truths of the Gospel; I mean, compared with what others possess, and what they themselves will possess afterwards. I seldom, indeed, like persons who all at once become so very clear and high; they remind me of those poor ricketty children, whose heads grow larger than their bodies; it is not the effect of strength, but of disease and weakness. I never think it well to see speculation going before expe-

rience. All God's works are progressive. We see first the blade—then the ear—after that the full corn in the ear. Our Saviour said to his own disciples, "I have many things to say unto you, but ye cannot bear them now." When will ministers, when will Christians, learn to follow His example? when will they be able to exercise patience towards the imperfect? You sometimes seem not only mortified, but even offended, because persons do not learn in a few weeks or months what God has been teaching you twenty or thirty years, and which you know but very imperfectly now. If the heart be broken (which is what I look for)—if the heart be broken for sin and from it; and if a man be brought on his knees, and humbly prays that God would lead him into all truth; if, as the apostle says, as far as he has attained he walks by the same rule and minds the same thing,—then, from him, I am authorized to conclude, "that if in anything else he be otherwise minded, God will reveal it unto him;" and though in such persons the work is often slow, I have often observed it is very sure; I have never found any of these persons carried away with the follies of the day; they have believed, and had the witness in themselves.

He makes darkness light before them, and crooked things straight.

2. *As to Experience.*—There are many things here which are often very perplexing to Christians; and nothing more than the temptations with which they are assailed. Perhaps there are persons here this morning who are ready to say, "Ah, no one knows so much of temptations as I do; they are the death of my comforts, and I often say, will prove the destruc-

tion of my soul at last." But as they go on, they are called to see and to understand, that while the strong man armed kept his palace, his goods were in peace; that Pharaoh pursued after the children of Israel before they had left his realms; that our Saviour was in all points tempted like as we are; and that the man who is a stranger to Christian conflict has no reason in the world to believe that he is a partaker of the Divine life; for every Christian tells us the flesh lusteth against the spirit, and the spirit against the flesh. Again: with regard to prayer, which is another source often of perplexity. The man reads in Scripture that God hears prayer, and, says he, "I have prayed, and he shutteth out my prayer." But, by-and-bye, he is enabled to distinguish between hearing and answering prayer; and to learn that the prayer of faith is immediately heard, but not immediately answered: that when God designs good to his people, He waits to be gracious: you would pluck the fruit while it is green, but He draws back your hand. It is the same with regard to the manner in which He answers prayer often. By strange, and sometimes even terrible things, in righteousness, does He answer His people, as the God of their salvation. Some of you are acquainted with the excellent language of Mr. Newton in his hymn:

"I ask'd the Lord, that I might grow
 In faith, and love, and every grace;
Might more of his salvation know,
 And seek more earnestly his face.

'Twas He who taught me thus to pray,
 And He, I trust, has answer'd prayer;
But it has been in such a way,
 As almost drave me to despair.

I hoped that, in some favor'd hour,
  At once He 'd answer my request,
And, by his love's constraining power,
  Subdue my sins, and give me rest.

Instead of this, He made me feel
  The hidden evils of my heart,
And let the angry powers of hell
  Assault my soul in every part.

Yea, more, with his own hand He seem'd
  Intent to aggravate my woe;
Cross'd all the fair designs I schem'd,
  Blasted my gourds, and laid them low.

"*Lord, why is this?*" *I trembling cried,*
  "*Wilt thou pursue thy worm to death?*"
"*'Tis in this way,*" *the Lord replied,*
  "*I answer prayer for grace and faith:*

"*These inward trials I employ,*
  From self and pride to set thee free,
And break thy schemes of earthly joy,
  That thou may'st seek thy all in Me."

So it is again with regard to *joy*. The man reads that religion is every way friendly to joy—that they return and come to Zion with songs, and with everlasting joy upon their heads; but, says he, I know so little of this that I am afraid I have no part nor lot in the matter; but he, by-and-bye, learns that saints are described in the Scriptures by their tears, as well as by their joys—"they shall come with weeping and with supplication." He mixes with Christians more advanced, and he learns from them that they are the subjects of the same alternations; and thus what proved a stumbling-block before becomes a way-mark to teach him that he is in the way everlasting. I remember —— Milner, in his last illness, said, "If some years ago I had been as destitute of comfort as I now am, it would have exceedingly perplexed me; but I have long learned that it is one important act of faith to hang on the bare word of God, and to trust in a God that hideth himself." This leads us to another article; and,

THIRDLY, WITH REGARD TO ASSURANCE, "He makes darkness light before them, and crooked things straight." Oh, say some, to know my interest in the everlasting covenant! Oh, then I would face a frowning world! Oh, then I would defy the king of terrors; but all is obscurity with me. 'Tis a point I long to know, but at present all I can attain is a kind of peradventure—perhaps I am right; but when trouble comes upon me—when the shadows of the evening are hastening on—to have no more certainty than this, what am I to do? Do as you are doing. "Wait on the Lord, and keep his way. Wait on the Lord, be of good courage, and he shall strengthen thine heart; wait, I say, on the Lord." "Them that honor me," says He, "I will honor." Keep at His feet, therefore, till you feel He has taken you into his bosom. Continue crying, "God be merciful to me a sinner," till you are able to say with Thomas, "My Lord and my God!" He will "make darkness light before you, and crooked things straight."

As to practical duty.—With regard to changes in your condition in life, the removal of your habitation, a transition from one business to another, or anything of this nature, you are at a loss to know what the will of God is: this genders in you many anxieties to which others are strangers; but you read that if you walk contrary to God, He will walk contrary to you; how much depends on one wrong step; consequences may arise from it that will give a complexion to all your future days, and quarter repentance upon you for life. Now here you are not to expect miracles, but you are to make use of sense and reason, and Scripture, and the advice of friends. You are to wait for God and you are to wait upon God. You are to remember the command, "Trust in the Lord with all thine heart, and lean not unto thine own understanding." "In all thy ways acknowledge him, and he shall direct thy paths."

"He will make darkness light before you, and crooked things straight."

5. *In the dispensations of his providence.*—Where is the Christian but has sometimes had reason to exclaim, "His way is in the sea, and his paths in the deep waters;" and where is the Christian but after a while has seen that He can turn the shadow of death into the morning? I see, says the Christian, why such a prop was taken away. I was beginning to lean upon it. I can see now why I was exercised with such a sorrow; it was to soften my heart, and to enable me to sympathize with others in distress; that sickness of the body was to heal the disease of the mind. So Job, although severely tried, saw before his death that the end of the Lord was very pitiful and of tender mercy. So David could say also, "It is good for me that I have been afflicted; for before I was afflicted I went astray, but now I have kept thy word;" that is, I was ill, and he bled me, and I recovered. He drew the ploughshare all along, but it was to break up the fallow ground, and to prepare for the reception of the seed. Take heed, therefore, that you do not draw hasty

conclusions from present aspects of providence. Take heed that you do not say, "All these things are against me;" but say with Paul, "I know that all things shall work together for my good." Follow the admonition of Isaiah, "Who is among you that feareth the Lord that walketh in darkness, and hath no light, let him trust in the name of the Lord, and *stay* upon his God." Now observe. If you were to travel with a guide when you came to a very dismal place, you would not only follow, but you would lay hold of, your conductor, and lean; and so says Isaiah, "Let him *stay* upon his God, and he will fulfil his word. I will bring the blind by a way that they know not; I will lead them in paths that they have not known. I will make darkness light before them, and crooked things straight." Then observe,

Thirdly. He is their never-failing FRIEND.—"These things will I do unto them, and will not forsake them." It will readily be allowed that they deserve to be forsaken, and they may say with the Church of old, "It is of the Lord's mercies that we are not consumed." And they also suppose frequently that they are forsaken—so did Zion. "Zion said, The Lord hath forsaken, and my God hath forgotten me." But it was not so. "Can a woman forget her sucking child, that she should not have compassion on the son of her womb; yea, they may forget, yet will not I forget thee." Asaph drew the same conclusion, and it was equally ill founded. "Will the Lord cast off for ever, and will he be favorable no more?" But how often do your ministers dwell on Divine desertion? We must, therefore, show how there may be a forsaking quite consistent with the truth of our text: "These things will I do unto them, and not forsake them." There are three ways in which God may be said to forsake his people:—

1. *As to outward comfort and condition.*—He may reduce them much; he may deprive them of their connexions and possessions. Remember what he said to the Jews: "I will *go*," observe he said, "I will *go* and return unto my place until they seek my face; in their affliction they will seek me early." We see what is intended by His going away and returning; it was leaving them to their embarrassments, and perplexities, and troubles, till He came to deliver them; but this is compatible with the real presence of God too: every condition is supportable while He is with us; and, with regard to trouble, if He leaves his people in anything else, He cannot leave them in trouble, for He has made a particular engagement there, "I will be with them in trouble." He may forsake His people,

2. *As to feeling spiritual comfort;* but while they have no sensible consolation, yet there is grace, and grace operating frequently with peculiar power in producing contentment of soul and humiliation before God. How was it with Cooper the martyr? He felt no consolation till he came to the stake, and then he exclaimed, "Now He is come, now He is come!" But He must have been with him before, (though now He came in a way of manifestation,) or he never would have come to the stake. What grace there must have been in Job to enable him to say, "Though he slay me, yet will I trust in him!" David says, "My soul followeth hard after thee; thy right hand upholdeth me." There seems a confusion of images. Here David is following hard after God, and yet God is up-

holding him at the same time. He was seeking God in one view, while God was supporting and sustaining him in another. He was seeking for consolation while he felt Divine support. Then,

3. As to grace itself He may forsake His people—not as to *habit*, but as to *degree*,—not as to existence, but as to exercise. The best way for ministers to teach, is to teach by facts, and history, and example. Remember the history of Hezekiah—howbeit in the affair of the ambassador God left him to try what was in his heart. "Weak as we are," says Newton, "we shall not faint." He may therefore leave you in three ways:—*First*, As to your outward condition:—*Secondly*, As to sensible spiritual comfort:—*Thirdly*, As to the degree and exercise of faith. But further than this we cannot go, unless we go without the Scripture. He never can forsake His people wholly; cast down but not destroyed. "Though ye fall," says David, "ye shall not be utterly cast down." He cannot forsake His people finally. Here 's His own engagement,—"This is as the waters of Noah unto me; for as I have sworn that the waters of Noah should no more go over the earth; so have I sworn that I would not be wroth with thee, nor rebuke thee. For the mountains shall depart, and the hills be removed, but my kindness shall not depart from thee, neither shall the covenant of my peace be removed, saith the Lord, that hath mercy on thee."

You know I have not time to argue this any further; otherwise how many passages of Scripture there are that would furnish us with materials enough. "He will not forsake his people, because it hath pleased him to make them his people." "Being confident of this very thing, that he which hath begun a good work in you will perform it unto the day of Jesus Christ." His people, therefore, may say without presumption, "I am persuaded that neither death, nor life, nor angels, nor principalities, nor powers, nor things present, nor things to come, shall be able to separate us from the love of God, which is in Jesus Christ our Lord."

It is a delightful spectacle that has been presented before us. It is always pleasing to see God at work; how pleasing and delightful to see His agency in the world of nature; how I love to stand on a hill and look down on the valley beneath, or to stand by the side of a brook, or to pass through a field of standing corn, and to see how He has prepared of His goodness for the poor.

I love to see His agency in providence, especially in a time of such trouble and disaffection as ours, and to remember that He is a God among the nations. But oh, to contemplate His agency in grace; to see God going and taking possession of a sinner for Himself; and forever to see Him detach him from his sins, and from the spirit of the world, saying to him, "Follow me;" to see Him taking the sinner in all the ruins of the fall, and making him an eternal excellency, the joy of many generations, and bringing him in triumph to endless glory! And oh, how often has He done it. "We speak that we do know, and testify that we have seen." I hail you, therefore, Christians, but I cannot pity you. I pity the poor, and I wish it were in my power to relieve them. I pity the wealthy who are destitute of heavenly riches. I pity the scholar who understands not a word of the language of Canaan.

I pity the astronomer who is familiar with stars, and knows not the way to heaven. Oh, these are all pitiable characters; pity them my brethren—pray for them; but as for you who are partakers of His grace, and are under His own guidance, I'll never pity you; whatever be your condition, however poor, however despised, you are not pitiable; you are enviable, and the only enviable characters in this world; and therefore we kneel in view of you and pray, Oh, remember me with the favor Thou bearest to thy people. And surely this should be an excitement and encouragement to you to seek for an interest in the same blessedness. "Therefore," says David, "they that know thy name will put their trust in thee." And you should apply this, Christians, as a remedy. You should take it as Paul did, and apply it as a cure for two things—covetousness and carefulness. Let your conversation be without covetousness. Be careful for nothing.

May you, therefore, take this promise with you from the house of God; and carry it along with you in all your succeeding journey. Make use of it as Solomon recommends, "Tie it about thy neck—write it upon the table of thine heart."

CONCLUDING OBSERVATIONS

ON THE

REV. WILLIAM JAY,

AS A PREACHER, AND AS AN AUTHOR,

BY

THE EDITORS.

CONCLUDING OBSERVATIONS, &c.

HITHERTO in these volumes the reader's attention has been mainly directed to Mr. Jay's own account of himself—his history, his progress, his recollections. The Editors have felt that their services to his memory ought to be chiefly regulated by the documents placed in their hands, and limited to such passing annotations, or supplemental matter, as seemed to be required for conveying a just view of their subject, and a complete narrative of his history.

But judging that so interesting and remarkable a character well deserves a separate sketch from another hand beside his own, and supposing that the reader will expect something of this sort, as a conclusion to the volumes, which in the main may be said to be his own representation of himself; the Editors have ventured to subjoin the following observations, on the two principal views of his public character for which he was admired by his contemporaries, and will be respected by future ages.

MR. JAY AS THE PREACHER.

A PREACHER who, from his first appearance in the pulpit, at the age of sixteen, till he retired from it when eighty-four years old, fixed and held the attention of the public; who, during this lengthened period, was heard with equal interest by the aged and the young, the learned and the illiterate, who always crowded, whenever he presented himself, to listen to his teaching; who was eulogized by such men as Wilberforce, Beckford, and Sir William Knighton; by Hall, Chalmers, and Foster; who, whether he preached in the city or in the village, drew after him his ministerial brethren, both of his own church and most others; who was esteemed and admired by all denominations of professing Christians; and who, when his sermons were sent forth from the press, raised for himself, in both hemispheres, a reputation such as few of his own day, or any other, ever obtained,—must have possessed elements of power, after which it is worth while to inquire, not only for the purpose of gratifying curiosity, but to prompt and guide the spirit of lawful emulation. Such a preacher was Mr. Jay; and it is the object of this Sketch to show in what his attractions principally consisted, and to what he owed his extensive and permanent popularity.

It may be stated, as a preliminary remark, that the arrangements of Providence, as regards his personal appearance, his physical endowments both of body and mind, the circumstances of his conversion, the peculiar nature of his professional education, as well as the state of the Christian Church when he first appeared in public, were all preparatory to his future eminence as a preacher of the Gospel. This, with a kind of instinctive sagacity, he perceived; and, from the commencement of his Christian career, fixed his eye exclusively upon the pulpit, and cherished a hallowed desire to excel as a minister of Jesus Christ. He clearly saw that, if he would do one great thing well, he must concentrate his powers upon *that*, and make everything else give place, or become subservient to it. He had from the beginning an almost intuitive perception of what constituted pulpit excellence; he studied the attractions and defects of other preachers—felt the promptings of a holy ambition after eminence and usefulness; and with that consciousness of power which usually attends genius, and inspires it with the foresight of success, he determined, by God's grace, to attain to distinction as a *preacher*. This, however, was not the mere yearning of youthful vanity, but the prompting of a heart throbbing with solicitude for the salvation of souls. True it is, that his attention was first of all directed to this subject by Mr. Winter. This excellent man discerned at once what a bud of ministerial promise there was in that mason-lad whom he saw among his hearers, and who afterwards came in his apron to converse with him on the subject of religion and of the ministry. But the boy Jay embraced with his whole heart the sublime object, as soon as it was presented to him, and consecrated himself to it from the moment that it arose in its full-orbed glory upon his mental horizon.

His academic curriculum was of too short duration, and too limited in its literary advantages, and too often interrupted by preaching, to allow much hope of his ever being a scholar, a metaphysician, or a philosopher. But preaching of a very high order he was assured could be attained without these things. And he was right. As a general principle, learning is of essential importance to the ministers of religion; and, other things being equal, *he* will make the best preacher who is most thoroughly educated. Nor should our young ministers suffer themselves too hastily to conclude, that they can never attain to eminence in literature; and be induced to abandon it under the notion that, as they have neither taste nor aptitude for it, they will concentrate all their attention upon preaching. Still, we contend that it is not indispensable that every preacher should be an eminent scholar. Where, as in the case of Mr. Jay, opportunities for literature are denied to the eager aspirant after ministerial labor, and yet there are all the other essential elements of a good preacher, there let a strong determination be formed by all possible diligence in the use of such means as are afforded, to excel in that holy career, to which the leadings of Providence invite, and the impulses of a longing heart prompt.

Mr. Jay's whole character, as a public man, may be summed up in that one word, THE PREACHER; and it is in this view he must be contemplated by all who would conceive of him aright. True, he was an author, and one of the most popular writers of his day, both in America and this country; yet nearly all his works consisted of Sermons, or what, as in his "Morning and Evening Exercises," bore a resemblance to them. So that he was still a silent preacher, even in his books. Such a mind as his could, however, doubtless, by dint of resolute determination and close application, have attained to eminence in any department of study. He himself tells us that his taste at one time led him to abstruse speculation; but that, finding it engrossed too much of his time, and interfered with more useful pursuits, he laid it aside, and addicted himself to matters which bore more directly upon his ministerial duties. We have no doubt, however, that while conscience had *something* to do with this, mental aptitude was not wholly unconcerned. What was practical was far more congenial with his order of mind than what was speculative; and his choice of the former was as certainly and, perhaps, as much the result of temperament as of principle.

Mr. Jay as a preacher owed not a little to his personal appearance, and undoubtedly much to his voice. In the earlier periods of his history, his countenance was eminently prepossessing. The portrait affixed to this work, copied from a painting taken when he was about forty-nine years of age, and which was considered a good likeness at the time, proves this. His black hair, dark eyes, florid complexion, and an expression of features in which intelligence and benevolence mingled with somewhat of archness, at once attracted and interested his hearers. As he advanced in years, he became much stouter, which, as he was never tall, destroyed in some measure the symmetry of his frame. A graphic writer thus describes his appearance in the decline of life:—

"It is not very long since," says Dr. James Hamilton, "we heard him with wonder and delight, and in our own as well as in millions of memories is still depicted that countenance whose sunshine furnished its own photograph; so wise and so witty, so wrinkled yet so radiant; with so much of youthful ardor welling up in the fountains of those deeply-fringed, softly-burning eyes; and with words so holy and so tender dropping from those lips in whose corners lurked all that was quaint or caustic; whilst like an oak-thicket on an old rampart-summit, that strong visage and firm brow rose and were lost in the shaggy wilderness which covered all with its copsy crown."

Mr. Jay's voice was certainly one of the charms of his preaching. It was sonorous but not loud—alternating between bass and tenor; strong yet soft; musical and flexible; and more adapted to give expression to what is tender, pathetic, and solemn, than to what is lively, impetuous, and impulsive. If it did not stir you as with the blast of a trumpet, it soothed and delighted you, as with the soft tones of a flute. This indeed was the general character of his preaching, in which the manner was suited to the matter. You sat in sweet stillness, luxuriating under those beautiful trains of quiet thinking, and gentle, holy, and evangelic emotion, uttered in tones so mellifluous, that you seemed to be listening to music which came from another world, and which lifted your soul to the sphere from which it emanated. An involuntary, unbidden tear occasionally suffused your eye, and a gentle emotion filled your heart, as some touching passage, in plaintive sounds, swelling like those of an Eolian harp, passed over your spirit and moved it, just as a summer's breeze ruffles the surface of a lake, without deeply or violently disturbing it.

He entered the pulpit in a grave, collected manner, apparently absorbed in his mission, and with a step rather quick, yet solemn, and without hurry, and after sometimes casting a glance round upon the audience, retired into himself, and seemed to be gathering up his thoughts and energies, to negotiate between God and man the weighty affairs of judgment and of mercy.

In the preliminary exercises of public worship, reading the Scriptures, and prayer, Mr. Jay never forgot that, in one of these, he was enunciating the words of the Most High; and in the other, that he was addressing himself to Him before whom the seraphim veil their faces. It has been sometimes thought and said that very little spiritual, at any rate saving effect, is produced by the public reading of the Scriptures. Is not this to be traced up to the careless, unimpressive, irreverent, and unfeeling manner in which the exercise is performed? The tones, emphasis, and accents of a good reader, who is neither elaborate, artificial, nor theatrical in his manner, convey both instruction and impression, and are a kind of exposition of the sacred text.

In prayer Mr. Jay was often singularly felicitous in his expressions, and always devout in his manner; his devotions were richly scriptural and strictly appropriate; perhaps occasionally a little too quaint in expression, and therefore liable to interfere with perfect composure and gravity. He was slow and solemn in his utterance, and his feelings were so far under control as never to hurry him into that rapidity and vociferation which, we regret to say, characterize those addresses to the Almighty which are made from some Nonconforming pulpits. If reform be necessary in the liturgical services of the Church of England, it is equally necessary in the extempore ones of some among the Dissenters. Occasionally there is too much of preaching in prayer; too much of theology; too little of petition and confession. There is a happy medium between that elaboration which, by its artificialness, represses religious feeling, and that negligence which disgusts good taste; between that muttering and trembling which betoken slavish dread, and the loud or even boisterous manner which indicates want of feeling and displays of unhallowed familiarity. We do not wonder that church people of refinement who occasionally attend Dissenting worship, complain of a want of solemnity and devout feeling in our prayers; yet were extempore prayer performed as it should be, they would retire with a conviction of its superior appropriateness, earnestness, and adaptation to the various classes of the congregation, and the changeful experience of the Christian heart.

In the selection of his texts, Mr. Jay was often very ingenious. His extraordinary acquaintance with his Bible gave him great advantage in this. His hearers were often surprised by a passage which was so novel to them, that they did not know there was such a verse in the Scriptures. His canon was, that to secure and hold attention, to produce impression and do good, the preaching must be something that will "*strike* and *stick*." Perhaps, in carrying out this, he sometimes erred on the side of quaintness, both in the selection of texts and in his illustrations. Yet a quaint text, if one may thus characterize any portion of God's word, if it contain an important lesson, and if it be fairly dealt with, and be not by an ingenious fancy tortured upon the rack, to extort from it a meaning which it would not otherwise acknowledge, tends to secure attention and enliven the preaching. But this must not be done too often, or it will lose its effect, and subject the preacher to the imputation of being a pulpit-jester.

Mr. Jay's introductions to his sermons were sometimes as striking as his texts. We remember once hearing him, when preaching on Pilate's question, put to Jesus Christ,—"What is truth?"—commence his sermon thus: "It is *A* truth, Pilate, that thou art a cowardly, guilty wretch, in surrendering Christ to be crucified when thou wert convinced he was an innocent man." This *ex abrupto* method of introduction is, however, a hazardous one, since it is somewhat difficult to keep up the attention to that altitude which it has reached by such an exordium. It is like spicing the first dish at a feast so highly as to render all that follow in some measure insipid.

The prevailing character of Mr. Jay's sermons, considered as to their matter, was the mixture of evangelical doctrine, experimental feeling, and Christian practice. His memoirs mention the fact, that on his first visit to London he had the character of several ministers described to him; one as a doctrinal, a second as a practical, and a third as an experimental preacher. With the good sense, tact, and discrimination belonging to him, he said to himself, "I will be neither exclusively, but all unitedly." So he was. His evangelism, so far as doctrine was concerned, was never very prominent, as a thing separate and by itself, in the form of a dogmatic statement, with proofs from Scripture and controversial arguments, but was held in solution in his general course of preaching. To borrow an illustration from his reminiscence of Mr. Newton, that good man, in speaking of his Calvinism, said it was in his whole preaching, as sugar in a cup of tea, that which sweetened the whole, but which is not to be taken in the lump.

We think Mr. Jay was a little deficient in not giving greater room and prominence to the chief truths of salvation in their dogmatic form. He acknowledged he was in early life, and it was perhaps also true to the end of it. When setting out in his ministry, he saw the errors into which many of the newly-formed evangelical school in the Church of England ran, in dwelling too abstractedly and exclusively upon dogmatic theology, and the bad effect it had in some instances upon their conduct;—and in avoiding this extreme he, perhaps, went over to another. He was in sentiment decidedly evangelical, and also in his preaching, but not formally and controversially doctrinal. It was his evangelism which constituted no small share of the attraction of his preaching. His confession of faith, if such it may be called, delivered at his ordination, though drawn up when only twenty-one years of age, is one of the most beautiful compends of evangelical truth in the English language.

He was, to a very great extent, an experimental preacher, but his preaching seemed to touch upon the experience of those only who were tried by the ordinary cares and sorrows of human life, and to suggest the usual topics of consolation adapted to such cases, rather than to analyze those deep workings of the human heart when struggling with all the powers of darkness, and all the strength of its own corruptions. It was the widow mourning over her bereavement, the mother weeping for her dead child, the man of broken fortunes, the orphan youth, the perplexed pilgrim, or the Christian troubled with the common temptations of our probation, that his preaching was calculated to help and comfort; and hence the wide range of his popularity. Hence, amidst the crowd of his hearers and admirers, were not so many of those who wanted the stronger consolation which a heart bruised and broken in the spiritual conflict requires. But equally true is it, that he never administered to inconsistent professors the ardent spirit of Antinomian comfort, which was but too common at the commencement of his ministry; or to imaginative believers, the cordials of a sentimental comfort, no less common at the close of it. It was, however, as a practical preacher that Mr. Jay chiefly excelled; and here his excellences were transcendent. No man knew more clearly the obligations of the Christian life, and no man urged them more earnestly or more attractively. It was his happy art to make men feel that wisdom's ways are ways of pleasantness, and that all her paths are peace.

Perhaps there is scarcely a single word which will more aptly describe Mr. Jay as a preacher than the term *naturalness.* This constituted, we are sure, no small part of the attraction of his *manner.* His voice, his tones, his action, were all inartificial, and displayed the gracefulness of nature. It was not an imitation of nature on the stage, but nature's self in her own walk and place of action. He spoke to you as you felt he should do, without any uncouth awkwardness or caricature which disfigures nature, or any studied affectations which destroys it. To much action in the pulpit, in the use of the hands and arms, he was strongly opposed, and seldom used any, except an occasional elevation of the hand. Here we think he was somewhat deficient, for nature prompts in strong emotion to bodily action. But this was the least part and the lowest manifestation of his naturalness. He spoke *from* his own nature *to* the nature of others. He was himself a most inartificial man. All his tastes, his habits, and his pursuits proved this. He knew human nature well. He studied it in himself and in others. He knew *man*, how he thinks, and feels, and acts. He drew his knowledge, not from copies in books, but from the living original. Men felt when they heard him, that they were listening to a preacher who knew not only books, and theories, and systems, but humanity, both in its fallen and in its restored state; in its wants, woes, diseases, remedies, and varieties; one who could sympathize with them as well as teach them. When, on a Sunday morning they came, worn and weary with the trials, toils, and cares of the six days' labor, and placed themselves under the sound of his mellifluous voice, they felt sure of not being tantalized and disappointed with a cold intellectualism, or a mere logical demonstration, or a metaphysical abstraction, or a wordy nothing, which would have been giving them a stone when they asked for bread; or with something religiously poetic, which would have been offering them flowers when they wanted meat;—but he fed them with food convenient for them, and satisfied the cravings of their nature with what satisfied his own.

This quality of his preaching was very strikingly displayed in the *illustrations* with which his sermons abounded. He never suffered the attention of his hearers to doze over dry abstract disquisitions, or dull, didactic, and prosaic harangues, but kept it perpetually awake by appeals to their imagination. His talent for illustrative allusion was extraordinary. His sermons were not only by his beautiful fancy illuminated, like the ancient missals, but illustrated, like modern books, by descriptive scenes. They contained all the glowing coloring of the one, with the more correct and graceful forms of the other. Here his naturalness constantly appeared, and in close resemblance to that of our Lord, who drew his similes and metaphors from the works of nature and the relationships of humanity. The great Teacher's discourses were replete with images borrowed from the beasts of the field, and the birds of the air; from rural sights and rural sounds; from the ties of parentage, and the reciprocal obligation of husband and wife, master and servant. So were Mr. Jay's. A natural simplicity and beauty, polished yet artless, pervaded his discourses. There was comparatively little of the grandeur and sublimity of the great masters of eloquence, but a constant succession of chaste, tender, and smiling allusions. His preaching did not produce the effect of the lofty and fervid utterances of Robert Hall, which, with their elegant diction, mighty conceptions, and glowing imagery, raised you into a fellowship of rapture with the speaker's own mind: nor did it bear any resemblance to the gorgeous language, exuberant fancy, and dazzling splendors of Chalmers, which overwhelmed you with such mental opulence. The eloquence of the two latter fell upon you as music from a full and perfect orchestra. It came with the rush of a mountain torrent, and sounded majestic and awful like thunder booming over the ocean; but the eloquence of Mr. Jay was as the gentle and noiseless flow of a majestic river, or like the deep, and solemn, and soothing tones of the organ. In hearing him you were brought near by a sweet and resistless attraction. You felt you could approach him, and be at home with him, and were in a state of affinity with him; while a feeling of awe came over you as you listened to the others, which at once fascinated you, and transported you with delight, and yet made you almost tremble. It seemed, in listening to Hall and Chalmers, as if you could no more always bear such mental excitement than you could always endure the roar of a thunder-storm, or the falls of Niagara; but to Mr. Jay you could forever listen, just as you never feel burdened by the waves of ocean gently breaking upon the shore on a summer's day, nor by the gurgling noise of a brook meandering among stones. Innumerable instances of this naturalness of allusion and illustration might be selected from his printed sermons, which, when uttered with all the effect given to them by the music of his pathetic tones, must have melted down the hearts of his hearers into a state of highly pleasurable emotion.

Mr. Jay was a master of the true pathetic. Ministers have too much neglected this. Some have thought to do all in religious teaching by forceful appeals of logic addressed to the intellect. The understanding is the only faculty they seek to engage. Their logic is clear, but it is cold. They deal with man in only one view of his nature, as a rational being, who has only to apprehend ideas, but forget that he is also an emotional being, who has a heart to feel, and who often needs rather to be moved than convinced. His sensibility, sometimes the best, the only, avenue to his soul, is left unobserved, unoccupied. If the *true* order of nature be for the head to guide the heart, yet, in our disturbed and disordered condition, it often happens that the heart is the avenue to the intellect. Men love to feel, as well as to think; and hence we speak of the luxury of tender emotion. Mr. Jay knew this, and entered very deeply into Christian æsthetics. His voice gave him great advantages here. His very intonations touched and opened the springs of feeling. When the people were in a prepared state of mind, he has sometimes melted them by his manner of repeating an interjection, or a single word. His pathos, however, was not all confined to his manner, but extended itself to his matter. In this there were often the most tender and touching allusions and descriptions. Who, that ever read, can forget that beautiful passage in his sermon to husbands and wives, in which he represents woman, pleading on the ground of her weakness and dependence, for sympathy, kindness, and protection? To have heard this passage uttered by his pathetic tones and plaintive looks, must have been followed by an effect more than dramatic:—

"Milton has finely expressed the difference in the original pair,—

> "'For contemplation he, and valor form'd;
> For softness she, and sweet attractive grace.'

Her bodily strength is inferior, her constitution less firm and vigorous, her frame more tender, her temper more yielding, her circumstances more generally depressing. A rose, a lily, allows of no rough usages. Tenderness demands gentleness; delicacy, care; pliancy, props. Has a condition few resources, and is there much in it of the afflictive and humbling?—the more does it need succor, and the more necessary is every assistance to maintain and increase the consequence of it, especially where so much depends upon the respectability of the character who fills it. Where is the man who is not alive to this consideration?

Where is the husband, who, reflecting on her peculiar circumstances, would not be disposed, by every possible means, to promote the dignity and the satisfaction of a wife? What is the language of these circumstances? 'Honor us; deal kindly with us. From many of the opportunities and means by which you procure favorable notice, we are excluded. Doomed to the shades, few of the high places of the earth are open to us. Alternately we are adored and oppressed. From our slaves you become our tyrants. You feel our beauty, and avail yourselves of our weakness. You complain of our inferiority, but none of your behavior bids us rise. Sensibility has given us a thousand feelings, which nature has kindly denied you. Always under restraints, we have little liberty of choice. Providence seems to have been more attentive to enable us to confer happiness than to enjoy it. Every condition has for us fresh mortifications; every relation new sorrows. We enter social bonds: it is a system of perpetual sacrifice. We cannot give life to others without hazarding our own. We have sufferings which you do not share—cannot share. If spared, years and decays invade our charms, and much of the ardor produced by attraction departs with it. We may die. The grave covers us, and we are soon forgotten: soon are the days of your mourning ended, soon is our loss repaired; dismissed even from your speech, our name is to be heard no more,—a successor may dislike it. Our children, after having a mother by nature, may fall under the control of a mother by affinity, and be mortified by distinctions made between them and her own offspring. Though the duties which we have discharged invariably be the most important and necessary, they do not shine; they are too common to strike; they procure no celebrity: the wife, the mother, fills no historic page. Our privations, our confinements, our wearisome days, our interrupted, our sleepless nights, the hours we have hung in anxious watchings over your sick and dying offspring.'"

There was an individualising effect produced by Mr. Jay's preaching. He not only preached *before* his congregation, but *to* them; and not only to the multitude, but to the individuals which composed it. His sermons formed a kind of mirror, which reflected the image of those who approached it, and in which every one saw himself as distinguished from others. Each of his hearers felt as if the preacher's eye were fixed on *him*, and his discourse addressed to *him*. This is a happy art in preaching, and, indeed, in all public speaking, and in order to which it is necessary to approach, without descending below ourselves or our subject, or even the more intelligent of our auditors, yet as nearly as we can to the easy comprehension of the mass of our hearers. When the preacher soars into the clouds where the understanding cannot track him, or diverges into a wood where they cannot find him, they will soon give over all attempts to follow him, and leave *him* to his wanderings. Mr. Jay's simplicity, clearness, and intelligibility to all, were most commendable, rarely equalled, and never surpassed. It were desirable that these qualities should be remarked, and, as far as possible, imitated, by all preachers of the Gospel. His beautiful conceptions, expressed in good plain Saxon words, were easily understood by the bulk of his hearers; in fact. none could misunderstand them, while the most cultivated and refined could not feel displeased with them.

It is recorded of Arago, the celebrated French astronomer, that he had a peculiar facility of bringing down the high parts of astronomy to the comprehension of ordinary minds,—a faculty so rare, that some of the most distinguished astronomers have failed in making their science intelligible or interesting to a public auditory. Arago adopted a method which we believe had never been tried before by any of his predecessors. When he began to give his course of lectures on astronomy, he glanced round on his audience to look for some dull aspirant for knowledge with a low forehead, and other indications that he was among the least intelligent of his hearers. He kept his eye fixed upon him; he addressed only him; and by the effect of his eloquence and powers of explanation, as exhibited in the countenance of his pupil, he judged of their influence upon the rest of his audience. When *he* remained unconvinced, the orator tried new illustrations, till light beamed from the grateful countenance. Next morning, when Arago was breakfasting with his family, a visitor was announced. A gentleman entered—his pupil of the preceding evening, who, after expressing his admiration of the lecture, thanked Arago for the very peculiar attention he had paid him during the delivery. "You had the appearance," said he, "of giving the lecture only to me." Shall it be the ambition only of the astronomer, and not also of the preacher, to be understood by the convert, and to make every individual feel *he* is the party addressed? Shall they who preach salvation think only of pleasing the cultivated few, to the neglect of the ignorant multitude? Let the minister of religion take a lesson, aye, and reproof too, from the lecture on astronomy. Mr. Jay had learnt this lesson, and practiced it well. It is not meant, of course, that the preacher is always to dwell on elementary truths, and even to accommodate his discourse to the poor and illiterate; but he ought never to forget that our Lord said, "the poor have the Gospel preached unto them;" and it was observed of his own preaching that "the common people heard him gladly." True, we ought not to be always in the nursery feeding babes with milk; but then the babes ought not to be forgotten or neglected.

The character of strong sound sense which pervaded Mr. Jay's sermons contributed very largely to his popularity, combined, as this uniformly was, with the practical. There seems to be in the public mind an intuitive perception that religion is not mere science or theory, but that it contains much that has to do with men's business and bosoms. There is an innate conviction that there is not only something to know, but something to do. They may not be always very willing to do what is enjoined upon them, but still they expect to hear it, and are dissatisfied if they do not. They are aware that it is a matter which has to do with all persons, states, and circumstances. Hence they feel somewhat of surprise, and even disgust, with the preacher who deals much in abstractions that lie remote from human nature and life. They expect to be told not only how they should think, but how they should act; and one good sound maxim of spiritual wisdom, which will guide them through the intricacies of life, and the perplexities of casuistry, will be far more valued than many an airy speculation, or elaborate investigation of some profound and abstract question in theology. Mr. Jay's practical directions possessed much of the terseness, the wisdom, and the force of proverbs. In a single sentence he often expressed what others would expand into a paragraph or a page. Few ever had, in such perfection, the happy art of saying much in few words. They who could not carry away a whole sermon could remember a single sentence, which perhaps contained the pith of the whole. They may not have been able to secure the entire string of pearls; but they could retain one which was complete in itself, and a specimen of all the rest. He always preached as if he wished his sermon to be remembered as well as heard; and it was this which led him to condemn the essay form of sermonizing, and to adopt so uniformly the methodical arrangement of his discourses into the usual divisions and sub-divisions of a sermon. He aimed not merely at present effect, but at permanent advantage; and his arrangement of his subject, which sometimes was fanciful,—aiming at antithesis and parallelism, and approaching almost to the metrical,—was intended to assist the memory, and thus to promote usefulness. Mr. Hall, a master and high authority on such subjects, speaks of the narrow trammels to which in these latter days discourses from the pulpit are confined, "so different from the free and unfettered airs in which the first preachers of the Gospel appeared before their audience. The sublime emotions with which they were fraught," he says, "would have rendered them impatient of such restrictions; nor could they suffer the impetuous stream of their argument, expostulation, and pathos, to be weakened by being diverted into the artificial reservoirs prepared in the heads and particulars of a modern sermon." The analogy, however, of the two cases will not hold. There are occasions, no doubt, when the sermon may with propriety and effect assume the form and character of an oration, though rarely of an essay, especially when concentrated impression, rather than instruction, is the design of the preacher; but as a general rule, considering the heterogeneous nature of our congregations, the plan of heads and particulars, if they are not too numerous, is most for edification; and it was certainly the method which Mr. Hall himself adopted: his Sermon on Infidelity, and on the death of the Princess Charlotte, being the only ones which are printed in which the usual announcement of heads and particulars is omitted. Mr. Jay's divisions, though always announced, were never unnecessarily multiplied; and thus, while he aided the memory, he did not burthen it.

Mr. Jay, though generally grave, chaste, and dignified in his composition, occasionally somewhat violated the law of propriety in regard to these excellences, by a quaintness of expression. This applies almost exclusively to his *preaching*, and was most probably purely extemporaneous. He has extruded nearly all of it from his printed discourses. This tendency to quaintness grew upon him in his declining years, when, perhaps, under some consciousness of decaying force, he thought he would supply the deficiency by what was fanciful and odd, or quaint. He was, perhaps, somewhat sensible of this when, in his preface to his "*Short Discourses*," he wrote the following sentence: "Though he does not wish to indulge a bad taste, the Author would ever remember that the preacher ought to have compassion on the ignorant, and on them that are out of the way. That which is too smooth, easily slides off from the memory, and that which is lost in the act of hearing will do little good. It is desirable to get something that will *strike* and *abide;* something that recurring again and again, will employ the thoughts and the tongue; and if this cannot be accomplished in certain instances by modes of address which perhaps are not classically justifiable, should not a minister prefer utility to fame?"

This great preacher threw a sacred charm over his sermons by a profusion of Scripture phraseology, and allusion to Scripture facts. They were adorned with the beauty and redolent with the fragrance of flowers culled from the garden of inspiration. Indeed the beauty and the perfume were almost in excess. The passages were not so much selected for proof as for illustration; they were brought forward, as classic quotations are by public orators, to grace a speech, and to convey the speaker's idea in the opposite language of a high authority. While listening to his discourses, and regaling themselves with his pleasing thoughts, his hearers were often surprised by his repetition of Scripture, so appropriate that it seemed as if it had been written for the occasion. He rarely ever referred to the book, chapter, and verse which he thus used, as he imagined that the hearers would be diverted from the subject, and disturb their neighbors by turning over the leaves of their Bibles, and the rustling noise, if many did so, which this would occasion. Here we think he was a little in error in point of excess. Fewer passages, some of them explicitly quoted as well as repeated, with a passing remark which would bring out and impress their whole meaning, must do more good than so many passages interwoven without reference or remark into the texture of the sermon.

Another excess in which he indulged in his later years, and in his ordinary ministrations, was, in the way of poetic quotation, especially verses of hymns. He was fond of poetry. His was a poetic mind; and though he rose not to the rank of a great lyric poet, yet he wrote some good hymns, as must be apparent to those who read this volume. In the last sermon he preached in Argyle Chapel, there are no less than thirteen of these poetic scraps. The greater part of them, however, he would no doubt have omitted had he prepared the sermon for the press.

Mr. Jay, through the whole of his ministry, was, as might be supposed, much in demand for public occasions. Few ministers were more frequently put in requisition for preaching at the opening of chapels, and for the various organizations of Christian zeal and benevolence. For such services he always carefully prepared, and rarely disappointed the expectation of his audience. He felt that it would be unworthy of himself, his subject, and his audience, to come forth with an ill-digested, crude, and hasty effusion of meagre thought, set forth in slovenly language. While, on the other hand, though aware he was surrounded by his ministerial brethren, he did not sacrifice the interests of the people to them, and, instead of producing sermons for edification, attempt to astonish by a display of profound and profitless speculation, or dazzle by an exhibition of rapid elegance, resembling the flash, the rush, the lofty flight and vanishing light of the sky-rocket, but withal as useless as that pyrotechnic exhibition.

He often surprised his audience by the ingenuity he displayed in the appropriation of texts to particular occasions. As specimens of this take the following examples:—On the death of George the Fourth—"Another King, one Jesus."—On the reopening of his chapel after a temporary closing—"A door was opened in heaven."—After an enlargement of the chapel—"Be ye also enlarged."—For a Communion address—"One of you is a devil." Who but he would have thought of such a passage as this, for the text of a funeral sermon for a great man: "Howl, fir tree; for the cedar is fallen?" From this passage he preached first, after the death of Mr. Hall; and then again at the death of Mr. Rowland Hill. How poetic, how striking, how appropriate to express the Church's lament over the grave of one of her illustrious pastors!

Mr. Jay considered it a solemn duty to take advantage of the times of public occasions to make nature and providence subservient to religious instruction. He generally preached on the seasons of the year; and on national mercies, calamities, and great political events;—but he did not bring politics, in the conventional meaning of that term, into the pulpit.

It need scarcely be said by those who knew Mr. Jay, that he made no use of notes in the pulpit, except occasionally at the very close of his ministry, when he could no longer so implicitly confide in his memory. In his earlier days he wrote his sermons pretty fully, and even where this was not done, most of the leading thoughts had passed through his mind in his previous meditations upon the text or the subject. He did not, however, so closely adhere to his prepared matter as to shut out suggestions that arose at the time; those "living thoughts," as Mr. Newton used to call them, which came warm and glowing from the heart while he was preaching. He very strongly reprobated the practice of pulpit readings, and lamented the growing disposition for this among the young ministers of the present day. Where is the practice of reading tolerated except in the Pulpit? Not on the Stage; not in the Senate; not at the Bar. In the time of Charles the Second it was forbidden by statute to the University of Cambridge, which says "the lazy way of reading sermons began in the time of the Civil Wars."

It will be seen, by this description, that we do not claim for this eminent preacher any dazzling brilliancy of genius, any profound originality, any power of philosophical analysis, any logical acumen, or even great theological research. To those who can only be pleased with such things, or to others who resolve all pulpit excellence into abstract generalizations, or lofty speculations, or subtle argumentation, Mr. Jay's sermons presented few attractions. His sound evangelism, his practical wisdom, his rich experience, his strong sense, his melting tenderness, his touching pathos, his beautiful illustrations, his sweet antitheses, his poetic fancy, which procured him while a living preacher such wide and continued popularity, and which in his published works will never cease to delight the readers who can be pleased with strong intelligence and true piety—were held in light esteem by those who love to soar in the clouds, or delve in the dark mines of German mysticism.

If Mr. Jay attained to such excellence as preacher,

it was not without great self-culture and laborious endeavors. No doubt there is some truth in the opinion, that there are natural tendencies which lead to distinction in any branch of human pursuit. We need not believe phrenology to admit this. In a qualified sense, Mr. Jay was born a preacher: person, voice, physiological temperament appropriate to this occupation, were all given to him in his physical constitution. But this was not all. If he owed much to those gifts lavished upon him by the hand of God, he owed much also to his own sagacity, diligence, and unwearied endeavors after improvement and distinction. He was a preacher from a boy. His choice of this line of action grew out of his religious convictions and emotions, and was sustained and stimulated by them. He longed to be useful in saving sinners from the condemnation which he had escaped; he saw the power of the pulpit as God's great instrument for accomplishing this end; and, almost from the time of his first entering it, he made it, as we have already said, the object of his hallowed ambition to excel there. In after-life, all his reading, his reflection, and his writing centred in that object. He studied the best models of preaching; learnt French chiefly to read the sermons of Bossuet, Bourdaloue, Masillon, and Saurin, in their own tongue; and attentively perused the Puritan and Nonconformist writers, together with more modern authors of sermons, the better to qualify himself to be a preacher. At home and abroad, when travelling or recreating himself at some watering-place, he was in one sense always sermonizing. He rarely returned to his own house, after a retreat for awhile to the coast, without bringing back with him some plans of sermons or texts that had struck him, in his reading or meditations during this season of innocent relaxation from pastoral duties. To be a useful preacher was his aim; and it was thus, by constant and unwearied effort, he became one.

And if this were the habitual study of all who are called to occupy the pulpit; if with an intense longing after the salvation of immortal souls, and an unwavering determination to know nothing among men, but Jesus Christ and him crucified; if with a true philosophical view of the adaptation of preaching to awaken attention and produce impression; if with a recollection of what has been done by the great masters in the art of preaching,—all ministers were to study the best models of evangelical pulpit eloquence, and were to take extraordinary pains to acquire, by the aid of Divine grace, a commanding and interesting style of pulpit address; and, while cherishing a sense of absolute dependence for efficiency upon the work of the Holy Spirit, they were to recollect the Spirit works by appropriate means; and took half the pains to make their speaking in the pulpit as impressive as the actor does to make his upon the stage; if concerning the powerful preaching of the Gospel, they said "*this one thing I do*," and called in all collateral aids to do it in the best manner,—we should not hear, as we sometimes do, of the declining power of the pulpit. It is for a wonder, a lamentation, and a reproach, that they who have to do the most momentous work under the sun, give themselves the least pains to do it effectually. Mankind are wrought upon by manner as well as matter—it is an interesting, earnest style of address, that engages attention, reaches the heart, and accomplishes the end of preaching; in the absence of which learning the most profound, and theology the most scriptural, will fail to secure popularity, or to obtain success. It will not do to say, we are so engrossed with the matter of our discourses as to be indifferent to the manner of them. The more important to men's interests is the matter, the more anxious should we be that in our manner there should be nothing to hinder, but, on the contrary, everything to aid, the success of the matter. That minister who feels called by the Holy Ghost to be a preacher of Christ's blessed Gospel, ought to feel himself no less called to take all possible pains to do it in the best possible manner.

How eminently Mr. Jay's efforts to excel in this matter were crowned with success, the reader of the foregoing pages has seen amply illustrated as he has advanced though this volume. We shall here, however, add one more testimony, which, from its impartiality and high respectability, is entitled to much weight. Bishop Shirley, in a letter to the Rev. C. Bridges, says: "I spent two days at Bath, and heard Mr. Jay preach. He is a very extraordinary man. There is a commanding energy in his manner, and a weight in his style, which gives authority to what he says, and secures attention; for he is evidently in earnest, and utters the result of much thinking and prayer." *

If the publication of Mr. Jay's life should serve no other purpose than to stir up the ministry to a more earnest and anxious endeavor to excel in this their momentous sphere of official duty, and to present to them

* Memoir of Bishop Shirley, p. 58. This letter is dated Ashbourn, February 18th, 1823.

a model which they shall aim to copy, then it will be subject of congratulation and thankfulness, that to the world has been given this memoir of one whom Foster designated, "*The Prince of Preachers.*"

MR. JAY AS AN AUTHOR.

AFTER having expressed our opinion of Mr. Jay as a preacher, we have felt some doubts whether our readers may not think it quite enough, without referring particularly to his authorship. But still there is a sufficient diversity in the two departments to justify a separate notice. The talents which secure success in the one can by no means be taken as a pledge of success in the other. It is a rare thing for a man to excel in both characters, even though the authorship may lie mainly in the line of sermons. Of this Mr. Jay himself seems to have been perfectly conscious; for he did little in the way of authorship, except in connection with his preaching, as he also did little in the way of public speaking, except from the pulpit. Under a just sense of the limitation of human faculties, he concentrated his upon one object; and that object gained so conspicuously and successfully supplied the first and chief inducement to appear as an author; and this rather as an extension of the preacher's office, or as an enlargement of his audience.

Mr. Jay's labors as an author were principally pursued at watering-places, during a *relaxation* of a few weeks in summer. He gives the following brief but interesting account of these labors, in an Advertisement to the last volume of the "Exercises":—

"At Sidmouth he began his 'Domestic Ministers'

Assistant,' and wrote many of the Family prayers. In the Isle of Wight, he composed 'A Charge to a Minister's Wife,' and 'The Wife's Advocate.' At Lynmouth, he finished his 'Christian Contemplated,' and wrote the Preface; with 'Hints on Preaching.'

"But this latter place must be a little more noticed. There, for several years successively, he passed a month, the most perfectly agreeable and happy he ever experienced in a life of loving-kindness and tender mercy.

"Linton and Lynmouth are nearly connected—the one being at the top and the other at the bottom of a declivity, covered with trees and verdure, interspersed with several houses. Linton has been remarked for its sublimity, and Lynmouth for its beauty, and their united aspects have been called Switzerland in miniature.

"Lynmouth was to the author the most interesting spot. Here, two narrow and craggy valleys, obviously once ruptured by a convulsion of nature, terminate; and down these, tumbling from rock to rock, two streams—one running from the east and the other from the south—unite, and then, at a small distance, empty themselves into the sea.

"At the time of his first going there it was hardly known or considered as a watering-place. It had not, therefore, as yet fallen into the corruptions of such receptacles; nor had the inhabitants been taught to make visitors a prey. The villagers were very respectful; and strangers felt a sense of perfect safety.

"Here the author fixed his residence. He took a whole cottage; it was far from elegant, but it was neat and agreeable; it wanted some accommodation and comforts; but he had what he more prized, rural and enchanting scenery and solitude. Yet not without some to hear the exclamation, 'How sweet this solitude is!' for he had society too; his company was small, but chosen, and suitable, and improving:—

> 'Where friendship full exerts her softest power,
> Perfect esteem, enlivened by desire
> Ineffable, and sympathy of soul—
> Thought meeting thought, and will preventing will,
> With boundless confidence.'

"His associates consisted of his wife and a female friend. It would be vain in him to extol the former; but as for the latter—especially as she was soon removed from our world—he may be allowed to say, we hardly could have had her equal in everything we wished. She was of a very respectable family; well educated, polished in her manners, intellectual, sprightly, witty, truly pious, full of sensibility and benevolence, and an entire stranger to everything like selfishness. What, with regard to this friend, before our first excursion together was acquaintance, was now rendered intimacy the most cordial; and she became a dear resident in the family till her lamented death. The cottage we occupied was near Mr. Herries' beautiful villa. It has since been spoiled by improvements, and is now a kind of tawdry little mansion; and the whole of Lynmouth itself, which taste might have altered, and yet left it a village still, is aping a paltry town.

"Here our party felt themselves at liberty to meet or to separate—to read or to write—or to converse or to walk—as inclination prompted. As to himself, the author opened his parlor, and spoke on the Sabbath-day evening to any of the neighbors who would attend. But having been struck with the design, and also having been urged to undertake something of the kind, he now began his 'Morning Exercises.' Of these, he here often wrote two, and sometimes three a day; and always read one of them in the morning and another in the evening devotion, and not often without the approbation of his companions, which most excited and encouraged him to proceed.

"Here he composed the greater part of these *Morning* Exercises, and here also, in after visits, he wrote the greater part of the *Evening*. He once thought of distinguishing by a final mark all he had written in this retirement; but not doing it immediately, his recollection soon became too indistinct for him to divide with certainty. The first 'Exercise' he wrote was that which is entitled, 'The Unlonely Solitude,'—John, xvi. 32: 'And shall leave me alone: and yet I am not alone, because the Father is with me.'

"He wished also to have marked those which he wrote as he journeyed to and from Lynmouth. At the 'Plume of Feathers,' Minehead, where he slept as he was going down, he composed the Exercise, called, 'The Pious Excursion,'—1 Sam. iii. 9: 'Speak, Lord, for thy servant heareth,' especially in reference to such a journey of recreation. At the same inn, as he returned, he composed the Exercise, entitled 'The Call to Depart,'—Micah, ii. 10: 'Arise, and depart hence, for this is not your rest.' He also wrote a third Exercise at the same inn, *viz.*,—'Changes in the wilderness not a removal from it,'—Numb. x. 12: 'And the children of Israel took their journeys out of the wilderness of Sinai; and the cloud rested in the wilderness at Peran.'

"The author cannot conclude without observing two things:—the *first* is, That relaxation is never so perfectly enjoyed as in connection with engagement.

> 'A want of occupation is not rest;
> A mind quite vacant is a mind distress'd.'

"Relaxation, indeed, can have no existence separate from employment, for what is there then to relax *from?* On the other hand, action prepares for repose, and labor not only sweetens, but justifies recreation; so that we feel it to be, not only innocent indulgence, but a kind of recompense. The *second* is, That, as of such a precious talent as *time* nothing should be lost, so, much may be done by gathering up its fragments."

The peculiar charm which his sermons derived from his oratory and elocution could not, of course, attend his publications, and yet, when divested of this fascination, they exhibited other charms and excellences, which secured for them, not only attention, but admiration, popularity, and usefulness. His compositions, when they came from the press, were greatly improved and chastened, both in thought and diction. What they lost of effect given them by his delivery, they gained in correctness, condensation, and point. Mr. Jay well understood that sermons printed must be skilfully prepared for the eye, which is a more critical judge than the ear. The single sermons which he first published were, no doubt, greatly aided in their success by the popularity of the young preacher. Moreover, his promotion so early to the pulpit of Surrey Chapel placed him on a pinnacle before the religious world of London; so that when he sent forth his first volume of sermons, which was as early as 1802, a wide circle of readers was anxiously waiting to peruse them. The moderation of sentiment these sermons displayed, as contrasted with the Antinomianism into which some were running, both in the Establishment and among the Dissenters,—their originality, simplicity, ease, and general adaptation to the state of the public mind, commanded for them a measure of success which rarely attends volumes of sermons in the present day, and still more rarely those from the pens of Dissenters. It may be fairly alleged, that, at the period when Mr. Jay first appeared as an author, there was a new and growing desire to peruse good and evangelical sermons; and that Mr. Jay's were eminently suited to the taste of the day; and it would be no disparagement to admit further, that in some respects they are less suited to the taste of the present day; or, indeed, that as good sermons are now so abundant from the pulpit, there is less need of supplying them from the press; and, in consequence, few volumes of sermons now obtain popularity, unless they are highly elaborate, or novel subjects, or characterized by eminent genius or transcendent eloquence.

There can be no doubt that Mr. Jay's sermons were happily suited to meet the increasing desire at that time for evangelical instruction. Whitfield and Wesley, with their co-workers and followers, had given the people a taste for something better than they had been accustomed to in the dry ethical essays of the clergy, as void of effect upon the audience as of heart and life in the preacher. Jay's sermons, therefore, were perhaps as much used in pulpits as in private houses, and might be heard in many a church, and found attractive to many a congregation of Churchmen. Some of the more liberal of the clergy recommended them to their brethren, and to their people; and this was especially the case with those who were alarmed at the spread of Antinomianism. The appearance of the successive volumes of Mr. Jay's sermons, and their increasing popularity, was a pleasing omen of the sounder views which were beginning to prevail. Indeed it may be stated, that the influence of the Antinomian preacher began to decrease about this time, and has been sinking till it can scarcely be said to retain an existence either in the Church or out of it. A few scattered individuals are all that can now be found, where formerly hundreds congregated to listen to high doctrine; and, among other useful works, no doubt Mr. Jay's have had a share of influence in promoting sounder views and a more Scriptural taste. An evidence of this is seen in the fact that Mr. Jay was singled out by Bishop Jebb, and recommended to his friend, Alexander Knox, as a pattern of sobriety and moderation of sentiment. He says in one of his letters:—

"It seems to me as if the more sober Calvinists, both in and out of the Church of England, were not a little alarmed by the prevalence of virtual, if not as yet practical, Antinomianism. There has been a good deal to that purpose, I mean expressive of that alarm, in the 'Christian Observer.' But the Independent minister at Bath, Jay, has lately published a volume of lectures, called 'The Christian Contemplated,' in the preface to which are some pertinent, and, I might say, happy remarks. It will be worth your while to get the book, were it only for the sake of the preface; but the book itself is worth looking over, for, though it has its defects and failings, it abounds in matter which tends to edify the reader, and do real honors to the writer."*

In speaking once upon this subject, he observed, that, though election was true, it did not appear to him a truth of equal importance with perseverance; and that, in preaching, we must not only distinguish between truth and error, but between truth and truth. It was a truth that our Saviour died under Pontius Pilate, and a truth that His death was an atonement for sin; but who would attach the same importance to both? So was it here. He did not conceive that there was any danger in preaching election in its effects; and that it must always be remembered, that perseverance was a duty enjoined by 2 Peter, i. 5–10, &c., and as a privilege promised in Phil. i. 6, &c.; and that this twofold view ought always to be remembered.

He said that Mr. Newton, at one of those breakfasts where he received ministers of all denominations, among other observations, made the following:—He said, that "Calvinism was one of the worst of systems preached theoretically, but one of the best preached practically." Mr. Jay added, that if he called any man master on earth, it would be Leighton or Newton.

This just and Scriptural moderation of sentiment which through life distinguished Mr. Jay, both as a

* Thirty Years' Correspondence between John Jebb, D.D., F.R.S., Bishop of Limerick, and Alexander Knox, Esq., M.R.I.A., vol. ii., p. 557.

preacher and author, commended him to the approval of the best part of the Christian body, both in the Established Church and among Dissenters. For this sobriety and comprehensiveness of view he was probably greatly indebted to his excellent tutor, whose large experience and acute observation, in the days when there existed considerable conflict and contention among theologians of adverse schools, in connection with his loving spirit and persuasive manner, qualified him to guard young minds against excess and extravagance. The same moderation of sentiment seems to have distinguished most of Mr. Winter's students. It is, moreover, a remarkable fact, that this sobriety was far from being associated with tameness or indifference. It was rather accompanied with eminent zeal, devotedness, and usefulness. It was very evident that Mr. Jay's supreme aim was to be Scriptural in all his religious sentiments. He bowed submissively to the Divine authority. Every statement is both illustrated and confirmed by the most apposite and striking quotations. Hence, too, Mr. Jay seems never to shrink from the appearance of paradox, when it arises from the strength of Scripture language in enforcing important truths separately. He had, from the commencement of his course, kept himself clear of the trammels of systematic theology; and was only concerned to bring the truth of God, as it appears in the Bible, to bear upon the hearts and consciences of men. Hence the constant interweaving of Scripture in every sermon—a practice which he avows and defends in the preface to "The Christian Contemplated," where he quotes, with warm approbation, the following judicious and beautiful defence of this practice, from the pen of Robert Hall, in his strictures upon Foster's Essay, which at that day stirred up no little controversy, and which was entitled—"On the Aversion of Men of Taste to Evangelical Religion." Mr. Jay hailéd this vindication of the use of Scriptural language, from so high an authority, though he suspects the same authority might censure himself for using it to excess; yet that he would still allow it was an error on the safer side.

"To say nothing," observes Mr. Hall, "of the inimitable beauties of the Bible, considered in a literary view,—which are universally acknowledged,—it is the Book which every devout man is accustomed to consult as the oracle of God; it is the companion of his best moments, and the vehicle of his strongest consolation. Intimately associated in his mind with everything dear and valuable, its diction more powerfully excites devotional feeling than any other; and, when temperately and soberly used, imparts an unction to a religious discourse which nothing else can supply. Besides, is there not room to apprehend that a studied avoidance of the Scripture phraseology, and a care to express all that it is supposed to contain in the forms of classical diction, might ultimately lead to the neglect of the Scriptures themselves, and a habit of substituting flashy and superficial declamation, in the room of the saving truths of the Gospel? Such an apprehension is but too much verified by the most celebrated sermons of the French, and still more by some modern compositions in our own language, which usurp that title. For devotional impression, we conceive that a very considerable tincture of the language of Scripture, or at least such a coloring as shall discover an intimate acquaintance with those inimitable models, will generally succeed best."

The copious use which Mr. Jay made of Scripture language, both in preaching and writing, gives his compositions a peculiar character. It is a feature which strikes every one as prominent, and we think, while it yields the highest satisfaction to every reader who peruses his books for edification and instruction, it can excite displacency in no one. There can be little doubt that the eminent success of Mr. Jay in all his publications is a sufficient vindication of his practice, especially when it is considered that the success of such writings must be taken as an indication of their usefulness. They minister nothing to the amusement of mankind; nothing to the gratification of a mere literary taste, or fondness for speculation; nothing to elegant scholarship, or dialectic skill, or a fervid imagination; but are the plain and forcible statements of evangelical truth, "not in the words which man's wisdom teacheth, but," to a great extent, "which the Holy Ghost teacheth;" and as such their extensive and continued popularity both vindicates the judgment of the writer and commends the taste of his numerous Christian readers.

Mr. Jay may not be an author suited to the taste of every reader, but he wrote for the many, and they have been his readers. He is not learned enough for some, nor profound enough for others; not critical enough for one, nor rhetorical enough for a second, nor imaginative enough for a third; but had he commended himself to the approbation of such readers, he would have had a much narrower circle than he has had, and still has. Nature, or rather the God of nature, formed his mind in one of its most current types, and to serve the greatest number, by exhibiting to them, in the most impressive, instructive, and successful forms, not the rarities of intellectual treasures, not the elaborations of human thought, nor the choicest and most sparkling gems of genius, but truths of universal importance and of daily practice. He aimed at the useful and substantial, and had little taste for the subtle, the recondite, or the profound. His mission was to preach the Gospel of the grace of God, which he had received, and to extend the benefit of what he had preached by books, for the service of those who had not the privilege of hearing him.

In his compositions, the critic may find many faults which passed unobserved from the pulpit. But though sometimes his style would admit of improvement in respect to refinement and polish, yet, in perspicuity, simplicity, and force, it is admirably adapted to the purpose of instruction. It is perfectly transparent and intelligible to all, and though occasionally, through his anxiety to be impressive, and to fix the truth in the mind, he indulges in an expression or a word beneath his subject, yet it is so obviously for the sake of *point* and *effect*, that good taste can hardly be offended, while the less fastidious reader is better pleased with the homeliness and point, and possibly feels the truth conveyed more effectually to his mind.

Eminently practical in all his views of Divine truth, he derives useful lessons from almost every part of Scripture; and places duties in new lights and relations, which impart fresh force and interest to them. He had no doubt profited much in his composition in later years by the long and extensive practice he had undergone, and which, from the advice of Mrs. Hannah More to write much and fast, he seems early to have adopted. Every Christian reader of Mr. Jay's works must be impressed with the pleasingly devotional turn of his mind. His reflections lead the pious and devout reader to the most elevated views of the Divine character, as a Father to be loved, and a Friend to be trusted. Every page seems to exercise over the mind an attraction to the Source of all wisdom, blessedness, and grace; and every sentiment seems bathed with the spirit of devotion, and designed to win the heart for God and truth.

Another feature in Mr. Jay's writings is the skill with which, without apparent effort, he throws light upon Scripture, and, by a few happy sentences, sets the sacred word in a new and interesting, and often strong, light. It is as if he placed the reader in a position from which he could discover new lustre in the jewel of Divine truth. He makes it flash its radiance upon the mind's eye with a power and beauty unperceived before. And, moreover, not simply as thus condensing the force of isolated truths upon the mind, but in the important and most useful capacity of an *expositor*, he is conspicuously successful. His large knowledge of the Divine word, and his intimate insight into its special import, and his holy ingenuity in discovering uses to which its facts and lessons may be turned, qualify him in a high degree to expound the sacred word. With an unrivalled force and effect could he bring out the hidden beauties of revelation, and enchain the mind to the truths of God's word. There was a startling originality sometimes in his application of texts, which interested and delighted the auditor, and fixed the attention more on the Word of God than on the preacher or the writer. But he never pursued originality for its own sake, nor sought, as many have done, and are still doing, to affect novelty of thought by mere novelty of phrase. The new idioms and the new terminology are found, when translated into pure English, to contain little more than old and common ideas; often they are a mere wrapper of grotesque or pompous phraseology thrown around poverty of thought and vulgar superficiality. But, in his own department, Mr. Jay was really an original thinker, and his thoughts engage, instruct, and delight the mind. His aim is always exalted, his means always legitimate, his motives always pure, and his success distinguished.

In confirmation of our own estimate of his publications, it will probably be interesting to the reader to be informed, upon the best authority, how his works have been received among the Christian bodies of the New World; and where, never having heard his voice, they judge of him exclusively as an author. Mr. Jay himself sometimes alludes to the extensive sale and usefulness of his writings in America, and we shall, therefore, here introduce some extracts from the pen of a distinguished American divine, who published an article more than twenty years ago in an American periodical, in which he reviewed the principal works of Mr. Jay, which had then been reprinted in that country. In pointing out these peculiar excellences, he thus concludes his review. (*The article is from the pen of the Rev. W. B. Sprague, D.D., and appeared in "The Quarterly Christian Spectator." It was afterwards published separately*):—

"If the estimate which we have formed of the character of Mr. Jay's publications be correct, it must be obvious to every one that they are designed to have an important influence in forming the religious character of the age; to say nothing of the more remote influence which they must exert upon posterity. We will consider, under a few distinct particulars, what are the effects which have followed, or may be expected to follow from the labors of this popular and excellent author.

"Mr. Jay's writings, if we mistake not, are peculiarly adapted *to promote the study of the Bible.* Not only are the 'Morning and Evening Exercises for the Closet,' directly of a biblical character, being designed as a sort of practical commentary on various portions of divine truth, but nearly all his other writings abound in scriptural illustration, and are pre eminently fitted to invest the study of the Bible with strong attractions. No writer of the present day makes a more copious use of Scripture than Mr. Jay; and we might say, that in his sermons he sometimes carries this to an extreme, were it not for the uncommonly felicitous manner in which his quotations are made. It would seem as if the whole Bible were in his memory, and he had the power, on every occasion, of selecting the very passage that is most to his purpose; and when a writer quotes Scripture with such an advantage, we can scarcely call any degree of quotation excessive.

"If Mr. Jay should be thought by some to urge to an extreme in respect to the direct use which he makes of Scripture in his public discourses, we are constrained to believe that there is a tendency among many preachers, in this country at least, to the opposite end.

We certainly do not wish to be brought back to the practice of some of our venerable fathers, who not only were accustomed to string together many passages of Scripture, often without much regard to connection, but detained their hearers by turning over the leaves of the Bible to look their passages out; but we do wish that every sermon should have so much of the Bible in it, either as it respects language or spirit, that it shall be obvious to every hearer that it is drawn directly from that sacred book. It were reasonable to expect that God should put special power upon his own word; and hence we find that the frequent introduction of Scripture language into a sermon imparts to it, in the view of the pious, a kind of unction which it can derive from nothing else. So, too, all experience proves, that there is no argument so strong as 'thus saith the Lord;' and many a mind which has warred through a long course of metaphysical reasoning, has been fixed in its convictions by one plain declaration of the Bible.

* * * * * *

"Mr. Jay's writings are also eminently distinguished for their *Practical Tendency* They are indeed by no means deficient in the exhibition of Scripture doctrines, but whenever doctrines are discussed, it is always in a practical way. They are not taken up as abstract propositions, but are presented just as they are found in God's word, and as they stand related to the experience and conduct of men. They are more commonly adapted to make men acquainted with their own hearts; to carry them back to the very springs of their actions; and to impress them with the conviction that the whole of religion is a practical reality.

We are not aware that Mr. Jay has written anything of a merely speculative character; whatever has come from his pen, so far as we know, has an important bearing upon practice, and is fitted to exert a benign and elevating influence upon human character.

"It has been a characteristic of some periods of the Church, that they have been distinguished by a rage for speculation. No one can go back to the time of the latter Christian fathers, or to the days of Thomas Aquinas, without being forcibly struck by the endlessly diversified and hair-breadth distinctions which were then resorted to, in illustration and defence of Scripture doctrine; and it were hardly necessary to say, that an age which had so much in its character that was speculative could not be distinguished by religious action. It was common, in those days, for men to exhaust all their powers in endeavoring to settle points which did not admit of being settled, and which, if they had been, would not make one hair white or black, as it respects the salvation of men, or the advancement of the kingdom of Christ. The lamentable result was, that, while men were spending their lives in metaphysical quibbling, the great cause for which the Saviour shed his blood seemed to stand still, if not to be on the retrograde; and the revival of the spirit of religious action did not take place until the rage for vain speculation had begun in some measure to die away. If we do not greatly mistake, wherever the doctrines of the Gospel are exhibited in connection with much of human philosophy, and encumbered by the technology of the schools, they will be found to a great extent inefficacious, and the Church will be found proportionably listless and inactive. But when these truths are presented in their naked simplicity, and brought home to the mind and heart as common-sense realities, without having their influence in any degree neutralized by foreign admixtures, they will be found quick and powerful; and it may reasonably be expected that in such a community there will be a waking from the dreams of carelessness, and a spirit of benevolent activity going forth to bless the world.

* * * * * *

"One great secret of the charm which pervades Mr. Jay's writings is, that he ranges through every department of human experience, and shows that the spirit has its appropriate teachings for every condition. Their tendency is not only to make man do right in all circumstances, but to do right intelligently, and upon principle.

"It is another characteristic of Mr. Jay's writings, that they are eminently fitted *to cherish a devotional spirit.* We have already had occasion to remark, that his 'Family Prayers,' while they show the fertility of his mind, the purity of his taste, and the originality and beauty of his conceptions, also breathe, in an uncommon degree, the spirit of genuine devotion. But most of his other writings, though they are designed primarily to instruct, and are indeed, in a high degree, instructive, are delightfully pervaded by the same spirit. His 'Morning and Evening Exercises' are particularly designed to be the companion of the closet; and it would seem scarcely possible that they should be used by any Christian, as they were intended to be, without bringing him into an appropriate frame for communion with God.

"It will be obvious to any one who reflects how much the present age is characterized by the spirit of active enterprise, that there is danger that it will suffer in its devotional character; danger that, while Christians have their hands full of work, their hearts will be comparatively barren of devout exercises; that their active efforts in building up the kingdom of Christ will be suffered to interfere with the more retired business of keeping their hearts and communing with God. We do not complain that the religious character of the age has too much in it that is practical; but we have much reason to fear that many Christians of the present day sometimes render apologies to their consciences for a partial neglect of their closets, on the ground that their time is so much engrossed by duties of a public nature that they have little left for anything else. Whenever this state of things exists, it is an evil which ought at once to be corrected; for not only does it indicate an approaching decline of the spirit of piety, but it looks as if the spirit of benevolent action would not endure; and whenever the Christian loses sight of his dependence on God, in his benevolent efforts, he may rest assured, either that his zeal will soon languish, or that his efforts will be unsuccessful.

"Another striking characteristic of Mr. Jay's writings is, that they exhibit, in the best sense, *a truly catholic spirit.* Not that there is anything in them that looks like lowering the standard of Christian doctrine or practice, or of yielding up anything that is essential in religion — far from it. The great doctrines and duties of the Gospel are constantly stated and urged in all their importance; and erroneous doctrines and practices meet with their deserved condemnation. But, after all, the author never seems to be trammelled by sectarian peculiarities; and scarcely ever occupies ground upon which he would not be cordially met by Christians of every evangelical denomination. This, no doubt, is one great reason of the universal popularity his writings have gained both in Great Britain and this country; and hence, too, we have found many who had been long conversant with his writings, who yet had never been able to discover to what denomination he belonged, and some who had always had the impression that, instead of being an Independent, as he actually is, he is a (Low Church) Episcopalian. No doubt he has his attachment to Independency; but it is so far from being a bigoted attachment, that he opens the arms of his charity wide to every evangelical Christian, let his denomination be what it may. Men may differ from him in many unimportant particulars, and yet, instead of standing aloof from them, as errorists, he cordially welcomes them as fellow-disciples of a common Master.

"The spirit of Christian catholicism which Mr. Jay's writings evince, is what we wish to see more and more extensively pervade the religious community. We are by no means disposed to plead for an annihilation of sects, or for any attempt to range all the followers of Christ under the same human banner. On the contrary, we fully believe that the division of the Christian world into various denominations is not without some important uses; and that, if its legitimate influence is not neutralized by unchristian jealousies and alienations, it may hasten rather than retard the ultimate triumph of the Church.

* * * * * *

"Let the delightful spirit which Mr. Jay has exemplified in his writings pervade all the different communities of the followers of Christ, and, though we may still have different denominations, yet it will be manifest that there is but one body. Under such an influence the world will be compelled again to the exclamations which were made in the early ages of the church, 'Behold how these Christians love one another!'

"In the writings of Mr. Jay there is a remarkable consistency, and they are fitted, in an eminent degree, to form *a consistent religious character*. One principal reason why most of the professed followers of Christ exert so little influence in favor of his cause is, that their Christian character is marred by such palpable inconsistency. This inconsistency results from the very estimate which they form of the comparative importance of different duties; and from the neglect of some, or other, or all of the duties of Christian life.

* * * * * *

"Now, if we do not mistake, Mr. Jay's writings are not more remarkable for anything than their tendency to counteract this evil. They bring before us with great felicity, and without any apparent reference to system, the various duties of men, just as they are inculcated in God's word, giving to each its proportionate importance. There is no elevating faith at the expense of works, or zeal at the expense of morality, or alms at the expense of prayer; but each duty stands forth with its own claims, holding its appropriate place. In short, we know of few writings which are fitted to make an impression more, in this respect, like that of the Bible itself, than those of Mr. Jay. Whoever reads them attentively, and imbibes their spirit, will not be punctilious in respect to one set of duties, and lax in regard to another; but he will be attentive to all; and, under such an influence, his Christian character, instead of being unsightly and monstrous, will develop itself in fair and beautiful proportions.

"After what we have already said of Mr. Jay's writings, we scarcely need add, that they are fitted *to form Christian character on the most lovely and attractive model.* It cannot be disguised, that, as the beauty of Christian doctrine has sometimes been marred by human philosophy, so the loveliness of Christian example has been obscured by what has almost seemed a cold and lowering melancholy. There have been those, and they are yet to be found, who appear habitually gloomy from principle; who set down the playfulness and buoyancy of the animal spirits to the account of an inveterate waywardness; and who never venture to speak on the subject of religion at all, but with what seems an air of affected solemnity.

* * * * * *

"If irreligious persons are liable to be confirmed in their irreligion, by the careless and trifling deportment of professed Christians, they are not less exposed to the same evil by seeing a Christian profession constantly associated with a morose and forbidding gloom. Let religion be exhibited in all its cheerful attractions, while yet it retains its appropriate seriousness and dignity, and it cannot fail to commend itself to the judgment, and conscience, and better feelings of all who witness such a manifestation.

"There are few men probably to whom the present age is more indebted for whatever of consistent cheerfulness its religious character may possess, than to Mr. Jay. Other writers, as we have already intimated, may have done more than he to rouse the slumbering conscience of the sinner, and bring him into the attitude of conviction and repentance; but few, we think, have done more to hold up religion to the world in all its divine and beautiful attractions. We cannot take leave of this interesting and popular writer, without commending his writings to every class of our readers. We would commend them especially to the young Christian, as being eminently fitted to form him to a high degree of religious enjoyment, activity, and usefulness. We would commend them to the men who would know most of the windings of his own heart, and would have maxims of true practical wisdom in his own mind, to regulate every part of his conduct. We would commend them even to the man who scoffs at religion as a fable; for if he can contemplate that view of the Gospel which these writings present, without acknowledging that it is consistent, beautiful, even glorious, then it is because he belies his own convictions, or because his infidelity has made him a madman."

Though this extract is long, yet it seemed the most appropriate, complete, and satisfactory testimony we could supply of the popularity and usefulness of Mr. Jay's writings in that extensive and populous country, where they are, to say the least, as extensively known and as much admired as in Great Britain. The long-established and well-earned reputation of the writer adds weight to his judicious and discriminating observations. Our own opinions and remarks, previously given, coincide, in the main, with those of Dr. Sprague. Mr. Jay studied, and preached, and wrote for the Christian community at large. He wished the whole world to hear and to read, in the most intelligible and impressive terms, the Gospel of the grace of God; and he wrote, therefore, in the *common dialect*, as the best vehicle for the truth of God; but this he wrought into a polished shaft, and gave it a direct and successful aim.

The admirers of sustained and impassioned eloquence, or of a magniloquent style, or even of a purely classic diction, will find little to satisfy them, much less to fascinate them, in the volumes of Mr. Jay's works; but all who desire to see the truths of Divine Revelation treated in their variety and comprehensiveness, their admonitions enforced in winning and persuasive words, with manly dignity, Christian simplicity, and apostolic earnestness; all who read religious books for instruction and improvement, to have the heart warmed, and the life corrected,—will find Mr. Jay's works a treasury which will never disappoint them, and which they will not soon exhaust. Beckford, of Fonthill Abbey, in a passage quoted in an early part of the Autobiography, compared Mr. Jay's mind to "a clear, transparent spring, flowing so freely as to impress us with the idea of its being inexhaustible;" and such is but a just description of those volumes which so powerfully affected that versatile and exquisite genius, considered the most accomplished and keen-sighted man of his day; but not him only, for thousands and tens of thousands, in almost every rank of life, are daily benefited, and will continue to be benefited, by the writings of William Jay. We can desiderate for them no happier or greater succcess than that which the man of taste, already mentioned, indicated as their characteristic—"the voice which calls us to look into ourselves, and prepare for judgment, is too piercing, too powerful, to be resisted, and we attempt, for worldly and sensual considerations, to shut our ears in vain."

Discourses on Truth.

By J. H. Thornwell, D.D., President of South Carolina College, Columbia, S. C. 12mo.

Quarles' Emblems.

EMBLEMS, DIVINE AND MORAL. By Francis Quarles. Illustrated. 16mo. $1.

"The quaint, suggestive, and beautiful Emblems of Quarles are here produced in a handsome volume, full of wisdom and sanctified wit, and impressive with the most spiritual and earnest views of Divine truth."—*Evangelist.*

May Dundas;

Or, PASSAGES FROM YOUNG LIFE. By Mrs. Thomas Geldart.

"Mrs. Geldart writes as one who understands and loves children—as all who write for children should write—in a gentle, pleasant style. Parents may safely trust the *hearts* as well as the *minds* of their children to her custody."

The Foresters. A Tale.

By Professor Wilson, author of the "Lights and Shadows of Scottish Life." 12mo. 75 cents.

Fritz Harold; or, the Temptation.

From the German, with Additions and Alterations by Mrs. Sarah A. Myers. Illustrated. 16mo. 60 cents.

A capital book for boys, and one which they will peruse with unbounded delight.

Florence Egerton; or, Sunshine and Shadow.

By the author of "Clara Stanley." Illustrated. 16mo. 75 cents.

"An affecting story for young readers, showing the beauty of piety and the fine moral effects of stedfast adhesion to duty. The heroine attracts the reader's sympathy by the simplicity of her character, while her life contains a rich and useful lesson."—*Evangelist.*

By the same Author,

Clara Stanley; or, a Summer among the Hills.

18mo. 50 cents.

Aunt Edith. A Story.

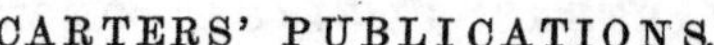

Vara; or, the Child of Adoption.

The Fifth Thousand, with four new Illustrations. 12mo. $1 00.

"It is a deeply interesting story. We hope every novel-reading young lady will procure and attentively read it. She will be made wiser and better by so doing, and will find it contains all the interest of the wildest romance."—*Pbn. Herald.*

"Its incidents are graphically and naturally told."—*Hampshire Herald.*

"There has no volume fallen into our hands for years with which we have been more interested '—*Sandy Hill Herald.*

"The writer is equally at home amid the picturesque scenes of the Pacific Isles, and the more familiar events of an American dwelling."—*Southern Baptist.*

"An affecting story."—*Jeffersonian.*

"A charming story: we read it with unbounded satisfaction."—*Lit. Standard.*

"Vara is of the same type as the gentle Eva."—*Democrat.*

"After perusing 'Vara' the heart seems hallowed with a holy spirit."—*Mercantile Guide.*

"One of the most charming books we have read in a long time, written in a most attractive style, and inculcating valuable Christian lessons."—*Religious Herald.*

"The tale is told in a strain of unaffected simplicity."—*Asmonean.*

"It is not often we become so deeply absorbed in a volume as we did in this book."—*St. Louis Presbyterian.*

Jeanie Morrison; or, the Discipline of Life.

By the author of the "Pastor's Family." Illustrated. 16mo. 75 cts.

A most fascinating, as well as instructive tale—the history of a little girl born in a primeval forest of the Great West—who, by the death of both her parents, while yet an infant, was thrown friendless upon the world. But the prayers of a pious mother on her behalf were answered; and she was well cared for by an excellent couple who adopted her as their daughter. The various trials to which she was exposed on the death of her kind guardians, and the power of Christian principle in sustaining her under them, are most strikingly illustrated in this beautiful narrative.

The Pastor's Family.

By the author of "Jeanie Morrison." 18mo. 25 cents.

"What an unpretending title; and yet what a history of joys and sorrows, trials and comforts, sunshine and shade, is gathered within its gilded covers. It is a painting of which there are many copies, variously colored, but all real and truthful in the history of ministerial life."—*Christian Advocate.*

The Brother and Sister; or, the Way of Peace.

By the author of "Grace Dermott." 18mo. 50 cents.

Infidelity;

ITS ASPECTS, CAUSES, AND AGENCIES. By Thomas Pearson, Eyemouth, Scotland. 8vo. $2. Cheap edition, 12mo, 60 cents.

"He writes like one thoroughly familiar with his ground; he has the confidence of one who has examined well the strength and manœuvrings of the enemy; who also knows well his own resources, and has no hesitation as to the side toward which victory will finally turn. He shows an uncommon degree of judgment and strong common sense. We feel assured that ministers and intelligent laymen generally, will read this work with no common interest."—*Presbyterian.*

"This work is written in a masterly style of argument, and with a beauty, as well as power of language, which makes it an eminently readable book."—*Observer.*

"We have no hesitation, without knowing anything of the author except from this work, in assigning to him a place among the most philosophical and discriminating minds of the age."—*Puritan Recorder.*

Jaqueline Pascal;

Or, A GLIMPSE OF CONVENT LIFE AT PORT ROYAL. With an Introduction by W. R. Williams, D.D. 12mo. $1.

"Jaqueline Pascal, the younger sister of the renowned Blaise Pascal, was a woman of surprising powers, of remarkable feminine attractions, and intellect and disposition in no respect inferior to her celebrated brother. The work before us gives a most delightful picture of this wonderful woman—of her sister, their eminent brother, and the members and connections of the family."

*The Self-Explanatory Reference Bible.

8vo. Half calf, $4 50. Turkey morocco $6. Morocco gilt, $6 50.

"The peculiarity of the edition is, that the marginal references are printed out in full, occupying the middle column of the page, so that, without the trouble of hunting out a reference, the eye may at once compare it with the text. This is a positive advantage, both for exposition in the family, for the preparation of the Bible Lessons, and for the purposes of the student. The type is clear, the paper good, and the whole page beautiful."—*Independent.*

*The Evidences of Christianity,

AS EXHIBITED IN THE WRITINGS OF ITS APOLOGISTS DOWN TO AUGUSTINE. A Prize Essay. By W. J. Bolton. 8vo. 75 cents

Wardlaw on Miracles.

12mo. Price 75 cents.

The Missionary of Kilmany.

18mo. Price 40 cents.

History of the Westminster Assembly of Divines.

By Wm. M. Hetherington, D.D. 12mo. 75 cents.

The Claremont Tales;

Or, ILLUSTRATIONS OF THE BEATITUDES. 18mo, with cuts. 50 cts.

A New Edition of the

Life and Times of John Calvin.

By Paul Henry. 2 vols. in one. Price $2.

John Howard;

Or, THE PRISON WORLD OF EUROPE. By Hepworth Dixon. New edition. 16mo. 75 cents.

The Lamp and the Lantern;

Or, LIGHT FOR THE TENT AND THE TRAVELLER. By the Rev. James Hamilton, D.D. 18mo. 40 cents.

"It is in Dr. Hamilton's best vein, and leaves a vivid impression of the grandeur, worth, adaptedness, and beauty of the Bible."—*New York Evangelist.*

Jacobus on the Gospels.

Vol. I., MATTHEW. Vol. II., MARK AND LUKE. Each, 75 cents.

*The Scripture Testimony to the Messiah.

By John Pye Smith, D.D. 2 vols. 8vo. English edition. $5.

Waters from the Well-spring.

By the Rev. E. H. Bickersteth. 16mo. Price 60 cents.

Evenings with Mamma.

Square, Illustrated.

Howell's Remains.

Hewittson's Letters and Remains.
2 vols.

Words to Win Souls.

Lectures to Young Men.
Delivered in London before the Young Men's Christian Association.

Bickersteth's Works.
16 vols. 12mo.

De Costa's Israel and the Gentiles.

Hours o Devotion.
From the German of Tholuck.

The Last Journey.
By the author of "Morning and Night Watches."

Cowper's Task.
Illustrated, by Birket Foster. 8vo. (Preparing.)

Matthew Henry's Miscellaneous Works.
2 vols. Royal 8vo. (Preparing.)

Malan's Switzerland.

Watson's Body of Divinity.
8vo.

A New Edition of Henry's Commentary.
In 6 vols. Quarto. Large type. (Preparing.)

Alford's Greek Testament.
Preparing.

Fletcher's Addresses.

Works of the Rev. John Angell James.

The Young Man's Friend,

AND GUIDE THROUGH LIFE TO IMMORTALITY. 75 cents.

The Young Woman's Friend,

AND GUIDE THROUGH LIFE TO IMMORTALITY. 16mo. 75 cents.

The Christian Father's Present to his Children.

75 cents.

Christian Duty.

A SERIES OF PASTORAL ADDRESSES. 16mo. 75 cents.

Christian Professor.

16mo. 75 cents.

The Widow Directed to the Widow's God.

18mo. 30 cents.

Christian Progress.

18mo. 30 cents.

The Anxious Inquirer Directed.

18mo. 30 cents.

The True Christian.

30 cents.

The Course of Faith;

OR, THE PRACTICAL BELIEVER DELINEATED. 75 cents.

Young Man from Home.

18mo. 30 cents.

Works of the Rev. William Jay.

The Autobiography and Reminiscences of the Rev. William Jay.

2 vols. Royal 12mo. $

This most interesting work includes, in addition to the Autobiography, sketches of Wilberforce, Cecil, Rowland Hill, Hannah More, and many other of Mr. Jay's contemporaries.

Female Scripture Characters.

Royal 12mo. $1.

"By all sincere Christian women the world over, this volume will be regarded as a spiritual treasure."—*Presbyterian.*

"They will be found unusually interesting in style and spirit, as well as in the skill and beauty of their portraiture, wise in their counsel, and excellent in their influence—worthy the fame of the distinguished author."—*Evangelist.*

"They bear all those characteristics of both mind and heart which have rendered all his productions at once so popular and so useful."—*Argus.*

The Morning and Evening Exercises.

A new edition, on large type, in *four* volumes, royal 12mo.
Price $4.

"This is a new edition of an excellent practical work, beautifully printed on large and fair type, and bound in cloth. The execution of these volume is in the best style, entitling them to a preference before all other editions. As the work is highly appreciated on both sides of the Atlantic, it is sufficient to say that we know of nothing more pure and scriptural in sentiment, nothing more elevated and devotional in spirit, nothing more simple and beautiful, than the reflections on the lessons from the Bible contained in this book."—*Christian Observer.*

"We doubt whether any work of modern times has been more blessed to the edification of God's people than Jay's Exercises. It has been the closet companion of tens of thousands of earnest Christians in all parts of the world, kindling anew within their hearts, with each day, the flame of devotion; instructing, cheering, and comforting them on their heavenward way."—*Presbyterian.*

The Same Work.

On smaller type, in 2 vols. $1 50.

The Christian Contemplated,

In a Series of Lectures. 18mo. 40 cents.

The Woodcutter of Lebanon and the Exiles of Lucerna.

By the author o "Morning and Night Watches. 18mo.

Mabel Grant.

A Highland Story. By Randall Ballantyne. 18mo. 50 cents.

Charles Roussel; or, Honesty and Industry.

By the author of "Three Months under the Snow." 18mo. 40 cents.

The Eternal Day.

By the Rev. Horatius Bonar. 18mo. 50 cents.

"This book is written and published for the joy and strength of those who are looking forward to an eternal day in heaven. The discussion is scriptural and full of unction and power. Many a weary pilgrim will read it with intense interest, and receive a new impulse in his journey toward that better land."—*Ch. Chronicle.*

Is it Possible to make the Best of Both Worlds?

By the Rev. T. Binney. 16mo. 60 cents.

"We wish that all apprentices, and young men entering on business, could be induced to procure and study this book. The happy results of future years would be the reward of attending to its counsels."—*Banner.*

Also a supply of the London edition of

Sir Thomas Fowell Buxton.

A Study for Young Men. By the same author. 16mo. 50 cents.

The Words of Jesus.

By the author of the "Morning and Night Watches." 16mo. 40 cts.

"They are like the precious words that introduce them, of a most tender and consolatory character, and especially adapted to strengthen the heart of the weary pilgrim."—*Puritan Recorder.*

Daniel, a Model for Young Men.

By the Rev. W. A. Scott, D.D. 8vo. $1 50.

Discourses and Sayings of our Lord Jesus Christ.

Illustrated in a series of Expositions. By John Brown, D.D.
2 vols. 8vo. $4.

"Where several conflicting opinions of the learned are detailed, his discrimination is admirable; when his own interpretation is given, it is set forth with so much clearness, and appears so reasonable, that the reader will seldom feel disposed to withhold his assent. As an able expositor—clear, candid, comprehensive—Dr. Brown is unrivalled among British divines."—*Kitto.*

The Right of the Bible in the Common Schools.

By George B. Cheever, D.D. 16mo. 75 cents.

"It is a question which in its decision is to influence the happiness, the temporal and eternal welfare of one hundred millions of human beings."—*Daniel Webster.*

By the same Author,

The Powers of the World to Come, and the Church's Stewardship, as invested with them.

12mo. Price $1.

"He makes the realities of the invisible world take on a living and substantial character. We seem to be in contact with the sublime scenes of the judgment, to breathe the air of the upper Paradise, and to listen to the wailings of the reprobate. If we were to characterize this work in a single word, we would say that it is a work of power."—*Puritan Recorder.*

"This is a solemn and stirring book. Many of the pages sparkle with gems of the richest lustre."—*Watchman and Observer.*

By Dr. John Brown,

Sufferings and Glories of the Messiah;

An Exposition of Psalm xviii. and Isaiah lii. 13; liii. 12.

"It is the ripe fruit of thirty years study of the deeply interesting passages on which it is founded. The learned author has spared no pains to make his examination thorough and satisfactory."—*St. Louis Presbyterian.*

Abbeokuta;

Or, Sunrise in the Tropics. An Outline of the Origin and Progress of the Yoruba Mission. By Miss Tucker, author of "The Rainbow in the North." Illustrated. 16mo. 75 cents.

Scotia's Bards.

Comprising the choicest productions of Scottish Poets, Illustrated with more than fifty elegant engravings in the highest style of the art, with Frontispiece and Vignette by Ritchie. 8vo. Cloth, $3; full gilt, $4; Turkey Morocco, $6 50.

"Scotland, rich in the treasures of Theology, History, and Philosophy, here stands before us with their long array of Poets, such as any country might be proud to acknowledge as its own."—*Watchman and Reflector.*

"An elegant volume, in the very best style of execution."—*Chrs. Intelligencer.*

"It is enriched with the most brilliant and costly poetic gems, from the mines of that land, which has been as fruitful in minstrels as in metaphysicians, heroes, and martyrs."—*Presbyterian.*

"This fine large octavo volume, printed in beautiful style, and enriched with many choice engravings, containing, we believe, the first extended collection of the best productions of the Scottish poets, that has ever been made. It cannot fail to be acceptable to all who can appreciate the finest creations of genius."—*Argus.*

"We predict that as 'Scotia's Bards' is one of the most superb books of the season, so it will be one of the most popular also."—*T. C. L.*

"A most excellent taste and judgment are displayed in the selection of this volume, and the biographical and critical notices prefixed to the poems, are happily written, in a chaste and simple style; the illustrations of the work will combine with its intrinsic value, to render it one of the most attractive of the season."—*Independent.*

Family Prayers.

By the Author of "Morning and Night Watches." 75 cents.

These prayers are conceived in a truly evangelical spirit, and are remarkable for the appropriate introduction of Scripture language. Besides morning and evening prayers for four weeks, there are a number of prayers designed for, and well adapted to as many different occasions. Those who are accustomed to use forms of any kind, will find this an excellent auxiliary to their family devotions.

Memoir of Richard Williams.

Surgeon. Catechist to the Patagonian Mission. By James Hamilton, D.D. 16mo. 75 cents.

"In all the history of Gospel Missions there is nothing that possesses such a fearful interest as that of the English Missionaries to Patagonia, the terrible sufferings and starvation of a portion of whom created such a shock a year or two ago. The subject of this memoir was the surgeon and catechist of that devoted band, and it is chiefly made up of his journal, which was continued by his own hand so long as he was able to put pen to paper. The annals of martyrdom contain few stories of a Christian heroism more noble than his and that of his associates."—*Bulletin.*

Christian Progress.

A sequel to the "Anxious Enquirer." By the Rev. John Angel James. 18mo. 30 cents.

The Law and the Testimony;

By the Author of the "Wide, Wide World," &c. 8vo, second thousand. Cloth, $3; half calf, $4.

"This is a great book, and manifestly the result of labor, patient and long continued. It is a complete collection, or at least a very extensive one, of all the passages in the Bible having a bearing upon particular specified subjects or points of doctrine, such as the Divine Nature, Divinity of the Saviour, God's Omniscience, Sovereignty and Justice, Christ's Office, Office of the Holy Spirit, Man's Freedom and Fall, Nature and Consequences of Sin, Nature of Faith, Repentance, Salvation, Judgment, Heaven and Hell, &c. . . . . A remarkable book, one that will take the shelf by the side of the most elaborate tomes and learned works of distinguished divines. The author has already acquired a wide reputation by two works of lighter literature, 'Queechy' and the 'Wide, Wide World;' but the 'Law and the Testimony,' we imagine, will be her most enduring work."—*U. S. Journal.*

"We welcome it as a fresh and worthy aid to the examination of the pure word of God."—*Watchman.*

"A delightful handmaid to the perusal and right understanding of the meaning, force, fulness, and harmony of the sacred text."—*Spectator.*

"A most valuable aid to all those who revere and study the Scriptures, as the only rule of faith and practice."—*Pbn. of West.*

"We commend this volume with all our heart. The Sabbath School Teacher needs it. Parents may well lay it on the table of the new married daughter. And aged Christians, as they follow on through these clear and well printed pages, will rejoice to find the foundation of their hope standing so strong."—*T. L. C.*

"We can commend it as a volume of great convenience in the study of the Sacred volume, and especially to the Ministers of the Gospel in their preparations for the pulpit."—*Pbn. Herald.*

Now completed, by the publication of the eighth and last volume,

Daily Bible Illustrations:

Being Original Readings for a Year on Subjects from Sacred History, Biography, Geography, Antiquities, and Theology. Especially designed for the Family Circle. By John Kitto, D.D.

Morning Series:—Vol. I. The Antediluvians and Patriarchs, Fourth Edition; Vol. II. Moses and the Judges, Second Edition; Vol. III. Samuel, Saul, and David, Second Edition; Vol. IV. Solomon and the Kings, Second Edition.

Evening Series:—Vol. I. Job and the Poetical Books; Vol. II. Isaiah and the Prophets; Vol. III. Life and Death of our Lord; Vol. IV. The Apostles and Early Church.

Each Volume is sold separately, price $1 each.

"One of the best books of the kind. Dr. Kitto brings to each reading curious learning, real information, and close argument, conveyed in a solid style."—*Spectator.*

"The series is admirable."—*Evangelical Christendom.*

"For family reading, these Illustrations are inestimable."—*Baptist Magazine.*

"We should wish to see this most useful work in every house."—*Church of England Magazine.*

BOOKS

PUBLISHED BY

ROBERT CARTER & BROTHERS,

285 BROADWAY, NEW YORK.

ABERCROMBIE (JOHN, M.D.)—**The Contest and the Armor;** to which is added, **Think on these Things.** 32mo. 25 cents.

ADAMS (THOMAS)—**The Three Divine Sisters;** or, Faith, Hope, and Charity. With an Introduction by the Rev. W. H. STOWELL, Rotherham. 60 cents.

"With the eye of a poet, the heart of a saint, and the tongue of an orator, he gives substance to abstractions, personifies the virtues, paints the beauties of holiness, and brings to the ear the voices of the distant and the dead."

Advice to a Young Christian, on the Importance of aiming at an elevated standard of Piety. By a Village Pastor. With an Introductory Essay by the Rev. Dr. ALEXANDER. 18mo. 30 cents.

ALLEINE (Rev. JOSEPH)—**Gospel Promises.** Being a short view of the great and precious promises of the Gospel. 18mo. 30 cents.

——— **Life and Letters of the Rev. Joseph Alleine.** 60 cts.

ALEXANDER (Rev. A., D.D.)—**Counsels of the Aged to the Young.** 32mo, gilt. 25 cents.

Ancient History—Containing the History of the Egyptians, Assyrians, Chaldeans, Medes, Lydians, Carthaginians, Persians, Macedonians, the Seleucidæ in Syria, and Parthians. In 4 vols. 12mo. $2.

ANDERSON (CHRISTOPHER)—**The Annals of the English Bible,** revised, abridged, and continued by Rev. SAMUEL IRENÆUS PRIME. 8vo. $1 75.

"The thrilling and providential history of our version of the Holy Scriptures, from its translation by Tyndale, in 1524, down to its final revisions and emendations at the close of the last century; the martyr fate of its early friends, and the desperate struggle through which it passed and in which it triumphed, are in these most interesting pages fully recorded."—*Zion's Herald.*

ANDERSON (CHRISTOPHER)—**The Family Book**; or, the Genius and Design of the Family Constitution. 12mo. 75 cents.

'We were not aware, before perusing his book, how abundantly the family state is recognized in the Bible, and how much of our inspired instructions are founded on our domestic relations."—*Observer*.

ANLEY (Miss C.)—**Earlswood**, a Tale of the Times. 12mo. 75 cts.

"This tale illustrates with great ingenuity the fearfully erratic tendencies that have been developed in latter years in the Church of England, and the paramount importance of a return to the simplicity of Gospel truth and Gospel usages. The characters are sustained with much spirit and interest, the style is simple and natural, and the general effect of the work highly favorable to vital and practical godliness."—*Puritan Recorder*.

Australia—A Narrative of the Loss of the Brig Australia, by Fire. Edited by the Rev. JAMES R. MCGAVIN. 18mo. 25 cents.

Assembly's Catechism of the Westminster Divines. $1 25 per hundred.

BAGSTER—The Genuineness, Authenticity, and Inspiration of the Sacred Volume. By the Editor of Bagster's Comprehensive Bible. 12mo. 60 cents.

BAXTER (RICHARD)—**The Saints' Everlasting Rest.** 12mo, large type. 60 cents.

A Call to the Unconverted; and other Essays. 18mo. 30 cts.

Bible Companion; designed for the assistance of Bible classes, families, and young students of the Scriptures. With an Introduction by Dr. TYNG. 18mo. 40 cents.

Bible Expositor; Confirmations of the Truth of the Holy Scriptures, from the observations of recent travelers, illustrating the manners, customs, and places mentioned in Scripture. 18mo. 50 cents.

"This volume contains much interesting information in regard to almost every thing peculiar to the habits and customs of oriental nations."

BICKERSTETH (Rev. EDWARD)—**A Treatise on Prayer**, designed to assist in a devout discharge of that duty. 18mo. 40 cts.

——— **A Treatise on the Lord's Supper.** With an Introduction, Notes, and an Essay by the Rev. G. T. BEDELL, D.D. Sixth Edition. 18mo. 30 cents.

——— (EDWARD HENRY, A.M.)—**Waters from the Well-Spring**, for the Sabbath hours of Afflicted Believers; a series of Meditations. 16mo. 60 cents.

Blossoms of Childhood By the author of the "Broken Bud." 16mo. 75 cents.

BLUNT'S Undesigned Coincidences in the Writings both of the Old and New Testaments, an Argument of their veracity. With Paley's Horæ Paulinæ, or the Truth of the Scripture History of St. Paul Evinced. 8vo. $2.

"A work of great value, and one which must attract the attention of every student of the Scriptures. The novelty of the investigation, the success with which it is prosecuted, and the confirmation it elicits, will impress the mind of any one who will give it an examination."—*Observer.*

BOGATZKY (C. V. H.)—**A Golden Treasury for the Children of God.** 24mo. 50 cents.

"This book consists of devout reflections for every day in the year. It is full of truth, and wisdom, and piety. It is a fitting companion for the Christian's closet."

BOLTON (Rev. C. W.)—**A Shepherd's Call to the Lambs of his Flock.** Square, illustrated. 50 cents.

"This is one of the most perfect religious books for children that we have ever seen. It contains six pointed lectures, so illustrated and exemplified that they are like stories for a child—easily understood and with a most obvious aim. Children will read and re-read them with delight, and its excellent teachings will be likely to be so thoroughly impressed upon their minds as to be obvious in their manners."—*Newark Daily Adv.*

BONAR (Rev. Horatius)—**The Night of Weeping;** or, Words for the Suffering Family of God. 18mo. 30 cents.

——— **The Morning of Joy;** a Sequel to the "Night of Weeping." 18mo. 40 cents.

——— **The Story of Grace.** 30 cents.

——— **Truth and Error;** or, Letters to a Friend on some of the Controversies of the Day. 40 cents.

——— **Man**—His Religion and his World. 18mo. 40 cents.

——— **The Bible Hymn Book.** 50 cents.

——— (Rev. Andrew)—**A Commentary on the Book of Leviticus;** Expository and Practical, with Critical Notes. 8vo. $1 50.

BONNET (L.)—**The Family of Bethany;** or, Meditations on the Eleventh Chapter of John. With an Introductory Essay by Hugh White. 18mo. 40 cents.

——— **Meditations on the Lord's Prayer.** 18mo. 40 cents.

BOOTH'S Reign of Grace. With an Introduction by Rev. Dr. Chalmers. 12mo. 75 cents.

BORROW (George)—**The Bible in Spain,** and **The Gypsies of Spain.** 8vo, cloth. $1.

BOSTON (Rev. THOMAS)—**Human Nature** in its Fourfold State of Primitive Integrity, Entire Depravity, Begun Recovery, and Consummate Happiness or Misery. 18mo. 50 cents.

——— **The Crook in the Lot.** 18mo. 30 cents.

BRETT (Rev. W. H.)—**The Indian Tribes of Guiana.** 18mo, illustrated. 50 cents.

BRIDGEMAN (ELIZA J. G.)—**Daughters of China**; or, Sketches of Domestic Life in the Celestial Empire. 16mo. 75 cents.

BRIDGES (CHARLES, A.M.)—**The Christian Ministry.** With an Inquiry into the Causes of its Inefficiency. 8vo. $1 50.

——— **An Exposition of the Proverbs.** 8vo. $2 00.

"The most lucid and satisfactory commentary on the Book of Proverbs that we have met with; and though it is of a popular cast, and quite within the scope of the general reader, it is a book which clergymen will find to their advantage frequently and diligently to consult."

——— **Exposition of Psalm CXIX.,** as Illustrative of the Character and Exercises of Christian Experience. $1 00.

——— **Memoir of Miss Mary Jane Graham,** late of Stoke Fleming, Devon. $1 00.

——— **Works.** Comprising all the above in three vols. 8vo. $5 00.

Broken Bud (The); or, Reminiscences of a Bereaved Mother; with a beautiful frontispiece. 16mo. 75 cents.

"This is a very touching and beautiful book. It is simply the treasured memories of a sorrowing mother, and there is in it so much tenderness, sweetness, and saddened resignation, that it is invested with an inexpressible charm."

BROWN (JOHN, D.D.)—**Expository Lectures** on the First Epistle of Peter. One thick 8vo volume. $2 50.

Of this work, the North British Review says:—"It is neither Scottish nor German, but sprung from the high and rare union of the best qualities of both schools in a single mind. It has the Scottish clearness, precision, orthodoxy, practicality; the German learning, minuteness of investigation, and disregard of tradition; and for certain qualities too rare in both—resolute adherence to the very truth of the passage—unforced development of the connection, and basing of edification on the right meaning of the Scripture, we have not met with anything in either country that surpasses it."

——— **Discourses and Sayings of our Lord Jesus Christ.** Illustrated in a Series of Expositions. 3 vols. 8vo. $6 00.

——— **The Sufferings and Glories of the Messiah**; an Exposition of Psalm XVIII. and Isaiah LIII. 12. 8vo. $1 50.

——— **Exposition of the Epistle of Paul to the Galatians.** 8vo. $2 00.

BROWN, (JOHN, of Haddington)—**Explication of the Assembly's Catechism.** 12mo. 60 cents.

Do. do. do. small one. 18mo. 10 cts.

——— **Concordance.** 32mo. 20 cents; gilt, 30 cents.

——— **Catechism for Children.** $1 25 per hundred.

——— (Rev. DAVID)—**On the Second Advent,** Will it be Pre-Millennial? $1 25.

BUCHANAN (JAMES, D.D.)—**Comfort in Affliction.** A Series of Meditations. 18mo. 40 cents.

"A fourth edition of an excellent work. We have before commended it in very decided terms, and again say to the afflicted, that a gentler, truer, and more sympathizing counseller could hardly be found than this author proves himself to be."—*Evangelist.*

——— **The Office and Work of the Holy Spirit.** 18mo. 50 cts.

"This work is to be commended alike for its simple and Scriptural views of religious doctrine, for its flowing and graceful style, and for its fervent and glowing appeals. The author is one of the most accomplished men in Scotland, and is a professor in the new College of Edinburgh."

BUNBURY (Miss SELINA)—**Glory, Glory, Glory,** and other Narratives. 25 cents.

BUNYAN (JOHN)—**The Pilgrim's Progress.** Fine edition, large type, with Illustrations by Howland. $1 00.

Do. do. close type. 18mo. 50 cents.

——— **The Jerusalem Sinner Saved**—The Pharisee and the Publican—The Trinity and a Christian—The Law and a Christian. With a Life of the author, by the Rev. JAMES HAMILTON, London. 18mo. 50 cents.

——— **The Greatness of the Soul,** and the Unspeakableness of the Loss thereof—No Way to Heaven but by Jesus Christ—The Strait Gate. With an Essay on Bunyan's Genius and Writings, by the Rev. R. PHILIP. 18mo. 50 cents.

BURNS (Rev. JABEZ, D.D.)—**The Parables and Miracles of Jesus Christ.** 12mo. 75 cents.

"This is an admirable volume, full of the loftiest truths, and the most valuable deductions and applications. It consists of sketches of sermons on the parables and miracles of Christ, explanatory and illustrative of the essentials of saving religion. It is warmly commended to all, but especially to ministers, who will find in it a fund of theological knowledge and pure scripture."—*Spectator.*

——— (JOHN, M.D.)—**Christian Fragments;** or, Remarks on the Nature, Precepts, and Comforts of Religion. 40 cents.

BUTLER—The Complete Works of Bishop Butler. 1 vol., 8vo. $1 50.

"The Analogy of Butler enjoys a reputation scarcely second to any other book than the Bible; to praise it would be a work of supererogation. As a specimen of analogical reasoning, we suppose it has never been equalled; and its influence, in promoting ministerial efficiency, can hardly be overrated. Some ministers are in the habit of reading it, carefully, once every year. The Analogy occupies about one half the volume; the remainder consists of Dissertations and Sermons."—*N. E. Puritan.*

——— **Sermons alone.** 8vo. $1 00.

——— **Analogy alone.** 8vo. 75 cents.

——— **and WILSON'S Analogy.** In one vol. $1 25.

CALVIN—The Life of John Calvin, the Reformer, by Professor Henry, of Berlin, translated by Stebbings, with a fine portrait. 2 vols. 8vo.

"Dr. Henry's large work, which has been repeatedly noticed by this journal, composed by one who has a high but not blind admiration of the reformer's character, and a cordial sympathy with those great principles, to the exposition and defence of which Calvin devoted all the energies of his noble soul, is very admirable. It contains the rich and ample fruits of the researches of many years; it is a well-stored repository of materials gathered from many sources."—*Princeton Review.*

CAMERON—The Farmer's Daughter. Illustrated. 18mo. 30 cts.

CECIL—The Works of the Rev. Richard Cecil, late Minister of St. John's Chapel, Bedford Row, London. 3 vols. $3 00.

"In Richard Cecil we see a man, combining the rich soil of strong native talent with a refinement of cultivation not surpassed by classic example; while in him the elegant and profound scholar and polished gentleman are only the subordinate characters of the humble-minded, devoted, and enterprising follower of the lowly Jesus."—*Baptist Advocate.*

——— **Sermons,** separate. $1 00.

——— **Miscellanies and Remains,** separate. $1 00.

——— **Original Thoughts on Scripture.** $1 00.

CECIL (Cath.)—**Memoir of Mrs. Hawkes,** late of Islington, including Remarks in Conversation and Extracts from Sermons and Letters of the late Rev. R. Cecil. 12mo. $1 00.

"The life and religious experience of Mrs. Hawkes is replete with interest to all who desire to study the grace of God as it is developed in the daily life, habits, and conversation of those who may be justly regarded as exemplifying the hidden meaning of the words—'the secret of the Lord is with them that fear him.' The records of her life are the more interesting because there are inwoven in them so many incidents connected with Cecil. But her own piety and opinions stand on its pages as fine gold purified in the furnace."—*Richmond Ch. Advocate.*

CHALMERS—**Sermons,** enlarged by the addition of his **Posthumous Sermons.** 2 vols., 8vo. With a fine portrait. $3 00.

——— **Lectures on Romans.** With a fine portrait. 8vo. $1 50.

——— **Miscellanies, Essays, and Reviews.** With fine portrait. 8vo. $1 50.

——— **Select Works;** comprising the above. 4 vols., 8vo. With portrait. $6 00.

——— **Evidences of Christian Revelation.** 2 vols. $1 25.

——— **Natural Theology.** 2 vols. $1 25.

——— **Moral Philosophy.** 60 cents.

——— **Commercial Discourses.** 60 cents.

——— **Astronomical Discourses.** 60 cents.

"So long as the eloquence of piety and truth, illustrated by the loftiest powers of intellect and the largest acquisitions of learning, shall have admiring students, so long will the sacred writings of Chalmers stand in the front rank of religious literature, and be valued among the treasures of the Church of God." —*N. Y. Observer.*

CHARNOCK (STEPHEN, B. D.)—**Discourses upon the Existence and Attributes of God.** With a Life of the author by the Rev. Dr. SYMINGTON. 2 vols., 8vo. $3 00.

"The sublimeness, variety, and rareness of the truths handled, together with the elegance of the composure, neatness of the style, and whatever is wont to make any book desirable, all concur in the recommendation of it (Charnock on the Attributes). It is not a book to be played with or slept over, but read with the most intense and serious interest."—*Adams & Veal.*

——— **Choice Works.** 18mo.

CHEEVER (GEORGE B., D.D.)—**The Powers of the World to Come,** and the Church's Stewardship as invested with them. 12mo. $1 00.

——— **Lectures on the Pilgrim's Progress,** and the Life and Times of John Bunyan. Illustrated. *Ninth* edition. Large 12mo $1 00.

"Dr. Cheever's name will go down to posterity conjoined with the immortal dreamer, in a union no less intimate, though more honorable, than that of Johnson and Boswell. As a commentator of Bunyan he stands without peer or rival. Scott has furnished notes for the text valued for their discrimination and piety; Dr. Hamilton and Robert Philip have contributed brilliant monograms in illustration of his genius; other eminent writers have labored in the same department, but Dr. Cheever has won the palm from all competitors. We can bestow no higher praise on the volume than to say it is worthy of its subject, and all readers of the charming allegory should not fail to read the Lectures."—*Ch. Chronicle.*

Child's Own Story Book, by Mrs. JERRAM. Illustrated with colored plates. Square. 50 cents.

Christian Retirement; or, the Spiritual Exercises of the Heart. From the Fourteenth London edition. 12mo. 75 cents.

Christian Experience; as Displayed in the Life and Writings of St. Paul. New edition, 12mo. 75 cents.

CLARK (JOHN A., D.D.)—**A Walk about Zion.** Revised and enlarged. Ninth edition. With two steel plates. 12mo. 75 cts.

——— **Gathered Fragments.** Fifth edition. Two steel plates. 12mo. $1 00.

——— **The Young Disciple;** or, Memoir of Anzonetta R. Peters. Sixth edition. 12mo. 88 cents.

——— **The Pastor's Testimony.** Sixth edition. Two steel plates. 12mo. 75 cents.

——— **Awake, Thou Sleeper.** A series of Awakening Discourses. Third edition. 12mo. 75 cents.

"Dr. Clark has for some time been known to the religious public as one of the most judicious and excellent writers of the day. His works are all characterized by good thoughts, well expressed in a graceful and appropriate manner, by great seriousness and unction, and an earnest desire to promote the spiritual interests of his fellow-men."

CLARKE (SAMUEL, D.D.)—**Daily Scripture Promises to Living Christians.** Now first arranged in Lessons for every day in the year. 32mo., gilt edge. 30 cents.

Clara Stanley; or, a Summer among the Hills, by the author of "Aunt Edith." 18mo. 50 cents.

'This little book, forming one of Carters' Fireside series, is full of delightful entertainment as well as useful instruction to the young. It not only inculcates a pure morality, but breathes a spirit of exalted piety."—*Argus.*

Claremont (THE) **Tales;** or, Illustrations of the Beatitudes. A Series of Tales. With engravings. 18mo. 50 cents.

Colliers (THE) **Tale**—A True History by James Bridges, Esq. 18mo. 25 cents.

COLQUHOUN—The World's Religion as contrasted with Genuine Christianity, by Lady COLQUHOUN. Uniform with her Memoir. 16mo. 50 cents.

Commandment (The) **With Promise.** By the author of the "Week." Illustrated by Howland. Fine copy, 16mo. 75 cts. Small copy. Do. Close type. 18mo. 40 cents.

Companion for the Afflicted. Consisting of Warnings, Prayers, and Promises in the Language of Scripture. In 2 parts. Each 15 cents.

COWPER'S Poetical Works. 2 vols., 16mo. Illustrated. $1 50.

CUMMING—A Message from God; or, Thoughts on Religion for Thinking Men, by the Rev. John Cumming, D.D. 18mo. 30 cts.

——— **Christ Receiving Sinners.** 18mo. 30 cents.

"A very attractive little volume, abounding in excellent thought, naturally and pointedly expressed."—*Presbyterian.*

CUNNINGHAM—A World without Souls. By the Rev. J. W. Cunningham, A.M., Vicar of Harrow. 30 cents.

CUYLER (Rev. T. L.)—**Stray Arrows.** 18mo. 30 cents.

Daily Commentary. Exposition of Select Portions of Scripture for every Morning and Evening throughout the Year; a Companion to "Family Worship." By One Hundred and Eighty Clergymen of Scotland. 8vo. Cloth, $3; half calf, $4; morocco, $5.

The work entitled "Family Worship; a Series of Prayers for every Morning and Evening throughout the Year, by One Hundred and Eighty Clergymen of Scotland," was published about a year ago. That volume, reprinted from the Glasgow edition, formed only a portion of the work issued in Scotland, each prayer in the Scotch edition being accompanied by a brief comment on some portion of Scripture. In order to render them more available, the Prayers were reprinted separately, and now, to complete the work, the Expository and Practical Comments on Scripture are embodied in this volume, uniform with "Family Worship."

This "Daily Commentary," however, is not only a valuable companion to "Family Worship," but it is also admirably adapted to the purposes of private devotion. It is believed, both on account of its variety and ability, to be unsurpassed, if not unequalled by any previous work of daily devotional exercise.

DALE (Rev. Thomas)—**The Golden Psalm;** or, an Exposition of Psalm XVI. 16mo. 60 cents.

D'AUBIGNE'S History of the Reformation. Revised edition.

5 volumes, 12mo.	Cloth	$2 50
" "	Fine edition	3 50
"	In one 8vo. volume	1 50
The fifth volume separate. 12mo.	Half cloth.	50
" " " "	Full "	60
" " " "	*Fine edition.*	75

The subject of this volume is the origin and early progress of the Reformation in England.

D'AUBIGNE'S Life of Oliver Cromwell. 12mo. Cloth. 50 cents.

——— **Germany, England, and Scotland;** or, the Recollections of a Swiss Minister. 12mo. 75 cents.

——— **Luther and Calvin.** 18mo. 25 cents.

——— **The Authority of God the True Barrier against Romish and Infidel Aggression.** 16mo. 75 cents.

DAVIES (Rev. SAMUEL, A.M.)—**Sermons on Important Subjects.** 3 vols., 12mo. Cloth. $2 00.

"I most sincerely wish that young ministers, more especially, would peruse these volumes with the deepest attention and seriousness, and endeavor to form their Discourses according to the model of our author."—*Thos. Gibbons.*

DAVIDSON (Dr. D.)—**Connection of Sacred and Profane History;** from the Close of the Old Testament till the Estabment of Christianity. New edition. 1 vol., 12mo. $1 00.

"This work is well executed. The historical plan is clear and unique, and the style is singularly attractive, on account of its purity and strength."—*Protestant Churchman.*

DAVID'S Psalms.	In metre.	12mo.	Embossed. . .		75
" "	"	"	"	gilt.	1 00
" "	"	"	Turkey morocco.		2 00
" "	"	18mo.	Sheep. . .		38
" "	"	48mo.	" . .		20
" "	"	"	Morocco. . .		25
" "	"	"	"	*gilt.*	31
" "	"	"	Tucks.. . .		50
" "	With Brown's Notes.	18mo.		Sheep.	50
" "	" "	"		Morocco.	1 00

DICK (JOHN, D.D.)—**Lectures on Theology.** 2 vols. in one. Fine paper, with a portrait of the author by Ritchie. Price $2 50. In 2 vols. $3 00.

"We recommend this work in the very strongest terms to the Biblical student. It is, as a whole, superior to any other system of theology in our language. As an elementary book, especially fitted for those who are commencing the study of divinity, it is unrivalled."—*Christian Journal.*

——— **Lectures on the Acts of the Apostles.** 8vo. $1 50.

"The style of the author is peculiarly adapted to a work of this description. It is uncommonly perspicuous, terse, nervous, and calm. His ideas are the production of a highly-cultivated mind, originally endowed with strong common sense. In many respects he has the characteristics of Andrew Fuller, with more of the polish of the school."—*Baptist Advocate.*

DICKINSON (Richard W., D.D.)—**Scenes from Sacred History**; or, Religion Teaching by Example. 12mo. $1 00.

—— **Responses from the Sacred Oracles**; or, the Past in the Present. 12mo. $1 00.

DILL (Rev. Dr.)—**Ireland's Miseries**; the grand Cause and Cure. 16mo. 75 cents.

"This is a book that will attract much attention."—*Commercial Advertiser.*

DODDRIDGE (Philip, D.D.)—**The Rise and Progress of Religion in the Soul.** 18mo. 40 cents.

—— **The Life of Col. James Gardiner.** To which is added **The Christian Warrior Animated and Crowned.** 30 cts.

DUNCAN (Rev. Henry)—**The Sacred Philosophy of the Seasons.** Illustrating the Perfections of God in the Phenomena of the Year. 4 vols., 12mo. $3 00.

"We know of no work more simple in its teachings, and of none that collects more glory about the revolving months, than this."—*Spectator.*

—— **Tales of the Scottish Peasantry.** Illustrated. 50 cts.

—— **The Cottage Fireside**; or, the Parish Schoolmaster. 18mo. Illustrated. 40 cents.

—— (G. J. C.)—**The Life of the Rev. Henry Duncan, D.D.,** of Ruthwell, Founder of Savings' Banks. 12mo. 75 cents.

—— **Memoir of George Archibald Lundie**; or, Missionary Life in Samoa. By Mrs. Duncan. 18mo. 50 cents.

—— **A Glimpse into the World to Come**; in a Waking Dream. By the late George B. Philips. With a brief Memoir by Mrs. Duncan. 18mo. 25 cents.

—— (Mrs. M. G. L.)—**Memoir of Mary Lundie Duncan.** By her Mother. 16mo. Fine edition. 75 cents.

—— **The Children of the Manse.** Illustrated. 18mo. 50 cts.

—— **America as I found it.** With portrait. 16mo. $1 00.

"A very readable book."—*Advocate and Guardian.*

—— (Mary Lundie)—**Rhymes for my Children.** Square. Illustrated. 25 cents.

EDWARDS (Jonathan)—**Charity and its Fruits,** as exhibited in the Heart and Life. Printed from the Original MS. 50 cts.

"A new work from the great mind and heart of Edwards, on such a subject as Christian Love, we hardly shall need to commend. We find in it the same exhaustive analysis, the same earnest spirituality, and wonderful familiarity with both the Bible and the human heart, which distinguish his great treatise on the Affections. How true to the high standard of gospel truth, and how affectionately severe to the reader's soul."—*Evangelist.*

EDGAR'S Variations of Popery. 8vo. $1 00.

"This volume is inestimable to the man who wishes to understand the Romish controversy."—*St. Louis Presbyterian.*

English Pulpit (The)—**A Collection of Discourses** by the most eminent English Divines. $1 50.

"This book contains thirty-two sermons by the most noted living preachers of England. Among the contributors to the volume are found Melvill, Bradley, Moore, Bloomfield, Cummins, Fletcher, Hamilton, Noel, Jay, Raffles, James, Newton, and Bunting. The Sermons are highly evangelical in sentiment, and set forth clearly and fervently the great doctrines of the Gospel."—*Watchman and Observer.*

ERSKINE (Ralph)—**Gospel Sonnets**; or, Spiritual Songs. With a portrait of the author. 18mo. 50 cents.

"This is a most delightful volume, full of beautiful thought and gospel gems, to comfort, cheer, and enrapture the believer travelling from earth to glory. These songs of Erskine will keep his soul in tune, and prepare him the better to join the full chorus of the redeemed in heaven."—*Am. Spectator.*

Evidences of Christianity; a Series of Lectures delivered at the University of Virginia, by eminent Clergymen of the Presbyteaian Church. With 13 portraits by Ritchie. 8vo. $2 50.

Among the contributors to this great work are Drs. Alexander, Rice, Breckenridge, M'Gill, Ruffner, Sampson, Green, Rev. T. V. Moore, &c.

"This is a noble contribution to sound logic, elegant literature, and pure Christianity. It consists of a series of discourses, delivered by some of the greater lights of the Presbyterian Church, illustrative of the divine authority of the Christian religion. Though one star in the volume differeth from another, yet there is not one that shines dimly or feebly, while their aggregate glory is very great. It deserves to become, and it can hardly fail to become, a standard work in this department of our Christian literature."—*Argus.*

Family Worship; a Series of Prayers for every Morning and Evening throughout the Year. Adapted to Domestic Worship. By one hundred and eighty Clergymen of Scotland. 830 pp. 8vo. Cloth, $3 00; half calf, $4 00; Turkey morocco, $5 00.

"This volume is a treasure of its kind. The prayers are simple, varied, and impressive; excellent in the grasp of their subjects, and fervent in the words of supplication. They were prepared by men of a prayerful spirit; and are such as may be usefully employed in the morning and evening worship of God's people."—*Watchman.*

Fanny and her Mamma. By the author of "Mamma's Bible Stories." Illustrated. Square. 50 cents.

Far off; or, Asia and Australia Described. By the author of the "Peep of Day," &c. Illustrated. 18mo. 50 cents.

"A charming little book, especially for juvenile readers."—*Savannah Repub.*

First Day of the Week. 18mo. 25 cents.

FISK (Rev. George)—**A Memorial of Egypt**; The Red Sea; The Wilderness of Sin and Paran; Mount Sinai; Jerusalem, and other principal localities of the Holy Land. With seven steel plates. 12mo. $1 00.

——— **An Orphan Tale**; told in Rhyme. 18mo. 25 cents.

FLEURY (Rev. C. M.)—**The Life of David.** A Series of Discourses. 12mo. 60 cents.

FORD (Rev. D. E.)—**Decapolis**; or, the Individual Obligation of Christians to save Souls from Death. 18mo. 25 cents.

FOSTER (John)—**Essays**; In a Series of Letters. Comprising the Essays, On a Man writing the Memoirs of Himself; On Decision of Character; On the Application of the epithet Romantic; On some of the Causes why Evangelical Religion has been rendered unacceptable to persons of cultivated taste. 12mo. 75 cts.

"As an Essayist, John Foster is a bright and shining light. As different as possible from Addison, Steele, and Johnson, he far excels them in the importance of his subjects, and in the originality, largeness, and vigor of his conceptions. Foster is one of those who apply to their topics the most critical analysis, and bring to their treatment a cultivated perception, and a rich store of varied knowledge.

——— **An Essay on the Evils of Popular Ignorance.** 75 cts.

"This Essay, by one of the most suggestive, awakening minds that has left its impress upon modern English Literature. We scarcely know how otherwise a young man could do more for the invigoration and quickening of his powers of thought, than by the study of this high Essay until he has mastered it."—*Independent.*

FOX—**Memoir of the Rev. H. W. Fox,** Missionary to the Teloogoo people. With an Introductory Essay by Bishop McIlvaine. Illustrated with a fine portrait, and seven highly-finished wood engravings by Howland. 12mo. $1 00.

"No appeal that I know of—not even the Memoir of Henry Martyn—has blown the trumpet in our Zion with so loud and so stirring a note, as that which sounds forth in this volume."—*Elliott.*

Frank Harrison. 18mo. 30 cents.

"An intensely interesting story, which no boy can read without profit."

Frank Netherton; or, the Talisman. Illustrated. 40 cents.

"A beautiful story, and fragrant with living piety."—*Recorder.*

FRY (Caroline)—**Christ our Example**; with Autobiography and Portrait. 16mo. 75 cents.

"These essays are rich and deeply instructive."—*Chr. Chronicle.*

——— **The Listener.** Illustrated from original designs by Billings, engraved by Howland. 16mo. $1 00.

"This is one of the most sensible, striking, suggestive, and truly useful books that can be placed in the hands of the young."—*Evangelist.*

——— **Christ our Law.** 12mo. 60 cents.

——— **The Scripture Reader's Guide** to the Devotional Use of the Holy Scriptures. 18mo. 30 cents.

——— **Sabbath Musings.** 18mo. 40 cents.

GAUSSEN'S Parables of Spring. 16mo. 40 cents.

Geological Cosmogony. 18mo. 30 cents.

GILFILLAN (George)—**The Martys, Heroes, and Bards of the Scottish Covenant.** Illustrated. 16mo. 60 cents.

"This is a book that we have looked over with great delight. The theme is one of the noblest that modern history has furnished, and it has found a fitting delineator in the polished pen of the brilliant author of the Literary Portraits, who has done his work with some of the fire and unction of a genuine child of the Covenant."—*Watchman and Reflector.*

God in the Storm. 18mo. 25 cents.

GOOD'S Better Covenant. 12mo. [illegible] cents.

GRAHAM (Mary J.)—**The Test of Truth.** 18mo. 30 cents.

GRAY (Thomas)—**Elegy** written in a Country Churchyard, and other Poems. Illustrated by Gilbert. Small 8vo. Cloth, $1 00; full gilt, $1 50; Turkey morocco, $2 50.

"To praise Gray's poems, and especially the Elegy in the Country Churchyard, would be little less than an insult to the intelligence of our readers. But there are some things about the book which we may afford to speak of, as they are not altogether a matter of course. The critical observations at the commencement, are a fitting introduction to the work, as they tell us who the poet was, as well as what he did. The illustrations are just about as beautiful as art can make them. The typography and the paper are both exquisite; and the copy which we have at least, has tasked the skill of the bookbinder to the utmost. It is every way a beautiful book."—*Puritan Recorder.*

GRIFFITH (Thomas)—**Live while you Live.** 18mo. 30 cts.

HALDANES—Memoirs of the Lives of Robert Haldane, of Airthrey, and of his brother, **James Alexander Haldane.** By ALEXANDER HALDANE, Esq. 8vo. $2 00.

"This is in all respects an extraordinary production. British biography presents nothing to be compared with it. * * * It is a book of facts, great and varied; it is a book of principles, most of them sound and important; it is a book of examples, shining and impressive; it is a book of lessons, full of encouragement and of caution; it is a book which will, in a future age, be considered as deserving a chief place in the biography of the first half of the nineteenth century."—*British Banner.*

——— **Exposition of the Epistle to the Romans.** By ROBERT HALDANE, Esq. 8vo. $2 50.

"It is clear and masterly in its development of principles. It is bold and decided in its tone, because the Word of God which it illustrates and defends is so. We recommend the work most cordially to the attention of ministers, preachers, students in theology."—*Edinburgh Christian Instructor.*

HALL—The Select Works of Bishop Hall. 12mo. 75 cents.

HAMILTON (JAMES, D.D.)—**Life in Earnest.** 18mo 30 cents.

——— **The Mount of Olives.** 18mo. 30 cents.

"Thousands, as they read this work, will find a new and holier impulse communicated to their religious thoughts and sensibilities."—*American Citizen.*

——— **Harp on the Willows.** 30 cents.

——— **Thankfulness.** 18mo. 30 cents.

——— **Life of Hall.** 32mo. gilt. 30 cents.

——— **Happy Home.** Illustrated. 50 cents.

——— **Life of Lady Colquhoun.** With portrait. 75 cents.

"'Life in Earnest,' stirs the soul like a bugle blast, and this beautiful memoir falls on the heart like the low, sweet wail of some magnificent dirge from the hand of a master. We know nothing finer from the pen of even Wilson, than the splendid picture of Loch Lomond, with which the second chapter opens, or the death and burial of the noble lady of Rossdhu, with which the last closes."

——— **The Royal Preacher;** Lectures on Ecclesiastes. With portrait. 16mo. 85 cents.

"There is so quick a sympathy with the beautiful in nature and art; so inexhaustible a fertility of illustration from all departments of knowledge, so pictorial a vividness of language, that his pages move before us like some glittering summer landscape glowing in the light of a gorgeous sunset."—*Observer.*

——— **The Lamp and the Lantern;** or, Light for the Tent and the Traveller. 18mo. 40 cents.

——— **Memoir of Richard Williams,** Surgeon in the Missionary Expedition to Patagonia, Terra del Fuego. By the Rev. JAMES HAMILTON, D.D. (In preparation.)

HAWKER (Robert)—**The Poor Man's Morning Portion.** Being a Verse of Scripture, with short Observations for every day in the year. 12mo. 60 cents.

——— **Evening Portion.** 12mo. 60 cents.

——— **Zion's Pilgrim.** 18mo. 30 cents.

HENGSTENBERG (E. W.)—**The Revelation of St. John.** Expounded for those who Search the Scriptures. Translated by Patrick Fairbairn. 2 vols., 8vo. $3 50.

"No living theologian is better acquainted with the Old Testament than the author of this able and elaborate work. He is, consequently, well prepared to expound those parts of the New, the imagery of which is borrowed from the Old. He has brought to his task, in the present instance, great learning, deep piety, and unquenchable ardor in the investigation of truth. That he has, in everything, written wisely and correctly, is more than can be said; but he has produced a work of great research, and of unquestionable value to those who search the Scriptures."—*Central Christian Herald.*

*__HENRY__ (Matthew)—**An Exposition of the Old and New Testaments,** largely Illustrated with Practical Remarks and Observations, with a Life of the author by the Rev. Samuel Palmer, and an Introductory Preface by the late A. Alexander, D.D. 6 vols., royal 8vo. Sheep. $10 00.

Do. do. *Fine Edition*, on larger and finer paper, and elegantly bound in half calf. $16 00.

"This work has now been before the Christian community for more than a hundred years, and has, from its first publication, been so well received, and is so generally approved, that all recommendation of the work seems now superfluous. Many other valuable commentaries, it is true, have been given to the public since this work was first edited, and have deservedly gained for themselves a high estimation and extensive circulation. But it may be safely said, that Henry's Exposition of the Bible has not been superseded by any of these publications; and in those points in which its peculiar excellence consists, remains unrivalled. For some particular purposes, and in some particular respects, other commentaries may be preferable; but, taking it as a whole, and as adapted to every class of readers, this Commentary may be said to combine more excellences than any work of the kind which was ever written in any language."—*Rev. Dr. Alexander.*

——— **A Method for Prayer,** with Scripture Expressions proper to be used under each head. 18mo. 40 cents.

——— **The Communicant's Companion.** 18mo. 40 cents.

——— **Directions for Daily Communion with God.** Showing how to begin, how to spend, and how to close every day with God. 18mo. 30 cents.

——— **The Pleasantness of a Religious Life Opened and Proved.** 32mo. Gilt. 30 cents.

——— **Choice Works.** With a Life of Henry by the Rev. James Hamilton, London. 60 cents.

——— (Philip)—**Life,** 18mo. 50 cents.

HERVEY'S Meditations and Contemplations. 18mo. 40 cts.

HETHERINGTON (Rev. WM. M.)—**History of the Church of Scotland,** from the Introduction of Christianity to the period of the Disruption in 1843. 8vo. $1 50.

"This is in every respect a work of great merit. It contains the history of one of the most interesting portions of the Christian Church, and is distinguished as well by its neat and graceful style, as by the fulness, perspicuity, and so far as we can judge, fidelity of its statements."

—— **History of the Westminster Assembly of Divines.** 12mo. 75 cents.

HEWITSON (Rev. W. H.)—**Memoir of.** By the Rev. J. BAILLIE. Portrait. 12mo. 85 cents.

"This is a book to make one sad, but only with that sadness that makes the heart better. It is sad to see a star so bright and beautiful in its heavenly track, blotted out of sight ere it reached its zenith; and sad to think how few such burning and shining lights are left behind."—*Watchman.*

HILL (GEORGE)—**Lectures on Divinity.** 8vo. $2 00.

"The candor and fairness of this author are remarkable. In stating the opinions of opponents he is singularly impartial, and states their arguments in their full strength—an unfailing indication of real greatness, and assured confidence in the soundness of his own. You feel yourself in a serene and refreshing atmosphere, as you follow him in these pages, and are everywhere instructed. His notices, or history of varying opinions in theology, are very valuable."—*Christian Mirror.*

HILL (ROWLAND)—**The Life of the Rev. Rowland Hill, A.M.** By Rev. EDWIN SIDNEY. 12mo. 75 cents.

"One of the best of men, and the greatest of preachers."

Historic Doubts regarding Napoleon Bonaparte; and Historic Certainties regarding the Early History of America. 16mo. 50 cts.

History of the Reformation in Europe. With a Chronology of the Reformation, by the author of "The Council of Trent." 18mo. 40 cents.

History of the Puritans in England. Ry Rev. W. H. STOWELL, Professor of Theology, Rotherham College; and **The Pilgrim Fathers,** by D. WILSON, F.S.A. In 1 vol. $1 00.

HOOKER—The Philosophy of Unbelief, by the Rev. HERMAN HOOKER, D.D. 12mo. 75 cents.

"This work is characterized by a lucid and agreeable style, by profound and discriminating thought, and by great strength of moral and religious feeling."

—— **The Uses of Adversity** and the Provisions of Consolation. 18mo. 30 cents.

"I can desire no higher satisfaction, and certainly there can be no truer honor, than to be the instrument of conveying comfort to the bereaved and desponding, and causing their grief to assume the aspect aud direction of celestial love."—*Author's Preface.*

*__HORNE__ (Thos. H.)—**An Introduction to the Critical Study and Knowledge of the Holy Scriptures.** By Thomas Hartwell Horne, B.D., of St. John's College, Cambridge. New edition, corrected and enlarged. Illustrated with numerous Maps and fac-similes of Biblical Manuscripts. 2 vols., royal 8vo. Half cloth. $3 50. In 1 vol. Sheep. $4 00. In 2 vols. Full cloth. $4 00. 2 vols. Library style. $5 00.

"To commend Horne's Introduction to the clergy, or other students of the sacred oracles, would be 'carrying coals to Newcastle.' It has long been regarded as an indispensable work for a theological library, and has acquired among Biblical scholars—at least English Scholars—a deservedly high repute. It is a work of gigantic labor. The results of the research and erudition of Biblical scholars of all countries, and in all time, are faithfully garnered, and, on the whole, well digested."—*N. Y. Evangelist.*

——— (Bishop)—**A Commentary on the Book of Psalms.** To which is prefixed an Introductory Essay, by the Rev. Edward Irving, of London. 8vo. $1 50.

"His style is lucid, and often terse; his reflections grow naturally out of the sentiments of the passage on which he comments, and there breathes through the whole so much sympathy with the Psalmist in his humble views of himself, and his exalted conceptions of Jehovah; there is such a heavenly, sweet frame of mind exhibited, so much spirituality, and such love for the Redeemer, as to render this commentary one of peculiar fitness for family reading."

HOWARD (John)—Or, the Prison World of Europe, by Hepworth Dixon, Esq. 1 vol., 12mo. $1 00.

"Of Howard, it has been said, 'He lived an Apostle, and died a Martyr.' He traversed the civilized world, and entered its gloomy prison houses, to reduce the sum of human misery."—*Chn. Observer.*

HOWE (John)—**The Redeemer's Tears Wept over Lost Souls;** Union among Protestants; Carnality of Religious Contention; Man's Enmity to God, and Reconciliation between God and Man. 18mo. 50 cents.

HOWELL—Perfect Peace. Letters Memorial of the late John Warren Howell, Esq., of Bath. By the Rev. David Pitcairn. With an Introduction by the Rev. John Stevenson. 18mo. 30 cts.

HOWIE (John)—**The Scots Worthies;** containing a brief Historical Account of the most eminent Noblemen, Gentlemen, Ministers, and others who have suffered for the Reformation. 8vo. $1 50.

"This is an old work famous in Scotch literature, and a worthy companion of Fox's Book of Martyrs. It is a circumstantial history of the principal sufferers of the Covenanters, and others, whose heroic devotion to truth and liberty are worthy of everlasting remembrance and admiration. There is not a name in this long catalogue that does not deserve embalming; their history and memory constitute the richest of Scotland's possessions. The perusal of such a work is well adapted to our times; and it affords, aside from its noble illustrations of Christian principle, a very clear history of religious liberty in Scotland."—*Evangelist.*

HUSS—Memoir of John Huss, the Reformer. Translated from the German. 18mo. 25 cents.

Infant's Progress (The)—From the Plains of Destruction to Everlasting Glory, by the author of "Little Henry and his Bearer." Illustrated with fine engravings on wood, from original designs. 16mo. 75 cents.

JACOBUS (Melancthon W., D.D.)—**Notes on the Gospels:** Critical and Explanatory. And incorporating with the notes, on a new plan, the most approved harmony of the four Gospels. With illustrations, by Melancthon W. Jacobus, D.D., Professor of Biblical Literature in the Western Theological Seminary, at Alleghany, Pa.

Volume I.—**Matthew.** 12mo. 75 cents.

"We are greatly mistaken in our estimate of this new work, if it does not become the general favorite in our country as the guide book to the study of the sacred volume. It appears, to our mind, the book we have desired; it embraces the marrow of all the best writers and commentators on the gospels, and the admirable style in which it is published enhances its value. We confidently predict a large sale and its rapid introduction to our Sabbath Schools." *Christian Alliance and Visitor.*

Volume II.—**Mark and Luke.** 12mo. 75 cents.

"We view with complacency every attempt to make the historical Scriptures, and especially the Gospels, more familiar as a subject of popular instruction. But we are particularly pleased to see this responsible work in the hands of those who combine the advantages of literary training and pastoral experience."—*Princeton Review.*

Volume III.—**John and Acts.** (In preparation.)

——— **The Catechetical Question Book.** Intended to accompany the same. $1 50 per doz.

JAMES—The Anxious Inquirer after Salvation. By the Rev. John Angell James. 18mo. 30 cents.

——— **Christian Progress.** A sequel to the "Anxious Inquirer." 18mo. 30 cents.

——— **The True Christian.** 30 cents.

——— **The Widow directed to the Widow's God.** 18mo. 30 cts.

——— **Young Man from Home.** 18mo. 30 cents.

——— **Christian Professor.** 16mo. 75 cents.

"He looks at the Christian professor in all his relations, difficulties, and dangers, from the public assumption of his high vocation, to his disappearance in the depths of the dark valley. We would gladly see a copy of this earnest and impressive Manual in the hands of every member of the church."—*Watchman and Observer.*

JAMES—Christian Duty. A series of Pastoral Addresses. 16mo. 75 cents.

"It is practical, heart-searching, solemn, affectionate, earnest."—*Spectator.*

——— **The Course of Faith;** or, the Practical Believer Delineated. 75 cents.

"We have ofttimes reviewed the works of Mr. James with personal and religious profit, but it has seldom been our pleasure to welcome and peruse a more sterling work from his pen than the one before us. Faith and its nature, its office and effects, is but faintly understood by even our most consistent Christians;—the author has succeeded in a most surprising manner, and with his usually impressive style, to demonstrate the nature of *faith* in its theoretical, practical and experimental influences upon the heart and the life. *The Course of Faith* is a rich treasury of piety, knowledge, boundless compassion, and vigorous thought."—*Baptist Memorial.*

——— **The Young Woman's Friend and Guide** through Life to Immortality. 16mo. 75 cents.

"We doubt very much if Mr. James has ever made a better book than this. Those traits of character which give beauty, strength, and power to youthful females are here set forth in that glowing and earnest language which mark this author's writings, and if we had it in our power we should be happy to lay this volume upon the toilet table of every young lady of our acquaintance." *N. Y. Observer.*

——— **The Christian Father's Present to his Children.** 75 cts.

Jamie Gordon; or, the Orphan. Illustrated. 18mo. 50 cents.

"A most absorbing story, fraught with valuable instruction."—*Chris. Mirror.*

JANEWAY (James)—**Heaven upon Earth;** or, Jesus the best Friend of Man. With a History of the Janeway Family, by the Rev. F. A. Cox, D.D., LL.D., Hackney. 18mo. 50 cents.

——— **A Token for Children.** 30 cents.

JAY (Rev. Wm.)—**Morning and Evening Exercises,** for every day in the Year. *New and elegant edition, on large type and fine paper.* In 4 thick volumes. 12mo. Price $

Morning Exercises. Common edition. 12mo. 75 cents.

Evening Exercises. Do. do. 75 cents.

——— **The Christian Contemplated.** In a Course of Lectures delivered in Argyle Chapel, Bath. 18mo. 40 cents.

——— **The Jubilee Memorial.** 18mo. 30 cents.

JERRAM—A Tribute of Parental Affection, to the Memory of my beloved and only daughter, Hannah Jerram. By the Rev. Charles Jerram, A.M. 18mo. 30 cents.

JOHNSON (Dr. Samuel)—**Rasselas,** Prince of Abyssinia. Fine edition. 16mo. 50 cents.

JOHNSON—Memoir of the Rev. W. A. B. Johnson, Missionary in Regents' Town, Sierra Leone. With an Introduction by the Rev. Dr. Tyng. 12mo. $1 00.

KENNEDY—Profession is not Principle; or, the Name of Christian is not Christianity. By Grace Kennedy. 18mo. 30 cts.

——— **Jessy Allan,** the Lame Girl. A story founded on facts. 18mo. 25 cents.

——— **Anna Ross.** Illustrated. 18mo. 30 cents.

——— **Decision;** or, Religion must be all or is nothing. 18mo. 25 cts.

——— **Father Clement.** 18mo. 30 cents.

Key to the Assembly's Shorter Catechism. Containing Catechetical Exercises: a Paraphrase, and a new and regular series of proofs on each answer. 18mo. 20 cents.

KING (David, LL.D.)—**The Principles of Geology** Explained and Viewed in their Relation to Natural and Revealed Religion. 16mo. 75 cents.

——— **The Ruling Eldership of the Christian Church.**

"Clear and pointed in argument, thoroughly practical in its tendency, candid, and courteous in the treatment of opposing views, and pervaded by a fervent sense of Christian obligation."—*The Scottish Presbyterian.*

KITTO (John, D.D.)—**Daily Bible Illustrations:** being Original Readings for a year on Subjects from Sacred History, Biography, Geography, Antiquities, and Theology, especially designed for the Family Circle.

Morning Series. 4 vols. 12mo. $4 00.

Vol. I.—Antediluvians and Patriarchs.
II.—Moses and the Judges.
III.—Samuel, Saul, and David.
IV.—Solomon and the Kings.

Evening Series. 4 vols. 12mo. $4 00.

Vol. I.—Job and the Poetical Books.
II.—Isaiah and the Prophets.
III.—The Life and Death of Our Lord.
IV.—The Apostles and the Early Church.

"The idea of the present work is excellent. In 'Readings' designed for each day of the year, but so brief that they may be read aloud in ten minutes, the author goes over the out-standing facts and incidents in the sacred narrative; and from his boundless acquirements, sheds over them a flood of charming illustration."—*English Presbyterian Messenger.*

——— **The Lost Senses**—Deafness and Blindness. 12mo. $1 00.

KRUMMACHER (F. W., D.D.)—**The Martyr Lamb**; or, Christ the Representative of his People in all ages. 18mo. 40 cents.

——— **The Last Days of Elisha.** 18mo. 50 cents

——— **Elijah,** the Tishbite. 18mo. 40 cents.

Last Day of the Week. 18mo. 25 cents.

Law and the Testimony, by the author of the "Wide Wide World," "Queechy," &c. 8vo. $3 00.

"Not a treatise nor an essay, neither hath it any human writing at all. It is simply a gathering of the whole Bible testimony on each of the cardinal points of Christian belief, there left to speak for itself. Beneath these grand general heads, about thirty in number, there are no sub-divisions and no artifices of arrangement or collocation; with only an instance or two of exception. Nothing of secondary or partial interest is touched upon. The end and aim of the work is towards the perfecting and beautifying of the faith of Christians, by enabling them to see not only 'the truth,' but the 'whole truth,' and towards establishing the faith of other Christians by setting forth the broad foundation laid for it. For many know but in part the curious articulation of the Christian system; here 'bone is joined to bone,' and the whole body of divinity stands in its full proportions and on its own feet."

LEYBURN (JOHN, D.D.)—**The Soldier of the Cross.** 12mo. $1.

"Like Wilberforce's 'Practical View,' it has the combined characteristics of the regular finished essay, and the rhetorical, heart-searching appeal. Sound practical instruction is here presented in a most attractive form. The original passage commented on, is singularly bold and beautiful, both in conception and in expression; and the ideas embodied within its imagery are, in this volume, admirably exhibited to the reader's mind. The work is valuable, not only as an instructive treatise for the perusal of the private Christian, but as a model of pulpit oratory in a walk now too seldom trodden."—*Presbyterian of the West.*

Life in New York. By the author of "The Old White Meeting-house." 18mo. 40 cents.

Life of a Vagrant. Written by himself. Or, the Testimony of an Outcast to the truth and value of the Gospel. 18mo. 30 cents.

"This is one of the most remarkable books of the day, and no one can read it without wonder and astonishment."—*Balt. Patriot.*

Lighted Valley (The)—or, the Closing Scenes in the Life of a beloved Sister. With an Introduction by the Rev. WM. JAY, of Bath. 16mo. 75 cents.

"There is an indescribable beauty and pathos running through every page of this volume, which makes us thankful that it has seen the light. Nature had combined with grace to make Abby Bolton one of the loveliest of her sex."—*Evangelical Magazine.*

Line upon Line. By the author of the "Peep of Day." 18mo. 30 cts.

Little Annie's First Book. In Words of One Syllable. With 70 cuts. 35 cents.

Little Annie's Second Book. A companion to the above. Colored plates. Square. 40 cents.

Little Lessons for Little Learners. Square. Col. plates. 50 cts.

Living to Christ. A Mother's Memorial of a Departed Daughter. With an Introduction by the Rev. Asa D. Smith, D.D. 16mo. 60 cents.

"Simple, beautiful, affecting and instructive, this little volume wins its way to the heart, with the freshness of a rill from the River of the Water of Life, clear as crystal. Let every parent read it, and see how early and how sweetly the love of Jesus may take possession of a child's heart. Let every child read it, and see and know the delightful example and evidences of youthful piety. It is a precious, useful book, encouraging, animating and delightful."—*Montreal Witness.*

LOWRIE (Rev. John C.)—**Two Years in Upper India.** 75 cents.

——— (Rev. W. M.)—**Letters to Sabbath School Children.** 25 cts.

LUTHER (Martin)—**A Commentary on St. Paul's Epistle to the Galatians.** 8vo. $1 50. With a portrait.

"This is a reprint of one of the noblest productions of the reformation. It bears the impress of the great mind of its author, and as a judicious, lucid exposition of Scripture, may be considered as almost unrivalled to the present day."

MACKAY (Mrs. Colonel)—**The Wickliffites;** or, England in the Fifteenth Century. 12mo. 75 cents.

MAGIE (Rev. Dr.)—**The Spring Time of Life.** Or, Advice to Youth. 16mo. 75 cents.

"We rarely meet with a volume prepared for youth, in this age of light reading, at once so attractive in style and so rich in evangelical truth. For purity, perspicuity, and beauty of expression and force of thought, it would be difficult to find its superior. It is just what we would wish to see in the hands of every apprentice, clerk, and student in the land."—*Newark Daily Adv.*

Mamma's Bible Stories, for Little Boys and Girls. Colored plates. 50 cents.

——— Sequel to the same. Colored plates. 50 cents.

MARSHALL (Walter)—**The Gospel Mystery of Sanctification** opened in sundry practical Directions; suited especially to the case of those who labor under the guilt and power of indwelling Sin. 18mo. 50 cents.

"The amiable and pious H· vey says of this little treatise, that, were he banished to a desolate island, with but two books beside the Bible, this should be one of the two, and perhaps the first that he would choose."—*Observer.*

——— (Mrs.)—**My Friend's Family.** 18mo. 25 cents.

MARTIN—A Brief Sketch of the Life of the late Miss Sarah Martin, of Great Yarmouth. With Extracts from the Parliamentary Reports of Prisons: her own Prison Journal, &c. 18mo. 30 cents.

MARTYN—Memoir of the Rev. Henry Martyn, D.D. By John Sargent, M.A. New edition. 12mo. 60 cents.

Martyrs and Covenanters of Scotland. 18mo. 40 cents.

"We do not remember that we ever read a little volume containing so much of deep and thrilling interest as this one.."—*Christian Alliance.*

McCHEYNE—The Life, Letters, Lectures, and Remains of the Rev. Robert Murray McCheyne. To which are added his Familiar Letters from the Holy Land. New edition. With a fine portrait. 8vo. $1 50.

——— **Sermons.** With portrait. 1 vol., 8vo. $2 00.

——— **Familiar Letters from the Holy Land.** 18mo. 50 cts.

——— **Complete Works.** Containing all the above. 2 vols., 8vo. $3 00.

"The tenderness of his conscience—the truthfulness of his character—his deadness to the world—his deep humility and exalted devotion—his consuming love to Christ, and the painful solicitude with which he eyed everything affecting his honor—the fidelity with which he denied himself, and told others of their faults or dangers—his meekness in bearing wrong, and his unwearied industry in doing good—the mildness which tempered his unyielding firmness, and the jealousy for the Lord of Hosts which commanded but did not supplant the yearnings of a most affectionate heart, rendered him altogether one of the loveliest specimens of the Spirit's workmanship."—*Rev. James Hamilton, of London.*

McCOSH (James, D.D.)—**The Divine Government, Physical and Moral.** 8vo. $2 00.

"If this work wants the attraction of previous literary reputation in the author, the disadvantage is compensated by the surpassing interest and peculiar seasonableness of its subject. The mere title of the book, as indicating an inquiry that must needs embrace some of the deepest questions that have ever exercised the human intellect, is sure to draw the attention of those who are addicted to speculative studies. A glance at its contents will satisfy such that it is deserving of a careful perusal; and once perused, it cannot fail, we should think, to leave an impression of wonder that, for the first time, the author should have become known to the public by a work of such pre-eminent merit. Nor do we fear to hazard the assertion, that he has thus, by a single stride, secured for himself a position in literature such as few ever reached by a first publication, and one which he might never have attained had he put forth in separate and more limited efforts the learning and thought which he has concentrated on this."—*North British Review.*

McCRINDELL (Miss R.)—**The Convent.** A Narrative founded on fact. 18mo. 50 cents.

"A well-wrought tale, with truth as its basis, and important usefulness for its aim."—*N. Y. Observer.*

——— **The School Girl in France.** Complete edition. 16mo. 50 cts.

McFARLANE (Rev. John, LL.D.)—**The Mountains of the Bible,** their Scenes, and their Lessons. With four steel plates. 12mo. 75 cents.

McGHEE (Rev. Robert J.)—**Expository Lectures on the Epistle to the Ephesians.** $2 00.

"These Lectures form a delightful and profitable running commentary upon this Epistle, so rich in experimental truth."—*Zion's Herald.*

McGILVRAY (Rev. WALTER, D.D.)—**Peace in Believing.** 25 cts

McLELLAND (ALEX., DD.)—**A Treatise on the Canon and Interpretation of the Scripture.** 12mo. 75 cents.

McLEOD (Rev. Dr.)—**True Godliness.** 12mo. 60 cents.

MEIKLE (JAMES)—**Solitude Sweetened;** or, Miscellaneous Meditations on various Religious Subjects. Written in distant parts of the world. 12mo. 60 cents.

MENTEATH—Lays of the Kirk and Covenant. By Mrs. A. STUART MENTEATH. 16mo. Illustrated. 75 cents.

"It is a long time since we have enjoyed such a treat as this volume has given us. No nation on the face of the globe has a history so full of interest to the Christian as that of Scotland. Her soil has been consecrated by conflicts, more noble than those immortalized in Homer's song. We are glad to find that Mrs. Menteath has the true spirit of the ballad—wild, plaintive and soul-moving, and we would say to all lovers of ballads, get this beautifully-printed and illustrated volume."

Michael Kemp—The History of Michael Kemp, the happy Farmer's Lad. A Tale of Rustic Life, illustrative of the Spiritual Blessings and Temporal Advantages of Early Piety. By ANNE WOODRUFFE. Illustrated. 18mo. 40 cents.

MILLER (HUGH)—**The Geology of the Bass Rock.** 16mo. 75 cts.

"This volume illustrates the truth that a very humble spot of earth may be invested with peculiar charms from clustering scientific and historic associations."—*Christian Observer.*

Miller (ROGER)—Or, Heroism in Humble Life. A Narrative. By ORME, with an Introduction by the Rev. Dr. ALEXANDER. 18mo. 30 cents.

"The reader who rises from this volume unmoved, and without a glow of new desires to be individually useful to the suffering and the wicked, must be made of sterner stuff than many to whom these pages have been submitted."—*Extract from the Introduction.*

Missionary of Kilmany (The)—Being a Memoir of Alexander Paterson, with Notices of ROBERT EDIE, by the Rev. JOHN BAILLIE.

"I should not be surprised if Alexander Paterson in his day and generation, shall be found to have turned more unto righteousness than many of the most esteemed and evangelical clergy of our Church."—*Dr. Chalmers.*

"A more delightful and instructive history than this we have very seldom read."—*Witness.*

Missions—The Origin and History of Missions. By Rev. J. O. CHOULES and Rev. THOMAS SMITH. 4to. Illustrated. $3 50.

MOFFAT (ROBERT)—**Missionary Labors and Scenes in Southern Africa.** With plates, and portrait of the author. 75 cents.

MONOD (ADOLPHE, D.D.)—**Lucilla;** or, the Reading of the Bible. Translated from the French. 18mo. 40 cents.

MORE (Hannah)—**Private Devotions.** Elegant edition. 18mo. 50 cents.

Small edition. 32mo. Plain. 20 cents. Gilt. 30 cents.

MORELL (J. D.)—**An Historical and Critical View** of the Speculative Philosophy of Europe in the Nineteenth Century. 8vo. $3 00.

"We have seldom read an author who can make such lucid conveyance of his thoughts, and these never of light or slender quality, but substantial and deep as the philosophy with which he deals. Even when not convinced by his reasonings, it is difficult to resist the impulse by which we feel ourselves carried along in the flow of his commanding and well-sustained sentences."—*Dr. Chalmers, in the North British Review.*

Morning of Life (The)—A Memoir of Miss A——n, who was educated for a Nun, with many interesting particulars, and original Letters of Dr. Doyle, late Roman Catholic Bishop of Carlow. By her friend, M. M. C. M. 16mo. 40 cents.

Morning and Night Watches. 16mo. 60 cents.

"Daily grace for the soul is as needful as daily bread for the body. This volume seems well adapted to lead the reader to meditate upon God's 'loving kindness in the morning,' and his faithfulness every night. Active piety will flourish under its guidance."—*Christian Advocate.*

MURPHEY (James, D.D.)—**Creation;** or, the Bible and Geology Consistent. 12mo. $1 00.

My School-boy Days. Illustrated. 18mo. 30 cents.

My Youthful Companions. A Sequel. Illustrated. 30 cents.

The above two in one volume. 50 cents.

Near Home, or, the Countries of Europe described, by the author of the "Peep of Day," &c. 18mo. 50 cents.

"This is really a charming book; and in this estimation we have no doubt every docile boy and girl will agree with us. Systematic knowledge, derived from geographies and histories, is, of course, indispensable; but the information conveyed in the familiar style of this book is received with more pleasure and eagerness, and becomes even more deep and enduring. We have here literally a picture of Europe."—*Ch. Intelligencer.*

NEWTON—The Works of the Rev. John Newton, of St. Mary's Woolworth, London. Containing an Authentic Narrative, etc.; Letters; Discourses; Olney Hymns; Poems; Messiah; and Tracts. To which are prefixed Memoirs of his Life, &c., by the Rev. Richard Cecil, A.M. Complete in one volume. New edition, with fine portrait by Ritchie. $2 00.

"If there is any name of modern times consecrated in the grateful remembrances and affections of the Christian, it is that of John Newton. His conversion to Christianity was scarcely less remarkable than that of Saul of Tarsus; and his subsequent course through a long and laborious life, was in many respects quite analogous to the course of the great Apostle to the Gentiles."

—— **The Christian Character** exemplified from the papers of M. Magdalen Jasper. 18mo. 30 cents.

New Cobwebs to catch Little Flies. Illustrated with sixteen fine engravings. 16mo. 50 cents.

NOEL—Infant Piety. A book for Little Children. By the Hon. and Rev. BAPTIST W. NOEL. 18mo. 25 cents.

OLD HUMPHREY—Works. 40 cents each. Viz.:

OBSERVATIONS.	OLD SEA CAPTAIN.
ADDRESSES.	GRAND PARENTS.
THOUGHTS.	ISLE OF WIGHT.
WALKS IN LONDON.	PITHY PAPERS.
HOMELY HINTS.	PLEASANT PAPERS.
COUNTRY STROLLS.	NORTH AMERICAN INDIANS.

"We know of no writer of the present day who seems to us more sure of meeting a cordial welcome from his readers, upon every fresh appearance, than Old Humphrey. His beautiful illustrations, both of nature and art, joined with a strong religious feeling, and a certain familiarity and quaintness becoming an old man, give to his works a charm to which few readers can be insensible."

Old White Meeting-house.—By the author of "Life in New York," &c. 18mo. 40 cents.

OLMSTED—Thoughts and Counsels for the Impenitent. By the Rev. J. M. OLMSTED. 18mo. 50 cents.

OPIE—Tales; or, Illustrations of Lying by AMELIA OPIE. 18mo. 40 cents.

OSBORNE (Mrs. D.)—**The World of Waters;** or, a Peaceful Progress o'er the Unpathed Sea. Illustrated. 75 cents.

***OWEN—The Works of John Owen, D.D.** 16 vols., 8vo. $20.

"This edition has been carefully compared with the earliest editions of Dr. Owen's Works, (who has been often and justly styled the 'Prince of Divines,') and no exertion has been spared to render it, in all respects, the *best edition* that has ever appeared."

——— **On Spiritual Mindedness.** 12mo. 60 cents.

PALEY—Horæ Paulinæ. By WILLIAM PALEY, D.D., author of "Natural Theology," &c. 8vo. 75 cents.

PASCAL—The Provincial Letters of BLAISE PASCAL. A new translation, with Historical Introduction and Notes by the Rev. THOS. MCCRIE. $1 00.

"It were superfluous to say anything in commendation of these world-famous letters. The translation before us is done by an accomplished scholar, and hence will give a better view of the wit and force of the original, than those that preceded it."

Pastor's Daughter (The)—or, the Way of Salvation Explained to a Young Inquirer, from Reminiscences of the Conversations of her late Father, Edward Payson, D.D. By LOUISA PAYSON HOPKINS. 18mo. 40 cents.

PATERSON—A Concise System of Theology on the Basis of the Shorter Catechism. By ALEXANDER SMITH PATERSON, A.M. 18mo. 50 cents.

"The Rev. Dr. Brewster, of Craig, Scotland—good authority on theological matters—describes this treatise 'as being one of the most beautiful, complete, and accurate expositions of the Shorter Catechisms which has ever appeared.'"

PEARSON (Rev. THOMAS)—**Infidelity**; its Aspects, Causes, and Agencies, being the prize essay of the British organization of the Evangelical Alliance. 8vo.

"It occupies a distinct field from most of the other recent volumes on this subject; for while these state the argument in defence of Christianity, or answer the principal objections of infidels, Mr. Pearson gives us a panoramic view of infidelity itself. We know not indeed any book which gives so full and so accurate a description of the various aspects which infidelity, in the present age, has assumed. To ministers of the gospel and to all who are brought into contact with the prevailing unbelief of the day, this volume will be peculiarly valuable, while it cannot fail to be deeply interesting to every thoughtful Christian. We congratulate the Church on having among its ministers one so able to do battle for the faith once delivered to the saints; and we congratulate the author on having produced a book which will win for him a high place in the estimation of all who love the truth as it is in Jesus."—*United Presbyterian Magazine.*

Peep of Day; or, the Earliest Religious Instruction the Infant Mind is capable of receiving. 18mo. 30 cents.

PHILIP (Rev. ROBERT)—**Devotional Guides**; comprising Guides to the Perplexed, Devotional, Thoughtful, Doubting, and Conscientious, to which is added, Redemption, or, the New Song in Heaven. 2 vols., 12mo. $1 50.

"These subjects are treated in a way that will be satisfactory to all serious minds. The author's style is evidently fitted to the work he has undertaken. It is simple, pure, terse, intelligible, occasionally highly beautiful and forcible, without affectation, labored effort or heaviness. I should regard the extensive circulation of these Guides as fitted to promote the spirituality of Christians, to make them acquainted with their own hearts, and with the power of the religion they profess to love."—*Rev. Albert Barnes.*

——— **The Young Man's Closet Library.** 12mo. 75 cents.

——— **The Love of the Spirit.** 18mo. 40 cents.

——— **Young Ladies Closet Library.** 4 vols., viz.:

MARYS, or, the Beauty of Female Holiness. 40 cents.

MARTHAS, or, the Varieties of Female Piety. 40 cents.

LYDIAS, or, the Development of Female Character. 40 cts.

HANNAHS, or, Maternal Influences on Sons. 40 cents.

"The fine discrimination of character, the sweet spirit, and just views of these works, we have always very much admired. We deem them among the most useful works for the reading of Christian females that we know of. There are but few varieties of woman's trials, fears, duties, and wants, which do not here find sympathy and counsel."—*Evangelist*

PIKE (Rev. J. G.)—**True Happiness.** 18mo. 30 cents.

——— **The Divine Origin of Christianity.** 30 cents.

POLLOCK (ROBERT)—**The Course of Time.** A Poem. Elegant edition. 16mo. Printed on fine paper. With a portrait of the author. Cloth. $1. Extra gilt, do. $1 50, Turkey morocco. $2.

——— **The Life, Letters, and Remains of Robert Pollok, A.M.** By JAMES SCOTT, D.D. With portrait. 16mo. $1 00.

——— **Tales of the Covenanters.** Containing Helen of the Glen; The Persecuted Family and Ralph Gemmell. Printed on large paper, uniform with the above. Illustrated. 16mo. 75 cents.

——— **Helen of the Glen.** Separate. Illustrated. 18mo. 25 cts.

——— **The Persecuted Family.** do. do. do. do.

——— **Ralph Gemmell.** do. do. do. do.

***POOLE** (MATTHEW)—**Annotations upon the Holy Bible,** wherein the Sacred Text is inserted, and various readings annexed; together with the parallel Scriptures. The more difficult terms are explained; seeming contradictions reconciled; doubts resolved, and the whole text opened. 3 vols. Imperial 8vo., printed on fine linen paper In cloth. $10; in half calf, $12.

"The late Rev. Richard Cecil said, 'If we must have commentators, as we certainly must, Poole is incomparable, and I had almost said, abundant of himself;' and the Rev. E. Bickersteth, amongst his 'Hints to Christian Students,' recommended it as 'judicious and full.' The Rev. Thomas Hartwell Horne, in his 'Introduction to the Critical Study of the Holy Scriptures,' remarks—'The Annotations are mingled with the text, and are allowed to be very judicious; and he who wishes to understand the Scriptures will rarely consult them without advantage. (This) the imperial 8vo edition, is very beautifully and correctly printed.'"

PORTEOUS—Lectures on Matthew. 12mo. 75 cents.

POWERSCOURT—Letters and Papers of the late THEODOSIA A. Viscountess POWERSCOURT. 12mo. 75 cents.

Precept on Precept, by the author of the "Peep of Day." 18mo. 30 cents.

Psalms in Hebrew. 32mo. Gilt. 50 cents.

PROUDFIT'S Counsels to the Young. Square.

Retrospect (The)—or, Review of Providential Mercies, with anecdotes of various characters. By ALIQUIS. 18mo. 40 cents.

RICHMOND (LEGH)—**Annals of the Poor.** Containing, the Dairyman's Daughter; Negro Servant; and Young Cottager. 18mo. 40 cents.

——— **Domestic Portraiture;** or, the Successful Application of Religious Principle in the Education of a Family exemplified in the Memoirs of three of the deceased Children of Legh Richmond, with an Introduction by the Rev. Edward Bickersteth. 12mo. 75 cts.

ROGERS (Mrs. G. A.)—**The Folded Lamb**; or, the Memorials of an Infant Son. Portrait. 18mo. 40 cents.

"A very touching little picture, which honors the gospel, and verifies some of its sweetest promises."—*Evangelist.*

——— (George Albert)—**Jacob's Well.** 18mo. 40 cents.

ROMAINE (Rev. Wm.)—**The Life, Walk, and Triumph of Faith.** 12mo. 60 cents.

——— **Letters on Important Subjects.** 12mo. 60 cents.

ROWLAND (Rev. Henry A.)—**The Common Maxims of Infidelity.** 12mo. 75 cents.

RUTHERFORD—**Letters of the Rev. Samuel Rutherford.** With a Sketch of his Life by the Rev. A. A. Bonar, author of the "Memoir of McCheyne." 8vo. $1 50.

"Rutherford's Letters is one of my classics. Were truth the beam, I have no doubt, that if Homer, and Virgil, and Horace, and all that the world has agreed to idolize, were weighed against that book, they would be lighter than vanity."—*Cecil.*

RYLE (Rev. J. C.)—**Living or Dead?** A Series of Home Truths. 16mo. 75 cents.

"A deeply practical and earnest address on personal religion, written in a pointed, taking style, and with a most commendable directness. It graphically paints the lost condition of the soul by nature, and the way of recovery; and then pungently addresses arguments to the sinner to flee the wrath to come."—*Evangelist.*

——— **Wheat or Chaff?** A Series of Home Truths. 16mo. 75 cts.

"Mr. Ryle is one of our most searching and earnest practical writers. He writes like a man who was not only familiar with the throne of grace and the Bible, but who also lived in close communion with the spirit and writings of such men as Baxter, and Flavel, and the older Puritans. Hence his words ring like the sound of a trumpet, and he speaks like a man awake. The present volume is in the same strain with its excellent predecessor, 'Living or Dead?' and is designed more especially for professed Christians."—*Watchman.*

——— **Startling Questions.** 16mo. 75 cents.

"Few writers hold a more vigorous pen than the author of this little volume. The questions are pressed home upon the conscience of the reader, and their consideration urged, by motives which make their appeal to the noblest feelings of our nature."—*Genessee Evangelist.*

——— **Young Man's Christian Year.** 15 cents.

SAPPHIR—**Letters and Diaries of Philip Sapphir,** a Converted Hungarian Israelite. 30 cents.

SCHMEID (C. Von)—**A Hundred Short Tales for Children.** Illustrated. Square. 50 cents.

SCOTT (Thos.)—**The Force of Truth,** an authentic Narrative. 18mo. 25 cents.

Scotia's Bards—Comprising the choicest productions of the Scottish Poets, accompanied with brief sketches of each. Elegantly illustrated. Cloth, $. Full gilt, $. Turkey mor. $.

This work comprises the most exquisite effusions of Thomson, Ramsay, Blair, Falconer, Beattie, Ossian, McNeil, Bruce, Logan, Burns, Graham, Scott, Hogg, Tannahill, Leyden, Knox, Campbell, Cunningham, Pringle, Pollok, Motherwell, Gilfillan, Bethune, Nicoll, More, Wilson, Mackay, Aytoun, Smith, and others. The poets of England and America, and even those of Germany, Italy, and France have been grouped together in many a graceful and fragrant wreath, while those of Scotland hitherto remain ungathered. It has been the desire of the Editor to give a selection—in most cases, complete poems—from each of the best or most noted poets. The selections have been the most copious from the minor poets—those least known in this country—among them will be found some of the most exquisite productions of genius. Accompanying the selections there is a brief sketch of each poet.

SCOUGAL—The Works of the Rev. Henry Scougal. Together with his Funeral Sermon by Dr. GARDNER, and an account of his Life and Writings. 18mo. 40 cents.

Scripture Truths. Square. Cloth. 15 cents.

Scripture Promises. Square. Cloth. 15 cents.

Select Christian Authors—Comprising Doddridge, Wilberforce, Adams, Halyburton, A'Kempis, &c., &c. With Introductory Essays, by Dr. CHALMERS, and others. 2 vols., 8vo. $2 00.

Select Works of JAMES, VENN, WILSON, PHILIP, and JAY. Eight complete works in 1 vol., royal 8vo. $1 50.

***Self-explanatory Reference Bible.** The Holy Bible of the authorized Version with Marginal Reading, and Original and Selected Parallel References PRINTED AT LENGTH. 8vo. Turkey morocco, $

"While the importance of *Reference* Bibles is admitted by all, it cannot be denied that their utility is much impaired by the time and labor required in turning to numerous passages. To remedy this defect the present edition has been prepared. Its peculiar object is to set before the reader, at a glance, the very words of those passages which are best fitted to illustrate the text, or to throw satisfactory light on its meaning."

SERLE (AMBROSE)—**The Christian Remembrancer.** 32mo. Gilt. 50 cents.

SHERWOOD (Mrs.)—**Clever Stories.** Containing "Think before you Act," "Jack, the Sailor Boy," and "Duty is Safety." 50 cts.

——— **Think before you Act.** Separate. 25 cents.

——— **Duty is Safety.** Separate. 25 cents.

——— **Jack, the Sailor Boy.** Separate. 25 cents.

Short Prayers in Scripture Language. 15 cents.

Sick Room (The). Square. 15 cents.

SIGOURNEY (Mrs. L. H.)—**Water Drops.** Illustrated with eight fine tinted engravings. 16mo. 75 cents.

"We know of nothing more appropriate as a gift book than this useful and entertaining volume."—*Chn. Secretary.*

——— **Letters to my Pupils,** with Narrative and Biographical Sketches. Illustrated with a fine portrait of the authoress, engraved expressly for this work by Ritchie. 16mo. 75 cents.

——— **Olive Leaves.** Illustrated. 16mo. 75 cents.

"This is a sweet book of delightful moral and religious tendency. History, biography, story and poetry are here intermingled in a manner both charming and instructive, making it one of the best of children's gift books."—*Indep'nt.*

——— **The Faded Hope.** 16mo. 75 cents.

"We have in this little volume a most touching account of the life and death of a highly promising youth, from the pen of his bereaved mother. Everything about the book bespeaks the smitten yet submissive heart. With the breathings of maternal love, it combines excellent taste, deep pathos, and exalted Christian feeling."—*Puritan Recorder.*

——— **Memoir of Mrs. Harriet N. Cook.** 16mo. 75 cents.

"This is a valuable little reminiscence of a devoted Christian lady, who died in the midst of her hopes, her enjoyments and usefulness. We see the tokens of Christian refinement, and excellence of character, which adorn the fireside, which fitly fill the place of wife and mother, and qualify for usefulness in every intelligent circle."—*Chr. Parlor Magazine.*

——— **The Boy's Book.** Illustrated. 18mo. 40 cents.

"We recommend the book most earnestly to our young readers, and hope that every parent who has a bright-eyed, joyous little boy, will try whether his eye will not grow brighter and his joy deeper, by the possession of such a volume as 'The Boy's Book.'"—*Watchman and Observer.*

——— **The Girl's Book.** Illustrated. 18mo. 40 cents.

——— **The Child's Book.** Illustrated. Square. 35 cents.

"A handsome little volume for the instruction and entertainment of children. Its pictorial embellishments and its easy lessons will delight them, while imparting to their opening minds some of the most salutary counsels."—*Ch. Obs.*

SIMEON—Memoirs of the Rev. Charles Simeon, M.A., of King's College, Cambridge. By the Rev. William Carus, M. A. Portrait. 8vo. $2 00.

SINCLAIR (Catherine)—**Modern Accomplishments;** or, the March of Intellect. 12mo. 75 cents.

"This is a brilliant narrative, written by a clever and popular writer, whose pen is ever ready for the illustration and enforcement of truth as well as for the revelation of error and sin. We entreat those who think that the ornamental should take the place of the useful in an education, to read this work, which cannot but command the attention of even the most desperate lover of romance."—*Spectator.*

——— **Modern Society,** a sequel to Modern Accomplishments. 12mo. 75 cents.

——— **Hill and Valley.** 12mo. 75 cents.

——— **Charlie Seymour;** or, the Good and Bad Aunt. 30 cents,

——— **Holiday House.** A Series of Tales. 16mo. Illust. 75 cts.

Sinner's Friend. From the 87th Edition, completing upwards of half a million. This work has been printed in sixteen different languages. 25 cents.

SMITH (Rev. James)—**Green Pastures for the Lord's Flock;** or, the Christian's Daily Remembrancer. From the 38th London edition. 12mo. $1 00.

SMYTH (Thos. D.D.)—**Solace for Bereaved Parents;** or, Infants Die to Live. With very full Selections from various authors, in Prose and Poetry. 12mo. 75 cents.

Songs in the House of My Pilgrimage. Selected and arranged by a Lady. 16mo. 75 cents.

"A scriptural text, containing a precious promise and an appropriate selection of poetry for every day in the year."—*Recorder.*

Sorrowing yet Rejoicing—or, Narrative of Successive Bereavements in a Minister's Family. Tenth American edition. 18mo. 30 cents. Also, 32mo. Gilt edge. 30 cents.

SPRING (Rev. Gard., D.D.)—**Memoirs of the late Hannah L. Murray,** or, a Pastor's Tribute to one of his Flock. 8vo. $1 50.

STEVENSON (Rev. John)—**Christ on the Cross.** An Exposition of the Twenty second Psalm. 12mo. 75 cents.

——— **The Lord our Shepherd.** An Exposition of the Twenty-third Psalm. 12mo. 60 cents.

"His style is highly animated, his sentiments eminently evangelical and devotional, and there is such a rich vein of spirituality pervading all his pages, that we read them with permanent profit as well as present pleasure."

Stories on the Lord's Prayer. By the author of "Edward and Miriam." 18mo. Illustrated. 30 cents.

"These are simple little stories, illustrating the different parts of our Lord's Prayer. They are in good keeping with the subject, which is giving them great praise."—*Evangelist.*

STUCKLEY (Lewis, 1640)—**The Gospel Glass.** Representing the Miscarriages of Professors; or, a Call from Heaven to Sinners and Saints. 12mo.

SUMNER—**A Practical Exposition of the Gospels of Matthew and Mark,** in the form of Lectures. Designed to assist the practice of Domestic Instruction and Devotion. By John Sumner, D.D., Canterbury. 12mo. 75 cents.

SYMINGTON—**The Atonement and Intercession of Jesus Christ.** By the Rev. Wm. Symington. 12mo. 75 cents.

"This work is the production of one of the most profound theological writers of the day. It takes up the general subject to which it relates, in its various bearings, and shows that the atonement, properly understood, connects itself with everything that gives life and value to Christianity."

TAYLOR (Jeremy)—**The Sermons of Jeremy Taylor, D.D.** Complete in one volume. 8vo. $1 50.

"This is a massive volume, printed in double-column, and embracing sixty-four not very brief sermons, from tho pen of one who, although a Lord Bishop, we better know under the familiar name of Jeremy Taylor. We should be very reluctant to endorse Jeremy Taylor's high churchism, with his no small spice of superstition, or to hold him up as a safe guide in religious matters; the reader must make abatement in these respects; yet, after all, who cannot relish his often fine and affluent thoughts, his no less striking and eloquent language, his poetical imagery, and his bright and picturesque painting, or afford to make up a theological library without reserving a niche for him?" —*Presbyterian.*

——— (Isaac)—**Loyola**; or, Jesuitism in its Rudiments, by Isaac Taylor. 12mo. $1 00.

"In its historic details it is fair, perspicuous, and sufficiently minute; in its reasonings it is luminous, ingenious, and to ourselves at least, generally irresistible."—*Argus.*

——— **Natural History of Enthusiasm.** 12mo. 75 cents.

"Every one will remember the 'enthusiasm' of delight with which this work and those belonging to the same series were greeted on their first issue. It was the discovery of a new '*placer*' of thought; and although severe tests have shown that all is not gold that glitters; and that some of the brightest surfaces of splendid thought were very thin, yet they have also shown that there was genuine bullion there."—*Watchman and Observer.*

——— (Jane)—**Limed Twigs to Catch Young Birds.** Square. 50 cents. Beautifully illustrated with colored plates.

——— **Hymns for Infant Minds.** Square. Illustrated. 40 cts.

——— **Life and Correspondence.** 18mo. 40 cents.

——— **Display,** a Tale. 18mo. 30 cents.

——— **Contributions of Q. Q.** Illustrated. 16mo. $1 00.

——— **Original Poems for Infant Minds.** 18mo. 40 cents.

——— **Essays in Rhyme.** 18mo. 30 cents.

——— **Mother and Daughter.** 18mo. 30 cents.

——— **Rhymes for the Nursery,** with sixteen colored plates.

TENNENT (Rev. Wm.)—**Life of.** 25 cents.

Theological Sketch Book; or, Sketches of Sermons. From Simeon's Sketches of Sermons; Pulpit Assistant; Benson's Plans; Preacher; Pulpit, &c. 2 vols., 8vo. Cloth, $3 00.

THOLUCK's Circle of Human Life. 30 cents.

Three Months under the Snow. The Journal of a Young Inhabitant of the Jura. Translated from the French. 18mo. 30 cts.

"The details of this little book, are of a most exciting character, and the spirit which it breathes, as well as the lesson which it teaches, is one of Christian trust and fortitude."—*Puritan Recorder.*

TUCKER (Miss E.)—**The Rainbow in the North.** Illustrated. 16mo. 75 cents.

"The emblem of the Rainbow, as applied to the Christian missionary, is peculiarly beautiful. This account of Prince Rupert's Land, and the arrival of the first missionary, Rev. John West, at Red River Colony, is exceedingly interesting. He is afterward joined by fellow-laborers in the great work of salvation—and amid trials by flood and famine, and many other difficulties and sufferings, they are at length rewarded by winning souls to Christ."—*Republican.*

——— **Abbeokutta**; or, Sunrise in the Tropics. 16mo. 75 cents.

TURNBULL (Rev. R.)—**The Genius of Scotland**; or, Sketches of Scottish Scenery, Literature, and Religion. 12mo. $1 00.

——— **The Pulpit Orators of France and Switzerland.** 12mo. $1 00.

TURRETINE—**Institutio Theologiæ Elenctiæ.** Authore Francisco Turretino. 4 vols., 8vo. $10 00.

TYNG—**Lectures on the Law and the Gospel.** By STEPHEN H. TYNG, D.D., Rector of St. George's Church, New York. Sixth edition. Large type. With a fine portrait of the author. 8vo. $1 50.

——— **The Israel of God.** A Series of Discourses. 8vo. $1 50.

——— **Christ is All.** 8vo. $1 50.

——— **Recollections of England.** 12mo. $1 00.

——— **Christian Titles.** 16mo. 75 cents.

"The design of this book is to exhibit in the most plain and practical way the various titles which are applied to Christians in the Holy Scriptures. Each one is found to be significant of some distinct privilege, or duty, or obligation. The work is an eminently experimental one, and is fitted to quicken and brighten all the Christian graces."—*Puritan Recorder.*

——— **A Lamb from the Flock.** 25 cents.

Very Little Tales for very Little Children. In large type. Square. First Series. 35 cents.

Do. do. Second Series. 40 cents.

WARDLAW (Rev RALPH, D.D.)—**On Miracles.** 12mo. 75 cts.

"A more thorough, profound and perfectly conclusive argument in favor of miracles than this work contains, is, so far as we know, not to be found; and one of its chief recommendations is, that it meets most triumphantly some of the most popular forms of infidelity at the present day. It is a work that will well repay an attentive perusal."—*Argus.*

WATERBURY (Rev. J. B.)—**A Book for the Sabbath.** 40 cts.

WATTS (ISAAC)—**Divine and Moral Songs.** Square. Beautifully illustrated with colored plates. 40 cents.

WAUGH—**Memoir of the Rev. Alexander Waugh, D.D.** $1.

Week (The). By the author of the "Commandment with Promise." Illustrated with eight beautiful engravings. 16mo. 75 cents.

Week Completed. Separate. 25 cents.

WHATELY—The Kingdom of Christ Delineated, and **The Errors of Romanism** traced to their Origin in Human Nature. By RICHARD WHATELY, D.D., Archbishop of Dublin. 75 cents.

WHITECROSS—The Assembly's Catechism. Illustrated by appropriate anecdotes. By JOHN WHITECROSS. 18mo. 30 cts.

WHITE (Rev. HUGH)—**Meditations and Addresses on the Subject of Prayer.** 18mo. 40 cents.

——— **The Believer.** A Series of Discourses. 18mo. 40 cents.

——— **Practical Reflections on the Second Advent.** 40 cts.

——— **The Complete Works of Henry Kirke White,** with an Account of his Life. By ROBERT SOUTHEY, LL.D. $1 00.

WILBERFORCE—A Practical View of the prevailing Religious Systems of professed Christians in the Middle and Higher Classes of Society, contrasted with real Christianity. By WILLIAM WILBERFORCE, Esq. Fine edition. Large type. 12mo. $1 00.

WILSON—Lights and Shadows of Scottish Life. By JOHN WILSON, Professor of Moral Philosophy in the University of Edinburgh, Editor of Blackwood's Magazine, &c. Illustrated with eight fine engravings by Howland. 16mo. 75 cents.

WILLIAMS—Memoir of the Rev. John Williams, Missionary to Polynesia, by EBENEZER PROUT. 12mo. $1 00.

WILLISON (JOHN)—**Sacramental Meditations and Advices.** 18mo. 50 cents.

Wine and Milk. Square. 25 cents.

WINER'S Grammar of the Idioms of the Greek Language of the New Testament. Translated. 8vo. $2 50.

WINSLOW (OCTAVIUS)—**Midnight Harmonies;** or, Thoughts for the Season of Solitude and Sorrow. 16mo. 60 cents.

——— **Personal Declension and Revival of Religion in the Soul.** 12mo. 60 cents.

WOODRUFF (ANNE T.)—**Shades of Character;** or, the Infant Pilgrim. 2 vols., 12mo. $1 50.

WYLIE—A Journey over the Region of Fulfilled Prophecy. By the Rev. J. A. WYLIE. 18mo. 30 cents.

YOUNG'S Night Thoughts. Elegant edition. Large type. With portrait. 16mo. $1 00.

Small edition. Close type. 18mo. 40 cents.

www.ingramcontent.com/pod-product-compliance
Lightning Source LLC
LaVergne TN
LVHW020114110826
845151LV00001B/158